Alpine Manual

Alpine Manual

Professional Ski Instructors of America Education Foundation

CREDITS

Education Director
Linda J. Crockett

Editor
Rebecca W. Ayers

Cover Illustration/Design Standards
Lee Reedy Creative

Graphic Design/Pre-press Production
Ken Grasman

Text Illustrations
Reata Bitter, Bitter-Sweet Studio

Still Images
Rodnunsky Arts, Ltd.,
Scott Markewitz

Digital Photo Design
Boulder Media Group

ISBN 1-882409-08-6

Library of Congress Card Catalog
Number 96-70407

Printed in the United States of America

Table of Contents

Foreword

Skiing is a marvelous and wondrous sport that is both fun and enlightening. Few physical endeavors match its form, substance, and extraordinary sense of freedom. Skiing gives you an unbridled and unrestrained feeling of being free for a moment in time. You are free to float down a powdery mountain meadow, fly across a broad and open dale, overcome a steep and icy chasm, and to glide over nature's white carpet. Through skiing, you discover, create, re-discover and re-create.

Our sport brims with experiences that help define and shape who we are. When we ski, we act on our perceptions, biases, beliefs, and moods. In doing so, we better understand our approaches and attitudes toward living and learning. Skiing is a metaphor for our lives—a true reflection of who we are and who we can be.

Skiing provides an element of risk, and by negotiating with this risk, by engaging yourself—intelligently—you stretch your abilities and come closer to reaching your potential as both an individual and a skier. Skiing reveals what you are made of: You understand your limits better and grow closer to realizing your own dreams and passions.

Sensations abound in skiing, and they can revitalize and rejuvenate. The weightless feeling of flying touches your stomach, the tug of gravity pushes and pulls on your muscles, the cold air burns your lungs, and the experience energizes you. Other sensations

include the rhythm of turning and the powerful, cutting feeling underfoot as you carve long and sweeping arcs from one side of the slope to the other. Then there is the sensation of a breakthrough—that indescribable elation you get upon improving your skills or accomplishing something for the very first time. At day's end, you bask in a state of euphoria, a buoyant and blissful feeling. Invigorated, enlivened, and re-energized, a day of skiing is a vital nutrient of a well-balanced diet for life.

To teach and coach this sport is a marvelous endeavor as well. In teaching, you have the opportunity to introduce others to skiing and share your passion with them, giving them this gift. Ski teaching offers a chance to interact with and engage another person, to impart and coach skills that go way beyond those that are inherent in our sport. It allows you to help others learn skills that enable them to enjoy this sport as you do.

To those new to ski teaching,

the profession at first seems quite simple. One quickly realizes, however, that teaching is a complex task, particularly in that it consists of continually re-educating oneself and applying all the innovation, experience, teaching methodology, and skiing technique accumulated over time. Those who stay with it will eventually mature as teachers. They emerge from the morass of perceived complexity and enter a realm where they can make sense out of knowledge and experience. They gain the ability *to make complex things easier.*

The goal of this manual is to provide you with the information and insights that will help you become a more accomplished skier and effective teacher. As you become more experienced, you will find new understanding and apply information in new ways. This is a part of the adventure. Try not to become obsessed with the outcome —as with skiing, it is important just to enjoy the journey.

The Spirit of Skiing

When the cold autumn winds blow,

a fire deep within me is rekindled.

With winter's first flurries,

this passion remembered starts to burn.

Skimming o'er the frozen white,

leaving life's ails behind in a cloud of icy smoke.

I'm free for a moment in time, free.

I dance the dance called skiing.

I fly this wingless flight.

Sensations abound, nourishing and

vitalizing my body and spirit.

I ride the wind, I fly, I ski.

It is a dialogue, a colloquy.

On the white canvas I paint and etch my every mood.

The shiny slope mirrors and I know myself better.

I share this passion with those I meet.

I give this gift, I pass on joy.

Hail skiing, hail teaching, hail ski teaching.

I love it so, for it makes me who I am.

I ride the wind, I fly, I ski.

Dave Merriam, PSIA National Demonstration Teams Coach

Acknowledgments

This manual reflects the combined expertise of many talented skiers, writers, and educators, and PSIA is greatly indebted to these individuals for their generous contributions.

It would be remiss not to extend a collective thank-you, also, to those who developed the American Teaching System and to those who have refined it over the years. PSIA owes a debt of gratitude to these pioneers of thought as the association continues to refine its fundamental education program.

The following list serves to credit those individuals who either wrote or helped develop the content for this manual:

- The Service Model chapter was written by Mark Dorsey, with significant contributions from Jack Copeland, Sue Spencer, Dick Tapply, and Weems Westfeldt.
- The Teaching Model chapter was written by Johanna Hall and contains contributions from Jim Taylor, Ph.D.
- The Skiing Model chapter was written by Jerry Warren and Jonathan Naughton, Ph.D., with contributions from Dave Merriam and Weems Westfeldt.
- The Ski Equipment chapter was written by Harald Harb and Dan Meldrum.
- The Quest for Skiing Excellence chapter was written by Dave Merriam.

- The Anatomy and Conditioning chapter was written by Melanie Holden and Robert Hintermeister, Ph.D.
- The Safety Awareness chapter was written by Michael Patmas, M.D.
- The Introduction to Mountain Ecology chapter was written by Allen Crockett, Ph.D.
- The expanded glossary was compiled by Johanna Hall and Ken Daly.

The following individuals served on the review panel for this edition and offered indispensable advice:
Jack Copeland
Johanna Hall
Megan Harvey
Dave Merriam
Mike Porter
Sue Spencer
Juris Vagners, Ph.D.
Jerry Warren
Calvin Yamamoto
Roger Zimmerman, Ph.D.

The following groups are due special thanks and recognition for their guidance and support:
- The PSIA Board of Directors
- The PSIA Alpine Demonstration Team
- The PSIA Education Steering Committee
- The PSIA Education Committee
- The PSIA Certification Committee
- The PSIA Ski School Management Committee

Also, Dave Merriam, head coach of the PSIA Teams, was a great source of information and perspective at every stage of development and review. At various times, he was pressed into service to write, read, and review text, and even volunteered to apply research on the hill! His insights and philosophy were not only practical but motivational.

Weems Westfeldt performed the technical review of this manual and the corresponding study guides. He was always willing to listen, edit rather than sleep, and offer invaluable creative solutions.

Jim Rogers, Ph.D., was responsible for the unenviable tasks of preparing an index and organizing material for the glossary. He was an efficient and cheerful innovator throughout the process.

Rebecca Ayers, PSIA communications director, edited the manual with the same high standards she applies to the association magazine, *The Professional Skier.* Many thanks to Rebecca for asking the tough questions and for her expert turns of phrase.

The greatest thanks goes to PSIA members, for it is through them that the American Teaching System is brought to life for skiers.

Linda J. Crockett
PSIA Education Director

Introduction

The Professional Ski Instructors of America (PSIA) is a nonprofit association dedicated to promoting the sport of skiing and other mountain sports and recreation. As a member of PSIA, you have distinguished yourself as an individual with an exceptional level of commitment and desire to pursue excellence in ski teaching.

PSIA offers numerous resources to help you achieve your fullest potential as both a teaching professional and a skier. The association provides education and training experiences to help you stay current in teaching techniques and learning theory, improve your skills, and enjoy your own skiing more—all of which enable you to provide the highest-quality lesson possible.

To help you navigate on your journey to ski teaching excellence, PSIA has created various "trail maps" in the form of education programs. These programs function as a support system with many reference tools that will guide you through the intricacies of teaching and the challenges of improving your own skills.

PSIA's *Alpine Manual* is one such tool. This textbook and its corresponding study guides focus on the American Teaching System (ATS), a comprehensive education program designed to augment your own experiences and impressions as a ski instructor.

The primary purpose of ATS is to show you specifically how you can share the wonderful sport of skiing with others. The system is

also intended to help you to identify ways in which you can improve your own skiing skills and enhance your professional development.

ATS and the other PSIA education programs are delivered through clinics, refresher courses, special-interest seminars, and the National Academy, an educational symposium on the latest ski teaching techniques and equipment

innovations. PSIA's education programs, offered through the association's geographical divisions, serve to encourage self-improvement, to gauge achievement through an examination/certification process and, consequently, help you advance in your career. This certification is recognized and respected throughout the United States.

The *Alpine Manual* is part of a

collection of PSIA educational materials that support association programs. Textbooks, study guides, handbooks, and videos are in a continuing state of development and revision, reflecting PSIA's responsiveness to the ever-changing dynamic of the snow sport industry. PSIA also publishes an award-winning magazine, *The Professional Skier*, which contains articles on teaching techniques, learning theory, communication methods, and industry news, among other topics.

PSIA has evolved into a sophisticated and influential entity since its fledgling beginnings some 35 years ago. The early days of ski instruction in the United States were typified by a variety of programs and techniques, many of which were brought to this country by European ski instructors. Teaching principles varied across the country as did the process of instructor certification, at that time bestowed by an assortment of regional associations. PSIA was founded in 1961 to develop a standardized system for teaching people to ski and to unify ski instructors throughout the country. In 1964, PSIA published *The Official American Ski Technique* manual, differentiating American technique from that of other countries. Since then, the association has continued to set the tone for U.S. ski instruction.

Today, PSIA is composed of nearly 25,000 members who serve skiers through the advancement of ski instruction. The association represents instructors of alpine and nordic skiing as well as snowboarding. Certification is available for alpine, nordic-track, and nordic-

downhill skiing, snowboarding, and adaptive skiing.

For more than 20 years, PSIA's national demonstration teams have helped deliver educational information to the individual member. These "teachers of the teachers" are top-flight skiers and ski educators who lead programs and offer training for other instructors across the country. Established PSIA teams include Alpine, Nordic, Snowboard, and the Junior Education Team (commonly known as the JETs, who specialize in children's instruction).

The association is represented regionally in the United States by nine geographic divisions. These divisions operate autonomously to handle membership registration, conduct training and examinations, and inform the members in their region of important association updates and events.

PSIA has several levels of membership. Registered members must have completed a training program offered by their ski school. With time, experience, and additional training, they can become qualified to seek certification, progressively working from Level I to Level II and then to Level III (also referred to as full certification). It may take an instructor a number of years to achieve Level III certification because of the depth of knowledge and skill proficiency this performance level requires.

As a member of PSIA, you obtain ski instructor certification from the geographic division in which you are registered.

Examiners who are appointed

by their divisions use nationally accepted standards to evaluate you based on your ability to teach, to ski, and to recognize what students must do to improve their skiing. You are also expected to answer questions about guest service and the basic workings of your home ski area. (See appendix B for a listing of PSIA's Education and Certification Standards for Alpine Skiing, revised in 1996.)

One of PSIA's objectives, aside from helping you improve your ski teaching ability, is to work with ski industry partners to promote skiing and ski instruction to the public. These partners include the National Ski Areas Association and the National Ski Patrol as well as tourism and recreation groups, manufacturers, and the media. PSIA and these groups work to keep the image of skiing alive in the public eye, and to welcome new and returning participants to skiing and other mountain sports.

PSIA's participation in the ski industry transcends national boundaries. Shortly after the association was formed it began sending representatives to Interski, an international educational event held every four years. This affiliation provides PSIA with a wonderful opportunity to exchange knowledge about teaching methods and skiing techniques with ski instructors in other countries. PSIA also is a long-time member of the International Ski Instructors Association (ISIA), which represents professional ski instructors throughout the world. PSIA members who have achieved Level III certification may join ISIA, an affiliation that may be useful when seeking employment with ski schools in other countries. Also, an ISIA card may qualify instructors for certain discounts at participating ski areas outside the United States.

One of the benefits of PSIA affiliation is that it provides numerous opportunities for professional growth. Within the organizational structure, you may aspire to influence the direction of the association itself by becoming elected to the national board of directors or by being appointed to serve on a committee. Or you may choose to help educate your colleagues about PSIA education programs and developments in ski teaching by achieving a spot on one of the demonstration teams. Each of these affiliations directly translates into practical and valuable experience, which may also be beneficial when seeking a management or training position.

As evidenced by the nature of its education programs, certification structure, and opportunities for self-improvement, the role of PSIA in the mountain sports and recreation industry continues to evolve with the times. Anyone who has skied for a number of years can attest to the fact that changes in equipment, clothing, and technique are ongoing, and occasionally demand that ski instructors reinvent what they teach and how they teach it.

One of the most recent and sweeping signs of change within the industry is the advent and increasing popularity of "shaped skis." PSIA, in its education

materials and association magazine, will continue to address the implications of emerging technologies to ski teachers and the ski industry at large. PSIA members must not only experience the new equipment for themselves, but they must understand how equipment may affect the teaching process and the ways in which people learn. Above all, members must translate their knowledge, experience, and insights into meaningful experiences for resort guests.

Ski instructors are increasingly required to be significant players in the entire resort operation and therefore serve as ambassadors for their area and their sport. Today's guests have high expectations. They demand high standards of products and services and often wish to master the sport in a limited time. Ski schools are competing for discretionary time and money that guests could spend on other recreation or leisure activities. As an instructor, you are challenged to create an experience for students that can rival the benefits they might gain from these other pursuits.

Mountain resorts reflect this trend as they expand and diversify their operations. Ski areas are increasingly open for year-round operation, moving from a focus on snow sports during the ski season to in-line skating, guided hiking, nature touring, and mountain biking during the warm-weather months. Instructors are challenged to play an active role in this larger arena.

In response to these changes, the PSIA Board of Directors in June 1996 expanded the scope of the association mission statement

to encompass not only ski instruction but the overall mountain sports and recreation experience. PSIA is poised to emerge as an international leader in this "umbrella" industry, and continue to elevate the demand for and professional recognition of its members.

As a member of PSIA, you have a wonderful opportunity to be a part of these exciting changes. At the same time, you must realize that the association cannot solve for you all the riddles of your profession, for each and every situation you face as a teacher or coach will be different. You cannot learn the most important lessons of skiing and teaching from a manual, either. In fact, you will make the most significant, insightful discoveries on your own—in daily interactions with students, as you strive to improve your own skiing skills, and through discussions with others in your profession.

By reflecting upon your experiences, your learning, and your development as both a skier and instructor, you will uncover the most meaningful aspects of your role as a ski teacher: to instill in others the elation of discovery, the satisfaction of learning, and the love of skiing.

chapter

The American Teaching System

The American Teaching System (ATS) is PSIA's own educational guideline to the three basic components of ski teaching: the instructional aspects (the Teaching Model), the technical, or skill-related, aspects (the Skiing Model), and the customer relations, or guest-service, aspects (the Service Model).

ATS is based on contemporary skiing techniques and mechanics as well as teaching and learning theory. Ski teachers use the system to evaluate their students' skiing ability and guide them toward improved skiing performance. Further, ATS provides the foundation for many ski school's training programs, and instructors refer to the system to improve their personal teaching and skiing skills.

As with all successful education programs, ATS evolves as it responds to the changing needs of PSIA membership, the ski industry, and the general public. It is designed to be adaptable because all students and teachers are individuals first, and therefore have different wants, needs, and motivations.

The system encourages creative decision-making, inviting you, the teacher, to augment textbook theory with your own intelligence and experience. ATS supports your autonomy and gives you the freedom and confidence to act on the many different situations you face each day as an instructor.

Those who have long been associated with PSIA will note that the teaching system has been identified by several titles throughout the years, evolving from the "American Ski Technique" to the "American Teaching Method" to the "American Teaching System."

The distinctions are subtle but reflect changes in focus. "Technique" connotes a more technical focus, or the "right" way to ski. "Method" indicates a prescribed process or body of skills and techniques for accomplishing the task. "System" implies a more comprehensive concept—a pattern for organizing information and developing a successful approach to instruction.

In the American Teaching System, represented in figure 1.1, ski teaching's most basic elements are shown as a triad of models—the Teaching, Skiing, and Service models.

Teaching and learning theories (Teaching Model), skiing mechanics

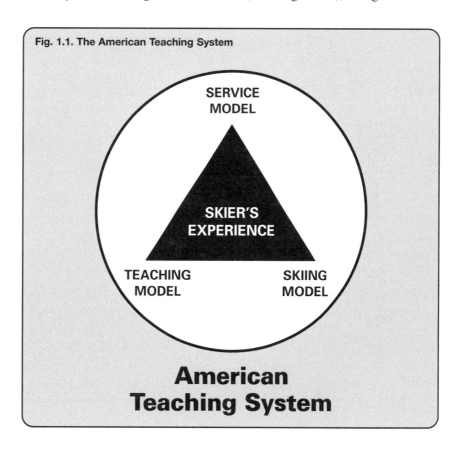

Fig. 1.1. The American Teaching System

SERVICE MODEL

SKIER'S EXPERIENCE

TEACHING MODEL

SKIING MODEL

American Teaching System

(Skiing Model), and service delivery (Service Model) all revolve around a nucleus that represents the skier's experience. The nature of this experience results from the interaction of the following components: the student's goals, aspirations, and expectations; the teacher's skills and abilities in leadership and service; and sound skiing fundamentals and mechanical progressions.

The Teaching Model represents the teaching pattern of successful instructors and is a framework from which instructors can organize their lessons. It addresses learning styles, how behavior affects learning, and how teachers can enhance learning by creating a learning partnership with every student in the group.

The Skiing Model represents the technical aspects of skiing. It provides the necessary background for understanding how turns are made and how to help students develop functional, elegant skiing. Instructors learn how to apply the fundamental skills of skiing to a variety of students and skiing situations.

Although the Service Model is the newest segment of the system, it represents concepts that good ski instructors everywhere have been practicing and delivering for years. These concepts include taking an active role in improving area operations by communicating with guests effectively, resolving customers' problems efficiently, and providing service that *exceeds* students' expectations. The Service Model is integrated into the system to emphasize the importance of helping students develop comfort with the whole idea of skiing, ski resorts, and ski lessons.

Note that the American Teaching System is not a rigid equation that should be applied to every student in the same manner; it will not produce the same results each time. Rather, it represents the many ways students learn, and it helps instructors strengthen their ability to create and deliver successful learning experiences.

The system was founded and developed by many contributors—it has no single creator. This seems fitting, since there is no single "type" of skier either. ATS, as it was conceived and as it is today, provides a flexible and pragmatic approach to instruction. This living, interactive system enables instructors to adjust each component based on the effectiveness and applicability of the other components.

ATS is characterized by the following qualities.

ATS is student-centered. This means that the students are the focal point of the teaching and learning process. In an instructor-centered process, the instructor has all the answers, sets the goals, and dictates the course of action. In a student-centered process, the instructor and students work in a collaborative manner. The instructor acts as guide and facilitator, working with students to create a learning partnership that is sensitive to each learner's unique needs.

ATS is outcome-based. ATS is based on the belief that all students can succeed, that success breeds success, and that all instructors contribute to the degree of success.

Instructors work with students to determine desired results for each stage of learning. Next, the instructor helps establish objectives and selects appropriate demonstrations, skill development, and concepts to present to students. This produces a creative, logical path to achieve desired results.

ATS is experiential. Learning by doing is an essential part of movement education. The instructor uses structured skiing, such as drills, games, and exercises in a variety of terrain and snow conditions, to create the desired learning. This experiential approach leads to improved awareness and understanding.

ATS is learning-partnership-based. The instructor creates a partnership with students by "reading" their behavior and then applying the appropriate educational techniques to help them improve their skiing. The instructor gathers clues from what students say and do and develops the presentation that will be most beneficial to them. This process involves active listening, feedback, checking for understanding, and adjusting the instructional plan to meet the students' needs.

ATS is guest-service-driven. The instructor is aware of the students' expectations for the experience and takes appropriate steps to ensure that the students have a positive interaction with area personnel and the services the resort has to offer.

ATS is delivered with sincerity. Sincerity refers to the respect and rapport all instructors must display toward their students. Ski teaching must be based on a true interest in helping others learn to ski and a genuine desire to help them improve their skills.

ATS draws together the many elements of ski teaching into a cohesive whole. The Skiing Model, the Teaching Model, and the Service Model each have an important and different purpose, but the applicability and effectiveness of ATS lies in the fact that the models function as a system. The elements draw upon and support each other to create illumination in ski teaching. Instructors see how to help others reach their goals in skiing, and how they, themselves, can reach their own goals in teaching and skill proficiency.

Educational Materials

The American Teaching System is supported by instructor training, education programs, and corresponding materials. These materials are arranged in way that is relevant to instructors at all levels in their careers.

The materials for alpine skiing are designed to work alone or in combination. The materials currently available include a manual, three study guides, a handbook, and a video.

The *Alpine Manual* contains material basic to ski instruction (such as the Teaching, Skiing, and Service models) and encourages further exploration into topics of special interest (such as psychology, behavior, conditioning, equipment, and mountain ecology). The additional topics are provided for

the reader's benefit and further study is encouraged. The list of suggested reading given at the end of this manual provides a starting point of references for study. Instructors who become knowledgeable in a number of areas, and perhaps in more than one skiing

discipline, are able to share this information with students.

The *Level I Study Guide, Level II Study Guide*, and *Level III Study Guide* are designed to accompany the manual, and they correspond with the certification levels I, II, and III, respectively. The guides introduce specific progressions and skill developments that become more complex with each higher level. They are produced in a workbook format so instructors can use them to check learning, develop personalized scenarios, and provide self-guided study.

The *Alpine Handbook* provides an on-the-hill file of exercise lines and valuable ideas for ski activities to try with your students. The activities are arranged according to skier level and supply information about the specific skills that the exercises target.

The *Alpine References* video supports the written materials with moving images. The video helps train the eye by showing skiing reference maneuvers, progressions, and upper-end, tactical skiing in a variety of conditions. *Alpine References* is indexed to the manual and study guides so they can be used together.

These materials explain how the American Teaching System works and how you can use this education program to become a more effective teacher. As you gain more experience, you will be increasingly capable of expanding upon this information and applying it to your own teaching in your own way. The true value of the American Teaching System is that it is flexible, allowing you to adapt it to any lesson situation for successful results.

chapter

2

The Service Model

For the first time in PSIA's history, the association includes a guest Service Model in an ATS manual—an inclusion admittedly long overdue. PSIA, in its teaching and training materials, traditionally focused almost exclusively on the technical and psychological processes of teaching. However, the most successful instructors normally satisfy the wants and needs of students in ways that go well beyond the educational aspects of the class. These deeply committed instructors serve guests as well as teach them, whether it be within the framework of the class or within the larger framework of the area itself.

Great guest service is part of the foundation of great teaching. Service is something you do in your job, every day on the hill. Since the recreation/resort industry is such a competitive service industry, instructors cannot afford to provide anything less than excellent service. The elements of good service are not self-evident, and that is why a broad overview of service is included in this manual. Instructors cannot afford to leave service issues to chance.

In this chapter the terms "customer," "guest," and "student" are used interchangeably. This is because ski school students pay to learn and therefore are customers. Customers in this day and age expect to be treated as guests, especially when spending hard-earned vacation dollars. You may be expected to provide an exceptional learning experience, show value for the dollars spent in providing services, and develop personal relationships, all in the same class. So it is irrelevant to try to decide if those who come to learn from us are customers, guests, or students. They are always all three.

The Ski Instructor's Role in Customer Service

Instructors spend more time with customers than any other employee on the mountain. Since customers return to businesses where they get good service, you are instrumental in creating return business, and this business benefits you and your employer.

Customer service, and good teaching, are founded on the idea of caring combined with common sense. If you emphasize these attitudes and practice your customer service skills in your training and exams you will be practicing skills that help students receive better lessons. They will have more fun and be receptive to learning. Through these skills you are supporting PSIA's mission of promoting the sport through good instruction while, at the same time, providing great guest service.

As you become more successful at providing good lessons and service, you will create a bond with your students, and returning students will be more likely to ask for you or come back to your ski school. As the pattern of requests grows, so, too, does your earning potential and the value of that student to your area. The Service Model provides tools that enhance your ability to create these bonds, so the model supports you and your area economically.

In short, there are a number of reasons to provide good customer service. First, as an instructor you are in a service business. Second, you want to create happy customers. But perhaps the most important reason is that good customer service can help build customer loyalty.

The Relationship Between Customers and Service

A number of publications cite statistics about customers and the effects of their complaints on business. The statistics may vary by a few percentage points, but they overwhelmingly arrive at the same general conclusions:

- 96 percent of customers who feel they were served poorly do not complain.
- 90 percent of those who feel they were served poorly will not return as your guests.
- Each person who feels as if he or she was served poorly will tell at least 9 other people, and 13 percent will tell at least 20 others.
- 95 percent of customers will return if their problem is resolved on the spot.

Surveys asking customers about why they took their business elsewhere revealed the following (*Customer Service Excellence,* by Debra J. MacNeil, Burr Ridge, IL: Business One/Mirror Press, 1994):

- 3 percent of the customers moved.
- 5 percent had developed other relationships.
- 9 percent left for competitive reasons.
- 14 percent were dissatisfied with the product.
- 68 percent left because of an attitude of indifference toward the customer by the owner, manager, or some other employee.

So much for the dark side. Rather than focus on what happens when you do not provide good customer service, take a look at what happens when you do provide it.

The Benefits of Providing Good Service

Providing good service is a building block to creating customer loyalty (*Building Customer Loyalty,*

by Barbara A. Glanz, Burr Ridge, IL: Business One/Mirror Press, 1994). Loyal customers

- give referrals about you,
- expand their business with you,
- come to you instead of going to competitors,
- willingly pay more for products simply because of the good service you provide, and
- are easier to serve because they are cooperative and more friendly toward you.

Management may set the tone for your area in terms of the marketing message, facilities, and the pricing and timing of products and services, but you are in the best position to influence customer loyalty because you have the most direct contact with customers.

The Relationships Between Teaching, Sales, and Service

Good customer service meshes well with the basics of both teaching and selling. In sales, the goal is to create a sale or transaction that fulfills a customer's need and yields a customer benefit. Any experienced salesperson will tell you that customers who realize the positive benefits of their choices do not disparage a product, service, or company. Likewise, in teaching, a student-centered partnership is now PSIA's professional standard. This emphasis is evident throughout the PSIA Teaching Model, which includes seven key points known as the Teaching Cycle. All of them relate to customer benefits:

1. Introduce the learning segment.
2. Assess the student.
3. Determine goals and plan objectives.
4. Present and share information.
5. Guide practice
6. Check for understanding.
7. Summarize the learning segment

Well-executed customer service, effective sales, and excellent teaching all focus on positively satisfying the needs of the intended audience to the benefit of the audience, and these behaviors are usually a function of common sense as well as courtesy.

Introduction to the Service Model

The Service Model is very simple at first glance (fig. 2.1). Customers come to you at your area to benefit from your expertise as a ski instructor. Their motivations are shaped by their background and the environment. Similarly, your actions are shaped by your background and your working environment. Your job is to try to understand the customer's needs and motivations, propose a plan to satisfy those needs and benefit the customer, and confirm that your actions have satisfied the customer's needs. If you do not meet the customer's needs, you begin the process again. If you do meet their needs, you send them on to a life of wonderful mountain experiences.

Ideally, you not only meet the customer's needs, but you exceed their expectations. Simply meeting needs is not enough to distinguish you from your competition.

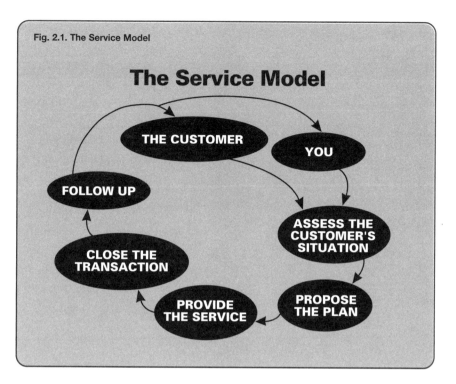

Fig. 2.1. The Service Model

The Service Model

- THE CUSTOMER
- YOU
- FOLLOW UP
- ASSESS THE CUSTOMER'S SITUATION
- CLOSE THE TRANSACTION
- PROVIDE THE SERVICE
- PROPOSE THE PLAN

The Service Model, essentially, is a framework that you can use to structure your lessons and make professional decisions about how to address students' wants and needs.

Here's how the model works. Both **you** and **the customer** begin with a set of experiences that shape you. These experiences come from your home and work environment as well as from your previous experience in sports, retail transactions, and other influences. The two of you also bring other personal experiences outside of business, plus impressions of the area. Finally, you, as an instructor, are influenced by training and interaction with other instructors.

One of the first things to do when you and the customer come together is to **assess the customer's situation**. You do this by trying to understand customers. You must ask questions about their attitudes about the area, lessons, and the

sport in general. Also ask questions about their motivation for being at the area and taking a lesson, their goals, and their personal needs. Pay close attention to body language as well as their verbal responses.

Once you feel as if you have enough information about the customer's motivations, **propose the plan** in the following manner.

- Confirm the customer's needs. (Restate them to the customer and ask if he or she agrees with your interpretation.)
- Formulate a plan of action that meets the agreed-upon needs and benefits the customer.
- Summarize the agreed-upon benefits and confirm that the plan indeed benefits the customer.
- Ask the customer if it is okay to proceed with the plan.

Now you are ready to go! **Provide the service** by executing the plan you propose. Be ready to reassess

needs and motivation as you proceed, and adjust your plan accordingly.

When you are near the conclusion of the lesson it is time to **close the transaction**. You do this by reviewing the key services and benefits provided, confirming that the customer indeed benefited, and checking for unmet needs. If you have time, move to meet any unmet needs. Once you have covered all these bases, propose the next steps to guide your customer's progress.

Finally, **follow up** with the customer about the next steps and his or her reaction to the service. Provide feedback to management if appropriate.

The resulting information will influence you and the customer and is sure to be a factor in the customer's next lesson or interaction with your area.

Customers and Your Work Environment

Customers bring a multitude of expectations into any transaction, and there are some general categories of qualities that customers have the right to expect from you and your business (MacNeil, 1994).

Reliability. Employees at your area can be counted on to do things right the first time and on time. Customers can depend on having access to the business or service when they need it, not only when it is convenient for staff.

Credibility. The product and service claims that you and your area make are honest, and the area's reputation is based on fact, not fiction. Area representatives are trustworthy and handle problems directly.

Appeal. Premises are clean and free of clutter. Staff are dressed appropriately and conduct business professionally. Product information is easy to find, displayed neatly, and easy to read. Products and services are priced fairly. Interactions with customers are pleasant and convey accurate information.

Responsiveness. Facilities and services are easily accessible. Personnel are helpful and available, and are able to solve problems in a reasonable time frame while keeping customers informed of the process.

Concern. Personnel treat customers as individuals and empathize with their concerns. Customer service literature (MacNeil, 1994) suggests the following reasons for most customer dissatisfaction: unkept promises; rude and inefficient service; conflicting messages or misinformation from employees; feelings of being victimized by the business or operations; delays and long waits; lack of communication between parties in dispute; treatment of customers as being uninformed; wrong, defective or inferior products; feelings of being dismissed or discounted by personnel; and business integrity or honesty that is questionable.

Remember, you do not have any control over how your customers react to dissatisfaction—you can only be responsible for *your* actions.

You can deal with customer dissatisfaction in basic ways. First, try to understand the primary cause of the customer's dissatisfaction. Second, to the best of your ability, alter the cause of the problem (rather than the customer's behavior) in such a way that you find a mutually acceptable solution.

Learning to Understand Customers

Your success in serving customers depends on your ability to understand and satisfy customers. This requires you to be flexible and not resort to a canned or scripted approach to your lesson or any other part of the service equation. A mechanical approach to service decreases the chance that you will genuinely connect with the customer, thus decreasing the chances that you will meet the customer's needs.

To forge a meaningful relationship with the customer, you will need to develop a strong partnership with the person by learning to identify customer expectations and motivations. There is no one set formula to accomplish this because there are so many variations of expectations and motivations.

Assessing Motivation

If you can assess customer motivations accurately, chances are you will be able to construct a successful lesson. Students will not alter their patterns or behaviors if they are not motivated to do so. And your desire to teach them does not constitute motivation on their part.

There is no advantage to presupposing motivations or the plans to address them, but there are advantages to keeping track of successful strategies you use to assess student motivations.

The following hints can help you keep track of your successes. (A more detailed discussion of this process is available in "Don't Let Your Bag of Tricks Become a Ball and Chain," *The Professional Skier*, Winter 1995, p. 24.)

1. Write down the methods you use to determine and list the customer's needs. Try grouping needs into the following categories: understanding (cognitive), motivation (affective), and physical movements (psychomotor). Each skier will be dominant in one of these categories, but an accurate description of that individual's needs will include all three.

2. Note all the methods you used to prepare students for information presented in a lesson. You might list ways in which you helped students discover new information, specific exercises that seemed to help students improve skills, and environmental conditions or experiences you helped create that fostered a strong learning experience.

3. List the questions you asked students and precise statements you made during the lesson that helped you gain the most information, confirmed your understanding of needs, or elicited positive learning behavior.

4. Identify and note the practice sessions that were successful during the lesson, including

what instructions you gave, the structure, and duration.

5. Look for trends and correlations, but be sure to pay attention to "exceptions to the rule."

Using Effective Communication Skills

In the process of trying to identify expectations and motivations, people have a tendency to generalize problems into broad categories, and, subsequently, create automatic responses to them.

Do not make stereotypical assumptions about people based on what they have told you initially. Instead, continue communicating with them throughout the lesson to make sure you are solving problems as they arise. You are in a position to work with customers one-on-one, and effective communication is your most effective tool in assessing expectations and motivation.

Communication is not something you do *to* someone, it is something you do *with* someone. Effective communication involves interaction, not a one-way lecture.

PSIA's American Teaching System is based on forming a learning partnership with the customer. The principles of effective communication and good customer service are also based on forming a partnership.

There are six key skills in communicating effectively:
1. Use open and closed questions.
2. Actively listen.
3. Provide/use effective feedback.
4. Be aware of verbal cues (e.g., tone of voice) and nonverbal cues (e.g., body language).
5. Avoid the use of jargon.
6. Confirm the proposed course of action or check for understanding.

Using Open and Closed Questions

In order to move from viewing customers as a generic group to meeting a customer's individual needs, you will need to master the art of asking questions. Your customers will come to you with different needs and individual problems, and you need to uncover those needs in order to solve problems and have happy, satisfied customers. By asking the right questions, you can determine what your customers want or need, and by paying careful attention to the answers, you can make educated recommendations to meet those needs.

Learning the art of questioning begins with formulating questions that elicit information from the customer to shed light on the customer's needs and expectations. The two basic types of questions are open and closed (MacNeil, 1994). The difference between open questions and closed questions depends on the type of response you want from the customer.

Answer the following question: Do you know what a closed question is? You probably answered this question with a simple yes or no. The question effectively limited the number of responses you are likely to give. *Any question that limits the respondent's choice of responses is a closed question.* Questions that ask for a numerical response (e.g., "How many days have you been skiing this year?") also fall into this category. These questions generally start with the words how many, when, and who. They limit discussion and are used to confirm agreement or understanding.

Now answer this question: What is an open question? Most likely, your answer to this question was a description of what an open question is, or you gave an example that provides insight into your understanding of an open question. *An open question is one that requires more than an answer of yes, no, or a numerical response.* Open questions usually start with the words how, why, which, tell me, or describe. They are generally used to start a discussion or gain information about the customer's insights, providing clues as to what the customer knows about your product or service, and what the customer needs from it.

The appropriateness of using one or the other type of question is dictated solely by the situation. There is a fine line in phrasing these questions that makes the difference between open and closed questions. For example, "May I help you?" is a closed question, whereas "How may I help you today?" is an open question. "Have you been snowboarding before?" is a closed question, whereas "Why did you decide to try snowboarding?" is an open question. Both types of questions have their place, and you should not rely exclusively on one versus the other.

Active Listening

Active listening means to become involved in the conversation, demonstrate interest, and pay attention to verbal and nonverbal messages. Are you familiar with the phrase "You hear me, but you aren't listening"? Active listening means that more is happening than sound waves hitting your eardrum.

It is very easy to slip into a passive role when listening. How often have you found yourself daydreaming or mentally composing your response while your customer was still speaking? Worse, how often have you stopped listening because you had the answer you wanted to give in your head, and you were simply waiting for the customer to finish talking just so you could give your opinion?

Succumbing to these temptations means that you cannot listen to the customer, and you cannot identify the customer's wants and needs. If you cannot identify these wants and needs you are going to have a difficult time satisfying the customer because you have, in effect, placed your agenda above the customer's. That is a fatal mistake in any service business.

How can you avoid these kinds of pitfalls? Simply put, take a *genuine* interest in your customer, and take an active role in meeting his or her needs. This does not mean that you monopolize the conversation, as some teachers are prone to do, or overpower your customer with your words. You demonstrate interest in what the customer has to say with a few very simple techniques that will

keep you actively involved in the conversation (MacNeil, 1994):
- Maintain eye contact.
- Smile.
- Do not interrupt.
- Use the customer's name.
- Articulate clearly.
- Stay focused on the conversation and eliminate distractions.
- Nod in acknowledgment.
- Repeat important points that the customer put forward.
- Probe for additional information.
- Take notes, if possible.

You are not actively involved in conversation simply because you initiated the conversation or discussion. It takes a minimum of two people to carry on a conversation, and conversation is an *exchange* of thoughts and feelings. To receive thoughts and feelings, you have to listen, and you cannot listen if you are articulating your own thoughts and feelings.

One quick note about the tone your responses: Positive versus negative language is an important factor in the communication process.

The number of agreements between two people increases the likelihood that you will move forward. It is difficult to gain agreement if your choice of questions, phrases, and feedback is consistently negative. Positive comments help create an environment that predisposes the customer to action and taking risks, while negative phrasing can reinforce feelings of inadequacy and rejection. One negative comment from you can mean that you will have to start over again, so pay close attention

to how you phrase your responses to customers. Gaining agreement is important if the customer is going to buy into your plan. And if the customer does not agree, why would he or she be motivated to change or go with you?

Being Aware of Verbal and Nonverbal Cues

Language is an important way to communicate with others, but it is by no means the only way. In fact, language is a small part of the way in which we communicate. Gestures, posture, facial expression, and vocal tone and inflection can change the intended meaning of a message. Because of this, customers may not always hear and understand what you intend for them to hear and understand.

Only 20 percent of your message is communicated face-to-face through words. About 45 percent is communicated through the quality of your voice tone and inflection. The balance of your message is communicated through body language, or nonverbal, communication, whether or not you want it to be (MacNeil, 1994). In fact, it is impossible not to communicate at all.

Attitudes are expressed in voice tone. Interactions that start out pleasantly can become difficult if one of the participants becomes tense or upset. Try to be aware of your tone of voice, especially if you are having a difficult day or are having trouble in class. Injecting tension, annoyance, or even a tinge of anger into your voice tone can cause your customers to react to this rather than your words.

Nonverbal communication is often undervalued in terms of its impact during a conversation. Negative gestures include frowning, offering a weak or limp handshake, slouching, keeping your arms crossed or your hands in your pockets, tapping your fingers, frequently glancing at your watch or the clock, and looking up, down, or away from your customer—all of which impart the impression that you either do not care about or are bored with what your customer is saying or doing.

Positive gestures include smiling, offering a solid handshake, sitting up straight, keeping your arms relaxed and open, maintaining eye contact, leaning forward to listen closely, and nodding your head in acknowledgment or encouragement (MacNeil, 1994). Positive gestures indicate your interest in the conversation and your concern for the customer, resulting in a positive, professional, and lasting image on that person.

Humans are emotional beings influenced by circumstances around them. With that in mind, think about your own emotions and how they factor into your customer interactions. If you can project an image of enthusiasm for your work, sensitivity to others, and concern for the happiness and pleasure of your customers as you do business with them, you are very likely to win their loyalty.

Avoiding the Use of Jargon

It is important to choose the right words to convey a clear and enthusiastic message—one mistake can inadvertently undo your best presentation.

Keep language with your customers clear, simple, and enthusiastic. Avoid the use of jargon, technical terms, and abbreviations at all costs. Jargon, which is language used inside the company, organization, or industry, is meaningless to the public. For example, the banking industry has CSRs, or customer service representatives, and the travel industry has CRSs, or computer reservation systems (MacNeil, 1994). One company's MIS system may be Management Information Systems while another company's MIS may be a Marketing Information System. Center Line means one thing to us as PSIA members but may mean a set of custom tire rims to an auto buff and absolutely nothing to someone else. These are examples of terms that have no meaning to your customers, so it is best to avoid using them.

Customers do not care about how much ski jargon you know or how impressive you were at the last division clinic. They care about what you are doing with and for them as human beings right here, right now. Relate to your customers as laypeople and human beings, not examiners, trainers, supervisors, or fellow instructors.

Proposing the Plan and Confirming the Course of Action

All the skills discussed in previous sections of this chapter are valuable in and of themselves, but they are only academic until you use them to meet your customer's wants and needs. In other words, you must *confirm* the customer's wants and needs through the use of closed questions. This helps you verify that the customer agrees with your plan.

As a teacher, you will formulate a plan of action with your guest in order to proceed with the lesson that addresses the customer's expressed wants and needs. To move forward, you will need to gain agreement with the customer about your plan of action.

You cannot presume that your plan will benefit the customer or meet the customer's wants and needs. You have to "close the sale" by asking the customer a closed question. If the answer is yes, you proceed. If the answer is no, the most logical response is to ask why, probe for more information, and work to formulate another plan.

Without confirming the course of action with the customer, any course of action you take is based on your agenda and yours alone. By confirming the course of action, you greatly increase the chances that the customer will come away from the experience happy and satisfied.

How to Uncover and Satisfy Needs

Concern for your customer only goes so far. Critical to the service process is your ability to uncover and satisfy customer wants and needs. The process for doing this is relatively simple and straightforward, but there are couple of pitfalls. The key is whether you can distinguish between a need and an opportunity.

A **need** is "a customer want or desire that can be *satisfied* by your product or service" (MacNeil, 1994). The customer's needs must remain the focal point of any transaction. But customers do not always state needs; rather, they often describe opportunities.

An **opportunity** is "a customer problem or dissatisfaction that can be *addressed* by your product or service." (MacNeil, 1994). However, opportunities sometimes act as a smokescreen, hiding the real need. Opportunities differ from needs in that they lack a clear statement of the customer's want or desire to solve the problem or alleviate the dissatisfaction (*Professional Selling Skills III, Unit 1: Need Satisfaction Selling*, Stamford, CT: Learning Intl., Inc., 1983).

The statement "I want to ski better in the bumps" indicates a need. The statement "I have problems skiing in the bumps" indicates an opportunity. In the former, the customer expresses a desire for change. In the latter, the customer may be making an observation and have no interest in improving his or her bump skiing, and for a variety of reasons (the customer has bad knees, likes to cruise, etc.).

If the customer does not state a desire to solve the problem, then he or she may be somewhat unhappy but not enough so to solve the problem. More important, the opportunity may stem from a different need you have yet to uncover, thus forming a smokescreen.

For example, a customer stating "I have problems skiing in the bumps" may not necessarily want to improve in the bumps. You need to ask the question, "Do you want to improve your bump skiing?" If the answer is yes, you can ask questions about what the customer wants to accomplish in the bumps. If the answer is no, then you should ask why.

You may find that the customer prefers to cruise, has trouble finishing turns, is intimidated, or is influenced by some other factor. You may find that the customer does not really want to ski bumps but wants to approach skiing with more confidence in a variety of terrain. You need to ask questions to uncover more information and get to the root issue.

A need *must* be confirmed verbally through key words and phrases (Learning International, 1983), such as need, like, want, interested in, looking for, and wish. Sentences that begin with the following phrases are examples of how a person states a need:
- "I need to find a way to..."
- "I wish we had a way to..."
- "I want to improve..."

Simply complaining about the situation is not the same as indicating a need. The fact that a customer may have a problem does not necessarily mean that the customer is looking for a solution. You must confirm the desire to change the situation or address the need in a way that benefits the customer.

Another part of satisfying customer needs is understanding the difference between features and benefits. A **feature** is a characteristic of your product or service (Learning International, 1983). Your knowledge of the products offered by your area, along with the technical knowledge you have as a teacher, constitute features.

Features describe functions. For example, a christie turn is a turn where the skis skid near the completion. A dynamic-parallel turn is a carved turn. These are features of the turn. Features, however, are not inherently valuable to the customer. They have value *only* if they benefit the customer *and* the customer agrees that there is a benefit.

A **benefit** is the value of a feature to the customer (Learning International, 1983) and is an interpretation of how the features meet the individual needs of the customer (MacNeil, 1994). Because of your product knowledge, it is probably very clear to you how certain features will satisfy a customer's needs. Just talking about features (e.g., a dynamic-parallel turn is a carved turn) does not mean your customers will share the same understanding, nor will they automatically conclude that the feature benefits them. In fact, they may come to the opposite conclusion.

To explain how your product or service will satisfy their needs, it is important for you to translate the features of your product into benefits. For example, you could tell your students, "The dynamic-parallel turn is a carved turn that will help you ski more smoothly and with less fatigue at the end of the day." At this point, you would frame a question to confirm their agreement as to whether learning this turn is beneficial. If they concurred, you would move on. If they disagreed, you would ask why and uncover more information about their needs. Remember, a benefit exists only if (1) the benefit meets the customer's stated needs, and (2) the customer agrees to the benefit.

To summarize, you start the process by **questioning** to gather information and uncover customer needs. You ask closed questions to confirm statements of need. You then satisfy customer needs by proposing a plan that yields a **benefit** that addresses the need. Finally, you **close** by gaining customer commitment to the course of action and the benefits.

What happens if you work through the process and the customer says no when you try to close the transaction? Then use an open question to find out why, and start the process again.

The final step in the process is to **deliver** on the promise. You must reward the customer for selecting your service or agreeing to your plan. If a customer comes to you or your place of business and his or her expectations are met and/or exceeded, that customer

will walk away feeling satisfied. If the customer's expectations are not met because his or her needs have not been uncovered or, worse, they have been uncovered but not matched with the appropriate benefit, the customer experiences a sense of loss. It is this perception of loss that often leads to complaints (MacNeil, 1994). The counter to this is your ability to successfully uncover and satisfy customer needs.

Providing Service and Exceeding Expectations

Understanding customers is only half of the job—satisfying customers is the other half. Even so, in today's environment, satisfying customers is not enough to get them to come back to you or your business. *Exceeding* expectations is what it takes, in part because customer's expectations are low, and satisfying a low expectation is not necessarily a good thing. Also, other competitors in the recreation industry are exceeding customer's expectations. The competitors for your customer's dollar are the movies, spectator sports, cruise lines, golf, diving, tennis, theme parks, shopping malls...the list goes on.

So what is one to do? Building loyal customers is a good start. Building customer loyalty comes from satisfying customers, and this means providing the following elements (Glanz, 1994):

Friendly and caring service. Customers want to be treated with courtesy and respect. They want to

feel that *they* are important.

Flexibility. Customers want you to jiggle the system for them and their individual needs. They do not want to hear no—they want you to figure out a way to get them what they want or need.

Problem-solving. Customers want the first person they speak with to solve their problem.

Recovery. When the organization or its employees have made a mistake, the customer wants them to apologize, fix the mistake, do something extra, and follow up. The customer wants the matter to be taken care of quickly and to his or her satisfaction.

The opportunity for you to make a difference by supplying quality work in a caring way exists at each moment of truth a customer has with you or your organization. Coined by Jan Carlzon of Scandinavian Airlines (in *Moments of Truth*, by Jan Carlzon, Cambridge, MA: Ballinger Books, 1987), a **moment of truth** is "any instance when a customer comes into contact with some aspect of your organization and has an opportunity to form an impression" about the organization.

These moments of truth reflect the customer's experience, and each one creates in the customer's mind a generalization about your *whole* organization and the quality of service you provide. As a ski instructor you may have many more opportunities to be a positive force during these moments of truth than other area employees.

Five Secrets to Success

Of course, you will not always know when a moment of truth will strike. Most can be anticipated, but others can come from out of nowhere. In either situation, it is best to be prepared, and there are five key secrets to success that can help you manage moments of truth when they appear.

1. *See yourself from the customer's perspective*. Put yourself in the customer's boots, mentally step away from yourself, and take a look at the role model you portray. Are you an ambassador of the sport, displaying professionalism and a fondness for healthy outdoor living? Does your appearance and demeanor express a feeling of being welcome, rather than the air of someone who is a member of an ego-oriented closed club? The image you project has a significant impact on how guests perceive you and your area.
2. *Be an active listener.* Do you use active listening to uncover wants and needs and to personalize the experience in your class? Do you use this skill to identify and confirm a proposed course of action?
3. *Positively exceed expectations.* Use your listening skills to help establish goals and provide the appropriate lesson expectation.
4. *Recover from service inconsistencies.* No matter how hard you try, there will be times when a guest becomes upset, irate, or out of control. At such

times it is important to remember: "The guest is not always right, but he or she is always your guest." Also, when a problem is brought to your attention, you "own" it, or are responsible for managing it, until it is resolved.
5. *Have fun doing what you are doing*. This last point is in some ways the one that makes all the others possible.

Tools that Help with the Five Secrets to Success

What tools do you have to manage moments of truth? Your most important tool is your personal communication style and awareness of how you interact with others. But there are other tools that can aid you in your quest to practice exceptional customer service. The remainder of the chapter will cover four issues: loyalty burners, loyalty builders, resolving problems, and how to create a positive, lasting impression. These tools will give you some practical ways to exercise your communication style, including how to work with customers who are upset or whose needs cannot be met by the area.

An important thing to remember is that it is impossible to positively exceed the expectations of 100 percent of the customers 100 percent of the time, much less satisfy them. Further, there are many factors that are beyond your control (e.g., the physical layout of the ski area, pricing, product development and marketing, lesson times). Do not worry about the

potentially negative consequences of the variables. Focus instead on providing the best service you can in the environment in which you have chosen to work.

It does not matter whether you work for a ski area with one rope tow or for the largest destination resort in the world, your attitude and behavior can and does influence every customer with whom you come into contact. These tools are meant for you as an individual, and it is hoped that your area will support you and your attitudes about providing a fun, meaningful experience for the guest.

Loyalty Burners

Loyalty burners are those attitudes or behaviors that can hurt the development of customer loyalty to your business. Karl Albrecht, in *At America's Service* (Homewood, IL: Dow Jones-Irwin, 1988), describes these behaviors in the following manner:

1. *Apathy.* An impression conveyed to the customer expressed in what comedian George Carlin describes as "DILLIGAD" ("Do I Look Like I Give A Damn?"). Many counter service people get this way when they get bored with their jobs, and nobody is reminding them that their job is to *serve* rather than stand behind the counter.
2. *Brush-off.* Trying to get rid of the customer by brushing off their need or problem; trying to "slam-dunk" the customer with some standard procedure that does not solve the problem but

lets the service person off the hook for doing anything special. For example, an instructor waiting for a class assignment sees what appears to be a confused group coming toward the lesson area, yet he ignores the people and instead waits for a supervisor to point them in the right direction.

3. *Coldness*. A kind of chilly hostility, curtness, unfriendliness, inconsiderateness, or impatience with the customer that says, "You're a nuisance—please go away." Think of the area restaurant managers who hire the most moody, depressed, hostile person they can find for the host, hostess, or cashier job, ensuring that the first and last moments of truth yield a negative impression.

4. *Condescension*. Treating the customer with a patronizing attitude, such as sometimes occurs in the health-care industry. For example, you address the doctor as "*Doctor* Jones," but he calls you by your first name and talks to you as if you are four years old. Ski instructors need to be particularly wary of this issue and avoid exhibiting the "I-know-what's-best-for-you-and-the-class" attitude.

5. *Robotism*. The "thank-you-have-a-nice-day-NEXT" approach. The fully mechanized worker puts every customer through the same program with the same standard motions and slogans, and with no trace of warmth or individuality. A variation of this is the smiling robot who gives you a fixed "Hollywood star" smile, but you can tell nobody's home upstairs.

6. *Rule Book*. Putting the organizational rules above customer satisfaction with no discretion on the part of the service person to make exceptions or use common sense. In ski teaching, this is often exhibited by a teacher's commitment to a scripted progression or lesson plan without regard to the customer's changing needs or ability levels.

7. *Runaround*. Trying to avoid dealing with the problem by referring the customer to someone else. ("Sorry, you'll have to call [or see] so-and-so. We don't handle that here.") The runaround experience is magnified when the customer is referred to a department that either cannot handle the concern or that refers the customer back to the department to which he or she was first referred. The effort here is to keep the problem on the back of the customer rather then have the organization resolve the issue, regardless of the nature of the problem.

These are proven ways to run customers away from your company, area, or even the recreation industry. Again, put yourself in the customer's shoes and try to see if your company creates an environment that fosters any of these seven sins or allows them to grow among the employees.

Loyalty Builders

The real cure for loyalty *burners* are loyalty *builders*. Loyalty builders are those behaviors that help customers build loyalty to your business. Critical to the success of any effort to build customer loyalty is how you view the customer. If you think of customers as a large, generic group, you are far more likely to exhibit behaviors that encourage loyalty burners.

In contrast, if you treat customers as individuals and are proactive and helpful, you are far more likely to exhibit behaviors that build customer loyalty. Loyalty is something that is earned—it cannot be mandated or commanded. And it is your job to earn it.

Each customer has individual expectations and needs. If you treat each situation exactly the same you will probably delight one customer while disappointing another. If the customer's perceptions of what actually happened in a transaction exceed expectations, that person is pleased or delighted. If perceptions are equal to what was expected, customers are satisfied. If perceptions fall below expectations, customers are disappointed or angry.

If you simply meet the customer's expectations, you may not be providing good service. Meeting expectations is like getting a "C" on your report card: Although you met the expectations of the class, you would rather have an "A."

What does it take to build customer loyalty (Glanz, 1994)?

• Trust the customer. This person comes to the transaction with a great deal of knowledge about what he or she wants—certainly more than you have.

- Go the extra mile for each and every customer.
- Recover when a mistake is made by acknowledging the customer and his or her concerns, and moving to solve the problem.
- Show appreciation for the customer.
- Take initiative to help the customer.

The last point is one of the most important. Too often, we expect the customer to embark on a course of action to solve the problem. If you take the initiative, you will reinforce your concern for the customer and for solving the problem.

Remember that even if you attend to each of these points, the key to building customer loyalty is to positively exceed expectations.

Resolving Problems

Try not to view customer complaints as an intrusion or a negative aspect of your job but as a challenge and an opportunity to salvage your area's relationship with that customer and create loyalty. Complaints tell you something that may affect more than one customer and can provide telling information about your products or services.

How can you handle a problem or complaint? The following five-step approach (MacNeil, 1994) is one of the best ways to handle (or recover from) a problem or complaint:

1. *Acknowledge the customer.* Greet the customer and indicate your availability to help. More important, use open questions to get the customer to describe the nature of the problem. Customers may be angry, defiant, or blame you, and your best recourse is to remain calm and listen. Acknowledge their feelings, that there is a problem, and that you want to help.
2. *Assess the situation.* Use your questioning skills to get as much information as you can. Be careful to listen, and avoid upsetting the customer further. Do not look for or offer excuses. Instead, seek to honestly find a solution to the problem.
3. *Affirm your understanding.* Paraphrase the customer's concerns and key phrases. Empathize with the customer.
4. *Analyze alternatives.* Work with the customer as you might work with a partner. Ask the customer for suggestions on how to solve the problem, and add those to your own. Use your questioning skills to find out the customer's preferred alternatives.
5. *Agree on a plan.* Propose a solution and ask the customer specifically if the suggested course of action would be satisfactory. Make sure you can deliver on what you agreed upon.

At times you will not be able to resolve the problem no matter how well you practice these approaches. Your customer may be too emotional to cooperate, or the action may exceed your authority or area of responsibility. Bring others into the process where appropriate or if the customer begins to become abusive. Know your organizational limits, and know where to go when you have reached them.

Finally, pay attention to patterns that may be emerging concerning your product or service. If there are items that are out of your realm of influence, you may want to bring them to the attention of management.

Closing the Transaction and Follow-Up

Most people tend to remember the first and last items presented to them in any given encounter. Consequently, bringing customer encounters to an effective close is as important as the greeting in creating a lasting impression.

Of course, there is always the possibility that a customer will upset you, despite your best efforts to address their concerns. When a particularly difficult customer upsets you, do not take it personally. Learn to step back mentally, and remember that to the customer you are the company, not an individual with feelings and emotions. Retain your professionalism and use the time after the customer has gone to deal with your emotions.

When the customer leaves, try to take time to regroup. At the very least, count to 10 or take several deep breaths before working with another customer. *It is critical that you not take the bad feelings generated from the previous encounter into the next one.* Take time to examine what happened and learn from it. Do not abandon your skills when you run into some difficulty or beat yourself up for mistakes you have made. Even though the goal is perfection in customer service, it is unrealistic to achieve that all the time, so do not hold yourself to an unreasonable expectation.

Near the conclusion of your transaction, make a point to

- review the goals or services you agreed upon with each other,
- review and confirm the benefits of following the plan to which you both agreed,
- check for unmet needs, and
- propose the next steps after addressing these issues.

Additionally, here are a few tips to help you make a positive lasting impression (MacNeil, 1994). The effective communication skills covered previously in this chapter are still your most effective tools, but the following tips are excellent ways to supplement these skills.

- Ask if there is anything else you can do for the customer.
- Smile sincerely.
- Shake the customer's hand.
- Offer your business card.
- Invite the customer to call, visit, or comment if he or she has questions or concerns.
- Use the customer's name.
- Make an appropriate comment or positive reinforcement for using your services.
- Thank the customer for his or her business.

Be prepared to follow up at another time to thank the customer for his or her business and ask for the customer's reaction to the services provided. If necessary, bring service issues to the attention of management.

Coming Full Circle

Your communication with each customer when closing the transaction and during follow-up can be invaluable. The information you gather at this time will shape your relationship with future customers and returning customers, and, ideally, make you more effective in your role at the area.

3

The Teaching Model

Every day, thousands of committed instructors help students enjoy their ski day a little more. What makes some ski instructors more successful at this endeavor than others? What is the secret of their success? Whether it is a natural or learned behavior, the ability to teach is arguably the most important skill a ski instructor can possess.

Attaining true expertise in teaching takes time and experience. To reach this level of proficiency you must accumulate the knowledge and insights derived from your failures as well as your successes in teaching. After you have identified your strengths, you will need to draw upon them to deliver information effectively. And, always, you will need to pay

attention to the reactions of your students to guide your professional decisions and behaviors.

Regardless of whether you are a new or experienced instructor, you must supplement your personal insights with a solid framework for structuring lessons. PSIA provides this framework in the form of the **Teaching Model**, one of the basic tenets of the American Teaching System (table 3.1).

The Teaching Model consists of behaviors that you follow, based on the student's needs, to ensure an effective learning experience. The Teaching Model helps you form, in essence, a **learning partnership**, or rapport, with each student so you can apply the appropriate educational techniques to maximize learning. This chapter discusses the elements of the learning partnership in detail.

A learning partnership is based on successful interaction between instructors and students. Instructors who are people-oriented and student-centered have a true flair for packaging all of their teaching and technical knowledge and ability into creative, interactive, and *fun* learning experiences for others. This proficiency reflects an approach to teaching that is both artful and scientific.

The *art* of teaching is reflected in your ability to present information in an interesting and creative way; introduce new concepts at just the right time; deal with performance frustrations and anxiety; elicit group participation; individualize each lesson; encourage play and work at the appropriate times; and orchestrate all these elements

into a cohesive ski lesson that produces results. In essence, the "artistic" qualities of your lesson are found in your willingness to devise a creative, customized, and, occasionally, unconventional approach to each lesson.

The *science* of teaching consists of drawing from your knowledge base to support the lesson content. This is reflected in your ability to break down movement patterns into component skills; develop and present exercises in the appropriate sequence; determine why a particular movement is difficult to develop; understand how ski equipment works; and apply learning and communication theory. These "scientific" aspects of teaching represent your ability to make justified, reasoned decisions about how to build a lesson plan and communicate it to your students.

It is essential to strike an appropriate balance between art and science in ski teaching—to support style with substance and vice versa. All instructors should continually work to refine their abilities in both areas, regardless of how many years of teaching experience they have or how proficient their skill level.

The Learning Partnership

The **learning partnership** refers to creating a rapport with students by "reading" their behaviors and subsequently using the appropriate educational techniques in your teaching.

This process begins as you

assess the **student profile**, those personal characteristics you become aware of during your initial interaction with each individual.

The student profile gives you cues about how to direct and modify the lesson. Your responses to this profile—the way you interact with the student and the types of educational techniques you use—are referred to as **instructor behavior**. Identifying the student profile and tailoring instructor behavior accordingly is known as the **learning partnership**. The student is not a passive vessel into which instruction is poured; rather, the student is always a partner in the learning process.

To ensure that the lesson is individualized, it is important to create a learning partnership with each person in the class. Even when there are 10 people in a class, the lesson has to offer something for everybody.

The learning partnership is one of the most important elements in any ski lesson because it helps you identify what people need and how to fulfill their needs. Each time a lesson unfolds, the success of the learning process is based on interactions with and reactions from students. The learning partnership guarantees that you will never teach the same lesson twice, because no two students are the same.

Creating the learning partnership is a basic and crucial skill in ski teaching. And, as with most other skills, if you do not have a natural ability for this, you can develop it through study and through practice.

Developing a Student Profile

Every student has a unique combination of individual characteristics, which is known in the context of ski teaching as the student profile. As an instructor, you generally identify each student's profile and lesson expectations when you introduce the lesson and assess the students. This individual assessment enables you to tailor the ski lesson for each student, even when teaching a group lesson.

The profile generally consists of the following.
• *Characteristics and background.* The student's personal attributes, e.g., experience with sports, physical attributes, physical challenges.
• *Learning preference.* The student's dominant learning style,

Table 3.1. The Teaching Model

The Teaching Model

STUDENT PROFILE	INSTRUCTOR BEHAVIOR	THE LEARNING PARTNERSHIP
• Characteristics and background • Learning preference • Motivation and desire • Emotional state	• Introduce the learning segment. • Assess the student. • Determine goals and plan objectives. • Present and share information. • Guide practice. • Check for understanding. • Summarize the learning segment.	• is creative, individualized, student-centered, interactive, experiential, and fun, • contributes to student success, • produces positive results, • provides ownership of skills, • creates lasting memories, • encourages pursuit of future learning, and • culminates in a great ski lesson!

i.e., doer, thinker, watcher, feeler.

• *Motivation and desire.* What prompts the student to learn, e.g., taking the lesson to please someone else, to achieve personal goals (realistic or unrealistic), to get "money's worth" from the lesson.

• *Emotional state.* The student's beliefs, attitudes, and values, e.g., is fearful, has high expectations, is receptive toward learning, has performance anxiety.

It is important to acknowledge and learn about each individual, taking note of similarities and differences between the people in the group. Carefully remember relevant facts about each person's profile, and make a special effort to follow up with people who need additional attention during the lesson. If one student is fearful, for example, reassure that person frequently. If another has unrealistic expectations for the lesson, be sure to discuss and agree upon goals right away, during a lift ride, perhaps.

Instructor Behavior (The Teaching Cycle)

Instructor behavior (fig. 3.1) consists of the steps you take to create valid lesson content (what to teach) and present that information in a style that is tailored to student needs (how to teach).

These steps, also referred to as the **teaching cycle,** describe the behaviors that help you determine (1) which activities to introduce to improve the student's skiing skills, based on proper analysis of his or her abilities; and (2) which presentation styles you will use to

Fig. 3.1. Instructor Behavior

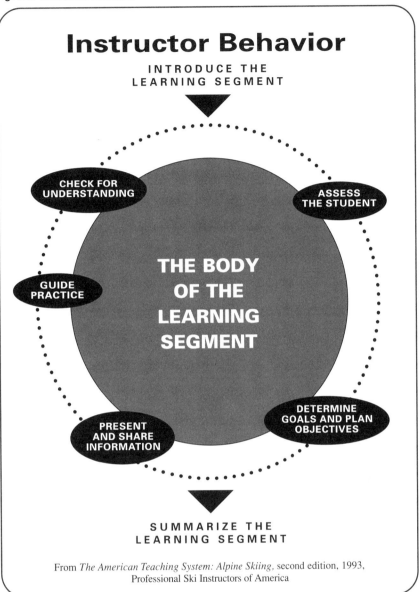

From *The American Teaching System: Alpine Skiing,* second edition, 1993, Professional Ski Instructors of America

communicate with your student.

The teaching cycle is designed to help you find your way through the always changing and often challenging process of conducting a lesson, regardless of your ability level and style. Whether you are more gifted at demonstrating good skiing, conducting movement analysis, or describing skiing images, it is important to work on your less-developed areas to

become more well-rounded as a teacher.

In this respect, the teaching cycle not only enables you to conduct a lesson that meets student needs, *it helps you identify your own strengths and weaknesses* so you can target your training appropriately. The teaching cycle provides the framework for you to develop the skills you need to be a ski instructor.

Throughout each lesson, you will find yourself cycling through these components and looking to your students for indications about what to do next.

For example, while presenting and sharing information, you might realize that the students are not responding to the activities you introduce. The teaching cycle encourages you to reassess the students to determine if your lesson is on track. You may have to alter the goals and plan the objectives differently to create a more successful lesson, but this flexibility is essential.

Knowing when and how to make appropriate teaching decisions is the difference between an average and exceptional instructor. The most effective instructors have highly developed skills in all aspects of the teaching cycle (see table 3.2).

The teaching cycle describes a pattern for instruction that is basic to all successful ski lessons. Clearly, a great ski lesson needs to contain these elements, and experienced teachers have learned to apply and expand on these concepts. The remainder of this chapter focuses on teaching and learning strategies that professional ski teachers use to deliver *great* ski lessons.

Teaching to an Outcome

The ability to work with students in a learning partnership is a necessary aspect of ski teaching, but obviously you cannot teach people to ski just by being fun or empathetic. Students pay premium prices for ski lessons and expect to see improvement in their skiing. If they get along wonderfully with you but do not learn something, you both will end up feeling as though the lesson has been a waste of time.

The American Teaching System helps you create lessons that lead to an **outcome**—the results that students take home with them. The system helps you develop a clear sense of how students progress in skiing, how to identify and develop skiing skills, and, ultimately, how to create a ski lesson with positive results.

To teach to an outcome, you must have a thorough understanding of the technical elements of the sport as well as the ability to apply that knowledge in a way that elicits results in the student's skiing. This technical knowledge and ability forms the foundation for the other important teaching attributes.

Technical understanding enables you to assess skiing ability. In turn, proficiency at assessment will help you establish priorities for what to work on during the lesson and how to narrow down the content to an attainable goal. If you target the right skills during the movement analysis, other skills will be positively affected, with dramatic overall results.

Although movement analysis entails watching students ski and determining what skills they need to develop, the delivery of your observations to students is crucial. To formulate an effective lesson plan and develop a solid learning partnership, apply variables such as the student's expectations for the lesson as well as the student's learning preference and attention span.

Analyzing Skiing Movements

Understanding the technical elements of skiing means that you understand how skiing skills develop. In other words, you have to be able to break skiing down into its components to identify a student's strengths and weaknesses. This is called **movement analysis**—determining how a student's skills compare with Center Line reference maneuvers of the Skiing Model, what skill deficiencies might exist, and what logical steps will produce the most desired results. (See chapter 4 for an in-depth discussion of the Center Line—the reference model for movement analysis.)

Specifically, movement analysis consists of four components that guide the development of a lesson plan:

1. Observing and defining the student's movement patterns and grasp of skiing skills
2. Determining cause-and-effect relationships
3. Prioritizing skill needs and identifying the lesson goal
4. Preparing a lesson plan that targets student needs

Your level of expertise in movement analysis will vary depending on your experience and technical understanding as an instructor.

The following section contains a description of basic steps you can use to guide your observations of students.

1. Set up a task for students to perform.
   a. Make sure they are warmed up and on terrain that is

Table 3.2. The Teaching Cycle

The Teaching Cycle

INTRODUCE THE LEARNING SEGMENT.
- Establish and continually build rapport with students individually and with the group as a whole.
- Create a fun, open, and supportive learning environment.
- Clearly define the general process and outcome of the learning segment.

ASSESS THE STUDENT.
- Inquire about previous experience with skiing and other sports.
- Determine ability level, expectations, goals, motivations, limitations, and concerns.
- Take students' learning preferences into consideration.
- Provide desired amount of information at any one time (low, medium, or high information).
- Find out the preferred type of feedback.
- Be sensitive to students' patience level.
- Decide whether to focus on a process or outcome orientation.

DETERMINE GOALS AND PLAN OBJECTIVES.
- Work with students to select appropriate goals based on individual and group abilities and expectations.
- Plan learning objectives relevant to individual and group goals.
- Formulate a logical lesson progression.
- Choose suitable terrain and snow conditions for lesson activities.
- Provide correct amount of practice time.
- State general (group) goals as well as specific (individual) goals.

PRESENT AND SHARE INFORMATION.
- Vary styles of presenting information to be suitable to the situation. Styles include (1) cognitive—explaining the rationale behind the technical, mechanical, and tactical elements in a logical and concise manner, (2) visual— creating clear and meaningful images of specific movements and patterns, (3) kinesthetic—developing body awareness and sensations associated with different movements, and (4) trial-and-error—allowing students the opportunity to experiment with new information.
- Adjust pacing of information according to students' capacity to receive it.
- Schedule in time for feedback and reinforcement.
- Address students' attitudes toward process or outcome orientation.
- Divide the lesson into appropriate portions of information delivery, practice, and skiing time.

GUIDE PRACTICE.
- Set practice tasks that are appropriately challenging.
- Include both process-oriented and outcome-oriented activities.
- Provide specific feedback to students.
- Reinforce student performance with appropriate comments.
- Use a variety of approaches to practice.
- Guide initial practice and prepare students for effective independent practice.

CHECK FOR UNDERSTANDING.
- Verify students' level of *physical* understanding based on skiing performances that are consistent with the lesson objectives.
- Determine the students' level of *cognitive* understanding by listening to and evaluating verbal statements and responses relating to the lesson objectives.

SUMMARIZE THE LEARNING SEGMENT.
- Review the learning segment goals and objectives and describe the degree of accomplishment to students.
- Preview the next learning segment and encourage further development.
- Establish independent practice guidelines for each student.

appropriate for their skill level.

b. Have them perform a task within their current ability. The task may be simple, such as skiing down to a stopping point, or more difficult, such as making short turns.

c. Either demonstrate the desired movement or simply watch the students ski for awhile to get an impression of their ability.

2. Observe students for overall performance.

a. Look for the students' degree of accomplishment.

b. Watch for timing, movement coordination, rhythm, and flow.

c. Determine the extent of turn shape and speed control.

d. Decide whether students are skiing competently at their skier level—they should exhibit balance and certain skill blends corresponding to the type of turn they make.

3. Compare the performances you observe with the Center Line reference turns.

a. Identify major differences first (i.e., turn shape, speed control, balance, large muscle movements).

b. Identify subtle differences next (i.e., how the student starts, controls, and finishes the turn; how the student uses the pole).

c. Determine specific skill usage and blending. Decide which skills are deficient and which are proficient.

4. Determine cause-and-effect

relationships.

a. Look for the obvious mistakes and try to determine where the problem originates.

b. One way to determine cause-and-effect relationships is to start at the end of the turn. "Back up" through the turn to determine the source of the problem.

c. Look at skill blends again. Problems can originate from either an overly dominant skill or a grossly lacking skill. For example, excessive skidding can be caused by too much rotary movement at the turn initiation (overly dominant skill) or by poor edge angle and leaning in at the end of the turn (grossly lacking skill).

5. Develop priorities for the order in which improvements should be made.

a. When teaching one student, set priorities based on that person's needs. When teaching a group of students, determine the highest priority skill need for the group.

b. Share your observations with students. Tactfully describe what you saw, and discuss problems they identify as well. Make sure the students understand some of the cause-and-effect relationships in their own skiing. If they understand the causes, they will be more focused when working on the solutions.

c. Determine a goal that the students will accept, and

provide them with a reason for their lesson. Create a partnership so they can relate to and benefit from the goal. Tie the goal into the movement analysis and let students know how they will benefit. Make sure the goal has been stated and understood, not just implied.

6. Create lesson activities that help students develop skills and change performance.

a. Determine what steps the students must take to change their performance. Create an objective, or mini-goal, that will help students move toward their overall goal.

b. Create fun, challenging, and attainable activities that make sense and fit together. Move from simple tasks to complex tasks.

7. Continue to observe students throughout the lesson.

a. Treat movement analysis as an ongoing process.

b. Interact with the students, always keeping in mind that people are more important than goals. Develop a strong learning partnership to ensure that students remain the focus of the lesson.

Goals and Lesson Planning

Lesson planning refers to establishing the lesson structure, considering relevant factors such as lesson duration, snow conditions, and the students' abilities and expectations. A lesson plan combines the art and science of teaching. It starts with determining **goals,** those broad target zones of desired accomplishment.

A lesson goal should be generic enough to encompass the needs of the whole group; however, different individuals within a group may need to hone different skills to achieve the same goal. There are infinite ways to reach goals in skiing—no two lessons need ever be the same because of differences in individuals as well as group dynamics. Patterns for teaching to achieve goals may be similar from day to day, but lesson plans are different every time. The personalities change, the situations change, and the conditions change daily.

To determine the lesson goal, you must combine the student's expectations with your professional analysis of his or her skiing and the information you have gathered from the student profile. Then, most important, you must communicate a goal that is tangible and attainable in the time allotted for the lesson.

For example, your student has indicated that he "wants to ski bumps." After talking with your student and evaluating his skiing, the two of you decide that his goal should be to improve confidence in the bumps. To do this, you determine that he needs to work on speed control in short turns and that the student is a watcher (see **Learning Preferences**, page 37), who will want to see many examples of turn shape.

You could express your plan for achieving the goal to the student this way: "Since we only have three hours, let's start by developing

your speed control out of the bumps. We'll accomplish this by creating a better shape in your turn, and then take what we learn into the bumps."

The steps you take to reach the goal are the lesson **objectives**, or mini-goals, that are skill-related. If the overall goal for the day is to learn short-radius turns with speed control, there might be five different objectives that can lead students toward the goal. Based on information from the movement analysis, you can choose those objectives that best match the skill needs of the group. If the weakest skill for the group is edging, one objective would be to focus on edging as it relates to speed control in short turns. The objective could then be met through a variety of exercises or **progressions**, which are those sequences of movements—from the least complicated to the most difficult—that help the student move toward an educational objective or goal.

Determining goals and planning objectives should always reflect the student's expectations, not just the instructor's opinion. It is important to verbalize the goals of the lesson to ensure cooperation from everyone involved. Too often, the goals of a lesson are implied a "secret" that only the instructor knows. Once you clearly articulate the goals, every activity in the lesson has a reason for being included. Students learn better and faster if they are given a sense of purpose and also if they are told when they have accomplished their goal.

Although students within a

group may have similar goals, they may end up with different results, because students learn at different rates. As long as you have established a good learning partnership with the students, goals can be molded and changed along the way.

After you have formed a partnership with the student, assessed his or her skiing, and verbalized and agreed upon the goal, the two of you can then embark on a fun journey toward the outcome of the lesson.

Missing any part of the goal-setting process can result in a teaching disaster. A student's dissatisfaction with a lesson usually can be traced back to miscommunication between you and the student during these crucial steps.

Table 3.3 provides an example of how to create a lesson plan. The steps consist of (1) determining the goal, (2) developing objectives to meet the goal, (3) designing progressions to improve skills, and (4) including activities to assist learning and understanding skills. These steps, if successful, result in the student acquiring the goal.

The table illustrates progressions that move from simple to complex movements, a basic but integral learning concept. Each progression acts as a mini-lesson that moves the student toward a specific outcome.

Sometimes students grasp a progression in only one run; other times they need to focus on it throughout the entire lesson. In all cases, be sure to give students the time they need to anchor their learning of each concept.

Table 3.3. Creating a Lesson Plan

Creating A Lesson Pla

SHARED GOAL

(Broad target zone of what can be accomplished during the lesson)

Student: "I want to ski parallel."

Instructor: "Let's smooth out your matching so you can match earlier in the turn. Before you know it, you'll be skiing parallel."

OBJECTIVES

(Specific skills students need to develop to reach the goal)

Objective 1: Attain a more balanced stance on the outside ski to allow smoother matching.

Objective 2: Isolate rotary movement of the inside ski. Create a smoother steering action during matching.

Objective 3: Attain earlier matching so it occurs directly at the turn initiation, becoming a parallel turn initiation.

PROGRESSIONS TO DEVELOP SPECIFIC SKILLS

(Mini-lesson of related activities for ski development)

Progression 1:
- Tighten the ski boots for better balance.
- Feel the shin in front of the boot for the entire turn.
- Lift the tip and tail of the ski while turning to find balance.

Progression 2:
- Feel the pressure change from the "big-toe side to the little-toe side" while matching the skis.
- Steer the inside ski from wedge to parallel—move the ski ahead.
- Pretend there are flashlights on the knees, and shine them in the same direction when matching.

Progression 3:
- Follow the instructor, matching when he or she does.
- Ski faster speeds on non-challenging terrain.
- Work on solid weight transfer— transfer and match right away.

The pace of the lesson and the specific skill progressions should be based on the students' response to activities and experiences. Blank stares or signs of frustration may indicate that it is time to let the group take a free run. This provides a break for those students who need one and a chance for others to try out their skills on the mountain. It is fine to combine drills and exercises with free skiing, as long as students are aware of what they are doing and why they are doing it.

It will only take you a minute or two to provide a group with a reason for an activity. Always explain why the students are doing a certain activity and how it ties into the goal. By sharing the reasons for activities during a lesson you can maintain the flow of communication, which keeps the learning partnership alive.

You may opt to give individuals in the group a different reason for doing the same activity. This is one way student-centered instructors individualize their lessons. For example, if angulation is the goal for the day, the entire group may participate in an exercise such as dragging the downhill pole to feel angulation, but each individual may conduct the exercise with a different purpose. One student may need the skill for better balance on the outside ski, but another student

LATERAL LEARNING ACTIVITIES TO CREATE OWNERSHIP OF SKILLS

(Activities to expand understanding and anchor learning)

- Match on small bumps and over transitions.
- Match quickly and slowly, on steeper and shallower terrain.
- Follow someone in class, and match skis when he or she does.
- Sideslip and traverse to anchor edging in the parallel position.
- Ski "J-turns" (straight in the fall line and then turn) without a wedge.

OUTCOME
(skills students take home)

Parallel turns

---

provide should be clearly tied to goals so the lesson makes sense to students.

Lateral Learning

A great way to provide a variety of learning activities while working toward a goal is through **lateral learning**. This concept refers to teaching students various skills within a skiing ability level so they can successfully progress to the next level.

Table 3.4 describes ways in which you can use lateral learning strategies to help students improve their skiing ability.

With the lateral learning approach, rather than focus on what type of turn your students are making, you isolate and develop the students' skills, and then provide students with the time, experience, and activities to integrate these skills into their overall ability level. Instead of moving students quickly from level to level, you give them the opportunity to fully develop skills at each level.

For example, the instructor who is unfamiliar with the merits of lateral learning might decide that the goal should be parallel skiing for those students who are at the beginning stages of making wedge-christie turns. With time, this is a realistic goal, but the student must attain many skills before moving from wedge-christie to parallel skiing.

On the other hand, the instructor who advocates the lateral learning approach would teach students all the necessary skills for the transition by using two mechanisms:

---

may need it to feel more secure with edging skills.

Exercises, games, and activities can be combined into a progression; however, you should know exactly which skills they develop. Some exercises are designed to develop one skill, whereas others address a number of skills. For example, one exercise with a specific edging focus is the "railroad track," in which students hold a strong edge in a traverse, leaving a

pattern like a railroad track in the snow. This activity might not be applicable to students trying to learn turn shape.

In contrast, you can have students focus on several different skills simply by having them tap the tail of their inside ski on the snow while learning to match. While tapping, they can concentrate on changing edges, on steering the inside ski, or on pressuring the outside ski. Every activity you

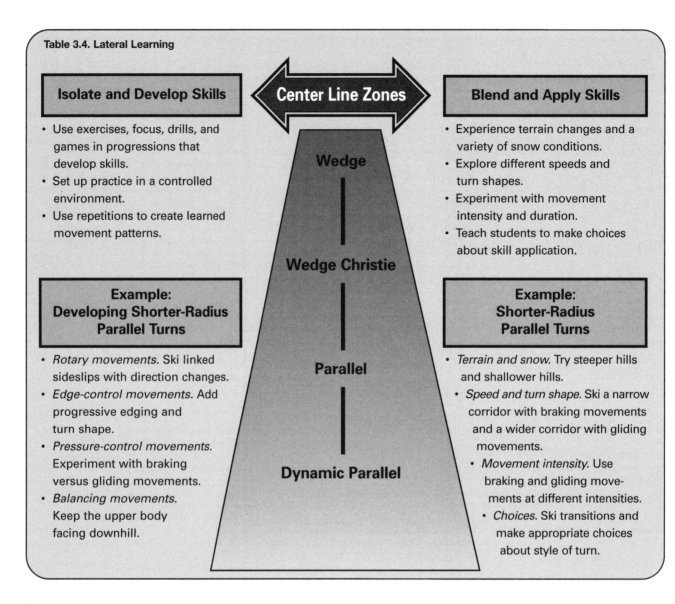

Table 3.4. Lateral Learning

Isolate and Develop Skills

- Use exercises, focus, drills, and games in progressions that develop skills.
- Set up practice in a controlled environment.
- Use repetitions to create learned movement patterns.

Center Line Zones

Wedge

Wedge Christie

Parallel

Dynamic Parallel

Blend and Apply Skills

- Experience terrain changes and a variety of snow conditions.
- Explore different speeds and turn shapes.
- Experiment with movement intensity and duration.
- Teach students to make choices about skill application.

Example: Developing Shorter-Radius Parallel Turns

- *Rotary movements.* Ski linked sideslips with direction changes.
- *Edge-control movements.* Add progressive edging and turn shape.
- *Pressure-control movements.* Experiment with braking versus gliding movements.
- *Balancing movements.* Keep the upper body facing downhill.

Example: Shorter-Radius Parallel Turns

- *Terrain and snow.* Try steeper hills and shallower hills.
- *Speed and turn shape.* Ski a narrow corridor with braking movements and a wider corridor with gliding movements.
- *Movement intensity.* Use braking and gliding movements at different intensities.
- *Choices.* Ski transitions and make appropriate choices about style of turn.

(1) isolating and developing skills, and (2) blending and applying skills.

A lateral learning activity to **isolate and develop skills** might focus on the different components of matching, for instance. You could combine several activities in a skill-related progression to focus on edge change, followed by another progression to focus on steering skills, and culminating with pressure-control activities to tie into the overall skills required in smoother matching. Any one

of these progressions could fit in during a lesson, as long as you are careful not to overload the student with too many activities.

A lateral learning activity to **blend and apply skills** might include a number of activities, such as variations of intensity, duration, or timing for matching in the turn. Or, the activity could include situation-specific variations, such as when to match when the terrain is flat versus steep, how matching feels when snow is ungroomed, and how matching changes in

response to speed variations.

With lateral learning, you must balance the time spent on the parts with that spent on the whole. If you spend too much time isolating and developing a particular skill, the pace of the lesson will be too slow and your students will leave the lesson feeling as though they never got to ski. On the other hand, if you spend too much time blending and applying several skills, your students will feel as though they did not learn any one skill particularly well.

Lateral learning is effective because students who gain skill and experience within a level move naturally to the next level. However, because movement patterns are more complex in advanced levels, more time and experience are needed as skills are isolated and developed, or blended and applied.

Teaching for Transfer

Along with lateral learning, another useful educational approach is **teaching for transfer**, that is, drawing upon a student's previous learning to help with present learning. By likening a skiing movement to another movement more familiar to the student, the process of transfer helps students learn. You accomplish this by pointing out similarities between the actions of various skills and by asking students to apply a particular strategy or concept to a new setting. This is also sometimes known as **positive transfer**.

Negative transfer refers to some previous learning or movement pattern that might hinder performance. Although you should be aware that some students may have negative associations with previous experiences, research indicates that positive transfer is far more common in motor skills training.

Learning Preferences

One aspect of a student-centered approach to teaching is awareness about the ways in which individuals learn. Students have different **learning preferences**, or styles.

That is, they have different ways of absorbing and processing information. (More information on this concept is available in the suggested readings section at the end of this manual.)

Many classification schemes have been developed to describe learning preferences. One scheme suggests that some students learn by **watching**, some by **feeling**, some by **doing**, and some by analyzing or **thinking** (table 3.5). Another similar scheme suggests that students are primarily either **visual**, **auditory**, or **kinesthetic** (feeling) in learning preference.

It is relatively simple to identify a student's learning preference. You may ask the student a question such as: "How do you like to learn: by watching, feeling, doing, or thinking?", then reinforce their self-evaluation with your own observations. The students' questions, comments, and behaviors in class provide clues to learning preference. By altering your presentation style accordingly, you can usually help the student more readily grasp the concepts you introduce.

Monitor the student's reactions throughout the lesson. Most people have more than one learning preference, and the one you are focusing on may not be effective all the time. For instance, visually dominant people usually also benefit from thinking about what they are doing and feeling. So, if the student is struggling to learn something, try presenting the concept in a way that targets a different learning style.

Instructors tend to teach most of their lessons in their own dominant

learning preference. For example, a highly cognitive instructor might teach with lengthy explanations as she draws vectors and angles on the snow. Students who are thinkers might love this type of lesson, but there could also be a doer standing just off to the side, tapping his pole.

You should take note of each student's learning preference so you can alter your presentation style accordingly when dealing with that person one-on-one. However, when dealing with students as a group, you will need to present information with a multi-media approach, in which you convey lesson activities in a variety of ways to address all the learning preferences represented. All students benefit from a well-rounded presentation that targets a variety of learning styles.

For example, to satisfy the thinkers in the group, you could provide a simple explanation for why you are presenting an activity. Then, you could follow up with a good demonstration, which would appeal to the visual learners. If you want to target the doers in the group, you could ask them to work on a specific item while they free-ski, then target the feelers by encouraging them to focus on the sensation of pressure in their ski boots.

You do not have to address each learning style every time you introduce an activity—that would make the lesson tedious. Plan to introduce these different approaches as the lesson progresses, and let the students influence decisions about presenting and sharing information. This will help you create a

Table 3.5. Presenting and Sharing Information

The following example illustrates ways to present information to students based on their learning preferences. Instructors should allow these preferences to guide their behavior and the activities they introduce throughout the lesson.

Sample Skill: Students are at the parallel level of skiing. They are learning to round out their turn shape for smoother turns.

Watcher

- The instructor demonstrates differences in Z-shaped and round turns.
- The instructor has students ski behind him or her to observe how to make round turn shapes.
- The instructor demonstrates and has students focus on turn initiations, showing students not to rush at the start of the turn.

Doer

- The instructor draws two huge "C" shapes in the snow, one in each direction, and has students try to ski in the shapes.
- The instructor has students follow in his or her tracks and initiate turn shapes.
- The instructor places cones on the snow, two for each turn, that dictate turn shape. The students turn around each set of cones.

Thinker

- The instructor describes differences in turn shapes, providing reasons for rounded turn shapes.
- The instructor has students ski both Z-shaped and round turns, having them compare the benefits and problems of each turn.
- The instructor uses a ski pole to draw a turn in the snow and discusses how gravity can help round out turns.

Feeler

- The instructor has students use flexion and extension to help smooth out turns. Students are instructed to flex progressively, instead of all at once, resulting in smoother, rounded turns.
- The instructor has students flex their ski boots a little forward and to the inside of the cuff. Students feel the increasing pressure that helps to round out turns.
- The instructor asks students to be aware of the lightness at turn initiation and heaviness at turn completion, then asks students to retain the lightness and soften the heaviness.

balanced presentation that addresses all the students' needs.

This is where teaching artistry comes into play—presenting activities that reflect your sensitivity to each student's needs while keeping the rest of the group engaged in a fun, dynamic learning experience. There simply is no absolute "right" way when it comes to presenting and sharing information.

The following guidelines are helpful when teaching students with visual, auditory, or kinesthetic preferences.

Visual learners. These students learn best by watching and imitating others. The following guidelines are helpful when teaching visual learners.

- Ski well-executed demonstrations that illustrate the point. Be careful not to exaggerate and destroy the picture of good skiing.
- Target the students' attention to a certain part of your body or to particular movements. Guide their viewing.
- Let students view demonstrations from different angles (front,

back, side). Provide stationary images or skiing images while students follow.

- Use video of the students' skiing as well as video of model skiing. Allow visual learners to make their own comparisons and visual connections.

Auditory learners. These students rely on verbal input to process information. The following guidelines are helpful when teaching auditory learners.

- Give clear, concise descriptions

of what students should do, see, and feel in their skiing, because auditory learners are typically thinkers and very cognitive.

- Be sure to explain why things happen so students can make connections between words and actions.
- Provide time for auditory learners to repeat the information in their own words. Listen for their interpretations and check their understanding. These learners will benefit from verbalizing their ideas.
- Pace interactions with verbal learners so they do not slow down other students in the group. Use lift rides and lunch time for in-depth discussions.
- Use descriptive words to paint accurate pictures of skiing movements. Let the students choose their own descriptive words, and be sure to mirror their choice of language.

Kinesthetic learners. These students learn best by feeling external sensations, such as feeling pressure of the shin against the front of the boot. (Note: All students can benefit from an awareness of what skiing feels like when it is done well. Repetitions of these sensations create learned movement patterns.) The following guidelines are helpful when teaching kinesthetic learners.

- Check the students' ski equipment for proper fit, adjustment, etc.
- Let students describe what they feel in their skiing. Be sure to mirror the choice of language they use to describe movement or sensations.

- Help students feel certain things by touching them in appropriate places. Ask permission first, and then move their bodies to help them feel something specific, such as the sensation of bending at the knees versus the hips.
- Demonstrate and describe what students should feel.
- Introduce new skills or movements on groomed terrain. If the terrain is too challenging, kinesthetic learners may become preoccupied with the sensations related to the slope rather than the task at hand.

Teaching Styles

Just as students have learning preferences, you, too, have preferences in terms of the teaching styles you call upon throughout the lesson to enhance group movement and learning. The style you choose will vary, according to class size, your students' ability level, their personalities, or just the need for variety. The teaching styles discussed here consist of the following.
- Command
- Task
- Reciprocal
- Guided discovery
- Problem-solving

When introducing a new movement or skill, you may want to use the **command style** of teaching, meaning that you are the main focus of the group while explaining and demonstrating the skill to students for the first time.

Once the students understand the skill and have tried it a few times, you might switch to the

task style of teaching. In task style, you step back and watch the students performing the activity. You are free to provide feedback and make sure the students are performing the task correctly.

The **reciprocal style** of teaching refers to pairing students up, with one student as the performer and one as the observer. This is a good class-handling technique if the students are proficient in a particular skill and you want to add depth to their understanding. Reciprocal style is a great way to encourage student interaction, however, you must carefully monitor them to make sure they are practicing skills or movements correctly. Reciprocal teaching is not a good way to present new learning because students need a baseline of knowledge before they can teach each other.

To present information in a reciprocal style, arrange students in pairs and give them tangible and specific skills or activities on which to focus. If the focus is too obscure, the exercise will not be successful. (Topics such as "pressure control" would probably be too general for students to grasp. Sub-topics of pressure control, such as "weight transfer" or "flexion and extension" are more specific.) Then give the team a task to evaluate and a prescribed area in which to ski.

You might introduce a reciprocal teaching segment as follows. "Number one, your job is to show skier number two exactly where you transfer your weight in the turn. Skier number two, your job is to watch skier number one and determine if the weight transfer is at the beginning, middle, or end of the turn. Be sure to stop and talk about what each of you saw and felt, and then switch roles."

Basically, reciprocal teaching allows you to step back and evaluate how students are progressing as they enhance their understanding and analysis of skiing through the enjoyable process of "peer teaching."

Some topics are best presented with the **guided-discovery style** of teaching, in which you take students through a range of activities that lead them to self-revelation about a concept or skill. This teaching style can work well with a large group of beginners.

For example, you might present a wide range of balancing activities that test the students' limits in their new environment. Through guided exploration, you lead the students to the right movements: "First try leaning far forward, then far backward. Find out where the best balance point is on your skis."

Guided discovery is not an effective way to teach specific skills or to handle a group of demanding learners. It is too time-consuming and might not show results that are specific enough for this type of learner.

To use the **problem-solving style** of teaching, set up a situation and then ask students to work through a problem and report the answers. Your role is to listen to the proposed solutions without judging the merits of the solutions. This approach helps students learn how to make decisions that will help them manage the problems

they encounter while skiing. Problem solving should be used after concepts have been firmly established. You must be careful to provide enough background information so the students can solve the problem on their own.

Here is one example of how to use problem-solving with students who are working on short-radius turns. During the lesson, they have learned how to make sharper, more braking turns as well as rounded, more gliding turns. Instead of layering on more learning at the end of the day, you use a problem-solving activity to encourage lateral learning and depth of understanding.

You choose a run that has a variety of pitches from flat to steep. Some portions of the ski run are smooth, whereas others have small moguls. You group the students into two teams—one with more aggressive skiers and the other with more timid skiers. You then tell the groups their assignment is to decide which type of turn works best in the different portions of the run. During the session, you hang back and do not interfere with the students.

At the end of the run, the teams discuss their choices. Both teams agree that it is most efficient to use braking turns on the steeps and gliding turns on the flats. However, the aggressive skiers prefer to make gliding turns in the moguls, while the timid skiers prefer to make braking turns.

As this example illustrates, the freedom to make choices helps students understand their decision-making and develop confidence in their actions.

Class Handling

Class handling refers to the organization and presentation of the lesson and starts the moment you address a group of students. The logistics of class handling are discussed in the following sections: how to evaluate students through the class split, how to arrange the class physically, and how to pace the lesson.

Class-handling choices and personal teaching style can either enhance or inhibit the learning environment. What works for one group may not work for the next, hence the important of acquiring class-handling skill.

Comfort and Safety

The comfort and safety of your students should be your foremost concern when conducting a lesson, and are therefore essential aspects of class handling. Always be aware of factors that either may contribute to or detract from the learning environment. If the stopping place is a very crowded slope, students may be distracted from learning, no matter how good the lesson content. If students are freezing cold, they probably will not pay attention to lines and vectors drawn in the snow or what you are saying.

Familiarize yourself with **Your Responsibility Code** (see chapter 8, Safety Awareness). Include concepts from the code into your thinking about class handling and into your lesson. You will have to constantly make decisions that are in your students' best interests, such as whether to ski in a line or one at a time, what makes a good stopping place, and what makes a good teaching area.

The Split

One way to provide a successful learning environment for people in group lessons is to make sure they are assigned to the right group. Often called the **split**, this process entails dividing skiers into classes or groups of similar interest and abilities, with attention to students' expectations, learning preferences, and skiing ability.

Class splits are handled in various ways at different ski areas. The split process may begin at the lesson sales counter as the student is questioned, or it may begin with prospective students viewing a video showing skiers at different ability levels so students can identify their own level of skiing proficiency. The instructor then evaluates each student's skiing to make sure that person has drawn an accurate conclusion. Ideally, you should make the final determination in the split for your class.

The visual aspect of the split consists of watching students ski so you can assess them on their speed and skill level. It is important not to overanalyze skiing mechanics at this point. Some of the best group lessons involve students of varying skill levels as long as they can travel around the mountain at the same speed. For example, a student who has a strong athletic ability and an aggressive nature but who over-estimates his skill level may benefit from a class that challenges his abilities. This

student might be bored and disappointed if you place him in a less-challenging class.

If there are not enough students to justify more than one class at a skill level, you will have to place students of various abilities together and be versatile enough to work with the group. However, with enough students, you may be able to further split the class according to differences in skill level or learning preference.

Pay close attention to individual student profiles so you can help narrow down the group. Fearful or timid students generally function better when placed in a group without aggressive, over-zealous students to distract them. You can then pace the class to their learning needs. This aspect of the split allows you to structure a relatively homogeneous group right from the start.

To support your visual conclusions when conducting the split, be sure to question students about their motivations, their learning

Fig. 3.2. Line-up

preferences, and their expectations. Some students at advanced levels of skiing may want a more experiential day—one with a lot of skiing, very little talking, and plenty of challenge. Other students may want a more structured learning environment—a lot of exercises, explanations, and feedback. If there are enough students of both types to warrant two classes, split the students into groups that will complement their skiing abilities and their expectations.

Class Arrangement

Formats for the physical arrangement of classes vary from lines to circles, and each one has merit, depending on the situation. The following are some sample **class arrangements**.

Line-up (fig. 3.2). In this formation, the students stand next to each other in a row and face you. This is a relatively formal arrangement that is best used in preliminary instruction. You can then organize the class on a more informal basis as the lesson develops.

Semicircular (fig. 3.3). In this formation, students form a semicircle around you. This formation allows for better visual contact and a slightly less formal arrangement than the line-up. An advantage to the semicircular arrangement is that students feel they are closer to one another.

Circle around the instructor (fig. 3.4). This formation, best used with a beginning class, consists of students forming a complete circle around you. This allows you to be close enough to each student to

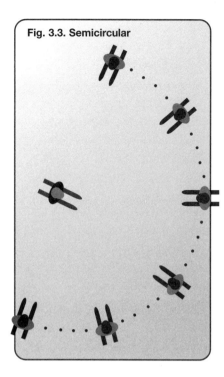

Fig. 3.3. Semicircular

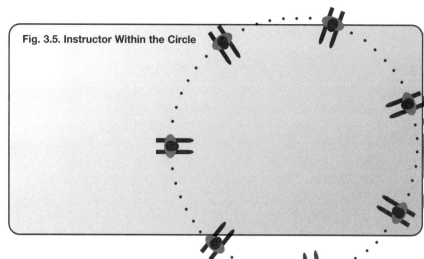

Fig. 3.5. Instructor Within the Circle

offer assistance and to be observed by all the students.

Instructor within the circle (fig. 3.5). In this formation, you join the class members in the circle. This helps establish a sense of similarity between you and the students. This class structure encourages students to feel less intimidated and to be more comfortable communicating.

Huddling up (fig. 3.6). This is the least structured-looking class formation. When students gather around you in a huddle, it is an indication that the general integrity of the class is good. The huddle works well when reinforcing student performance, drawing the class together as a unit, and getting students excited about the skiing they are doing.

Follow me (fig. 3.7). In this formation, the students ski behind the instructor. Instructors often use this technique when moving their class from one place to another. Follow me can be very effective when establishing the

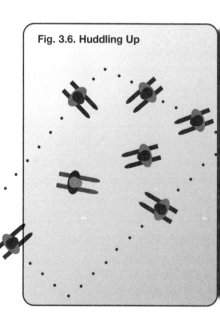

Fig. 3.6. Huddling Up

path of descent, when the terrain is hazardous, when students need to control speed, when the path of descent over particular terrain can enhance the learning process, and when following you can help to ingrain a particular movement pattern.

The follow-me formation may not work well when students are learning a new skill, when traffic is dense, when students need to make decisions, or in very challenging

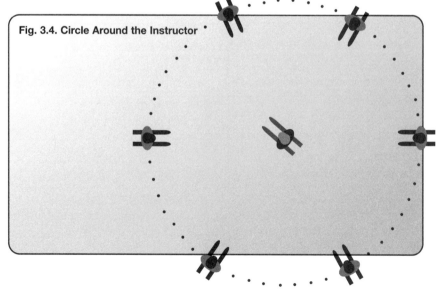

Fig. 3.4. Circle Around the Instructor

Fig. 3.7. Follow Me

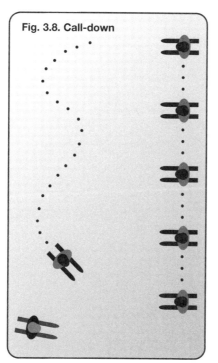

Fig. 3.8. Call-down

students. They encourage interaction and active participation in the learning process. After determining a focus, the class breaks up into smaller practice groups. Students help each other, and you move from group to group, helping as needed and listening for cues about the students' needs.

Demonstration (fig. 3.11). Instilling a good image of a task is critical to teaching. As the instructor, you need to reinforce the desirable skiing image over and over again, and you do so by demonstrating almost constantly. The focus of demonstrations changes to highlight specific elements as students' development dictates.

terrain. The decision to use this approach should be based on the terrain, conditions, and needs of the students, and it should not be overused when alternative patterns are available.

Call-down (fig. 3.8). In this formation, you have students ski down to you one at a time. This format is a popular way to observe and critique individual skiers. It works well when class members support one another and are not worried about falling or making mistakes. Call-down is best used as an assessment tool and should not be overused.

Free practice (fig. 3.9): This is another viable working format if you have established good control over the class. In free practice, after you and the students have determined the focus, the group works without further direction from you. The class reconvenes at a pre-determined landmark after

they have had some practice time. If a short lift is available, you may position yourself on the hill and have students practice and ski on their own while you observe, give encouragement, and hold mini-lessons for those who need input.

Micro-teaching and peer input (fig. 3.10). These are effective practices to use with experienced

You may be quite proficient at teaching students in any of these formations, but your class-handling skill will be tested whenever you work with a group of students who have different levels of skill, speed, and endurance. Therefore, you will need to be creative and willing to try any of these formations during the lesson.

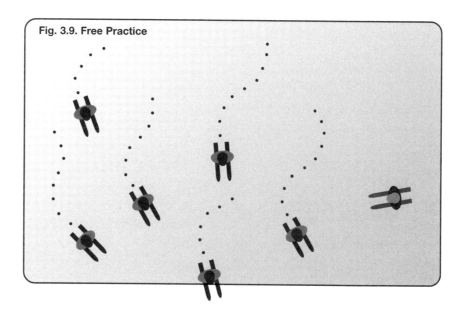

Fig. 3.9. Free Practice

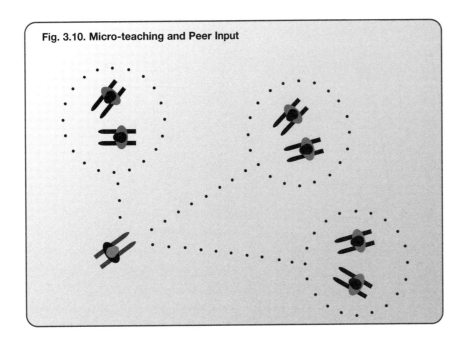

Fig. 3.10. Micro-teaching and Peer Input

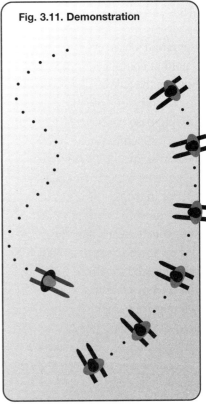

Fig. 3.11. Demonstration

With students who ski at variable speeds, for instance, it may seem as if the only solution is to pace the lesson for the slowest person in the class. Instead, you might provide activities that target the fastest skiers (such as follow me) while having the slower skiers take a rest or a practice run to give them a short break (free practice). Or, team up fast students with slow students and have them learn from each other (micro-teaching and peer input).

Pacing

To keep students interested and motivated in the learning process, you will need to pace information appropriately with respect to the students' changing energy levels.

Pacing involves orchestrating appropriate amounts of focused skill development, practice, free skiing, and application of skills on new or harder terrain. This variety will help you anchor learning much more effectively than if you have students work only on acquiring new skills all day.

Students display many different behaviors that provide clues about how to pace the lesson and which activities to present. Signs of restlessness such as pole tapping, shuffling feet, and looking around at passing skiers may indicate that it is time to get the group moving. In contrast, a marked drop in performance, more falls than usual, or a noticeable lack of concentration may signal that the group is getting tired.

Most people have a regular energy flow that roughly corresponds to the timing of meals. Typically, students warm up in the morning, reach their peak around mid-morning, and start losing their energy a bit before lunch.

After lunch, the group may be slow to warm up as their food is digested, have an energy peak at mid-afternoon, and an energy drop-off again at the end of the day.

Hence, it is best not to have students ski the hardest run at the end of the day.

Being aware of your group's energy flow will help you know when to push students and when to back off. You can elicit amazing performance results in your students if you pace their lessons in an appropriate manner.

Psychological Factors Affecting Learning

There are four psychological factors that impact ski lessons in particular and skiing in general: (1) motivation, (2) confidence, (3) intensity, and (4) focus. These four factors can be thought of in the context of a pyramid, with motivation as the wide base upon which the other skills are built (fig. 3.12).

Motivation

A pyramid's base is its most important component because it supports the entire structure. So, too, is motivation the critical, underlying base of learning to ski—without it, confidence, intensity, and focus have no foundation.

Students who are motivated will put in the time and effort to get the most out of their lesson time, which means they will be well prepared to ski their best. The well-prepared student is more likely to have confidence about skiing well under a variety of conditions. Intensity does not turn into anxiety and fear, and the student is able to stay relaxed even when challenged. This attitude helps the student stay focused on skiing well rather than be distracted by negative or irrelevant variables.

Motivation is the desire to initiate and persist at a task. Applied to skiing, motivation means having the interest to take up the sport and the desire to continue to ski and improve. This is motivation that comes from within (intrinsic motivation). As the instructor, you can influence the student's motivation by identifying, reinforcing, and expanding his or her desire to ski and improve. Your influence is defined as outside motivation (extrinsic motivation).

When students lack motivation they often display low energy, put forth little effort, give up easily, are inattentive toward your feedback, and remain generally uninvolved in the lesson. Try to be sensitive to these and other signs of a loss of motivation, and use this information to alter the lesson plan accordingly.

You can reinforce the student's desire to improve during a lesson by motivating that person in the following ways.
- *Act as a role model.* If you model desire and enthusiasm for skiing, students are more likely to be motivated similarly.
- *Provide fun.* One of the most common remarks from motivated students is that they enjoyed themselves in their lesson.
- *Set goals.* The types of goals that students have coming into a lesson can dictate the kind of lesson experience they will have. If student goals are realistic, you can help refine them or describe how they will be achieved. If the goals are unrealistic, you can help students create attainable ones. As a result, students will view the lesson positively and will want to have another lesson in the future.

Confidence

Second to motivation, confidence is the most important psychological factor in skiing. **Confidence** is how strongly skiers believe in their ability to learn or execute a particular technique.

Here are some ways to encourage confidence in students.
- *Act as a role model.* As with motivation, you can be a powerful role model of confidence. If you are positive and confident about yourself and your students, the students are also more likely to believe that they can ski well. Refrain from making negative

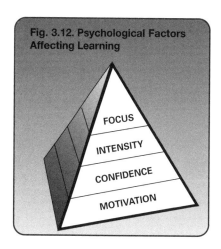

Fig. 3.12. Psychological Factors Affecting Learning

FOCUS

INTENSITY

CONFIDENCE

MOTIVATION

statements to students, and try to be as supportive as possible.
- *Help students be successful.* You can structure positive experiences that will help students feel successful for the majority of the lesson. Failure—whether real or perceived—is the quickest way to defeat confidence. To help students experience success you must understand their physical, technical, and mental capabilities so you can challenge them with the lesson and ensure a significant number of successes.

Intensity

Intensity refers to states of mental arousal from very low (e.g., sleep) to very high (e.g., terror). To ski well, you must have a correct level of intensity—too much or too little will impair skiing performance.

Skiers with too little intensity have low energy, feel lethargic, and have difficulty narrowing their focus. Under-intensity in skiing is rare because of the ongoing need for skiers to be alert to the challenge of the slopes.

More common among skiers is over-intensity, typically labeled as anxiety, nervousness, or fear. Here are some of the causes of over-intensity and some steps you can take to help manage it.

Extreme thinking. Some students imagine catastrophic events that might happen to them if they attempt to ski. Students with low confidence may come to a new trail that is moderately steep and regard it as if it were a cliff—if they try to ski on it, they will fall off and get seriously hurt.

You can monitor extreme thinking in much the same way as you would negative thinking. If you hear an extreme reaction, do not let it pass or laugh it off. Instead, examine why students have these unrealistic thoughts, provide some realistic perspective about the thinking, defuse the extreme thinking with accurate information (e.g., "there is a skier on the trail and she is not falling off"), and encourage students to be more realistic and positive.

Unfamiliarity. Some people have a hard time establishing positive expectations and predicting realistic outcomes when they are in unfamiliar situations. For example, at a first encounter with a relatively challenging mogul run, students may not expect to ski well—they will likely expect to ski poorly and fall.

You can head off this reaction by providing regular and detailed information about what lies ahead in the lesson and by assuring the group that the new demands are not really new; rather, they are a natural progression from what the students have been working on.

Feeling out-of-control. Students

may *feel* out of control because they are learning a new skill, or they may actually *be* out of control on their skis. By providing them with better skills for controlling their skis, they will gain more control, and these feelings should subside.

Information overload. During their first ski lesson, students may feel overwhelmed as they try to process and integrate information while contending with the new terrain and snow conditions. Remember, it is always better to give too little information at first, then more as needed, rather than present too much information and too many demands all at once.

Although you usually can have a positive effect on how your students react to new or challenging situations, it is valuable to teach students how to reduce the negative effects of over-intensity on their own. Here are some useful techniques to share with them.

Deep breathing. Have students manage their breathing in a calm, controlled manner, which will relieve many of the symptoms of over-intensity, including muscle tension, shaking, and loss of coordination.

Active muscle relaxation. Skiers tend to accumulate tension in different parts of the body, mainly the legs and shoulders, which can clearly inhibit performance. Active relaxation is a great way to relieve tension before a run. (And, you can teach it to them on the lift ride, making this time a useful part of the lesson plan.)

Ask students to notice where

they feel tension. Have them tense those muscles for five seconds, relax, then take a slow, deep breath. Repeat the exercise as needed, following the same procedure for each tense muscle group. During these exercises, say "tight" just before the students tense their muscles and "loose" before they relax. This encourages students to condition their bodies to these key words so that when they feel over-intensity, the students themselves can say "loose" and the word will inspire an automatic relaxation.

Relaxing and smiling. You can help set students at ease by smiling often and keeping the tone of the lesson light and fun. Encourage your students to smile frequently. Smiling causes the brain to release neurochemicals that have a relaxing effect.

Despite your best attempts to identify the causes of over-intensity and prevent this anxiety from occurring, most students will nonetheless experience this feeling from time to time. Always try to acknowledge, respect, and respond positively to what they are feeling. Never belittle or dismiss their fears, regardless of how irrelevant or irrational these feelings may seem to you. Avoid making statements such as "Relax, there is nothing to worry about," which is not only ineffective but may sound disrespectful.

Fear is not imaginary—it *is* real. If you take the time to help students defuse it, you will help them overcome a major barrier to learning and enjoyment.

Focus

Students must be able to focus so they can be aware of internal (e.g., thoughts and feelings) and external (e.g., sights and sounds) aspects of the environment. Good focus should feel natural, effortless, and flexible. Students should be able to focus on the instructor at times and on their skiing at other times.

Good focus occurs when students concentrate only on those things that enable them to ski their best, such as technique, terrain, or snow conditions. Also, it means focusing on the present, not on what happened during the last run or what will occur on the next run.

You can help your students focus by not letting them become distracted by anything that might interfere with or be irrelevant to their performance. Common barriers to focus include the following.

- *Distraction by external cues* (e.g., difficult snow conditions)
- *Distraction by internal cues* (e.g., negative thoughts and over-intensity)
- *Distraction by making mistakes* (e.g., falling and losing control)
- *Lack of attention* (e.g., simply forgetting the technical feedback you have given them)

As an example of focus, just before taking a run, students are focused on your feedback. But as soon as they begin the run, their focus shifts to distracting cues. Suddenly, there are more important things to think about: staying in control, not falling, and avoiding injury. Here are some ways to help students stay focused.

Use key word progressions. Key words are simple yet highly descriptive words that remind students to focus on the instruction (e.g., "forward," for keeping weight forward, or "press," for pressure on the outside ski).

The first step of the technical key word progression is called **cueing**, which involves repeating the keyword out loud for the students as they ski. That way, students do not have to focus on what you said previously because you provide it for them constantly. The students can simply practice the technique.

The second step of the progression is for students to say the key word out loud as they ski. This prompts them to focus on the instruction and helps them more easily block out interference.

The third step is to have students repeat the keyword silently. Eventually they will need less focus to remember to do the technique. Students know they have learned the skill when they can execute it without using the key word. If they become distracted, they can use it again to regain focus.

Use a key object reminder. Another way to improve focus is to use a key object rather than a key word during a run. For example, students can plan their route through a mogul field, then focus on that or on squeezing their pole grips at the start of each turn to remind them to make a good pole touch.

Encourage deep breathing. Suggest that the students concentrate on their breathing for awhile to give themselves a break from

information overload or from focusing on a skiing technique. This is a great way to relax, particularly since skiing requires such intense mental and physical effort. It also counteracts the tendency to hold one's breath or breathe shallowly, which are common reactions to stress.

Skiing Imagery

Skiing imagery, which means repeatedly imagining a good skiing performance, is one of the most powerful tools you have at your disposal as an instructor, because it involves both the mental and the physical aspects of skiing.

With skiing imagery, you mentally reproduce an actual skiing performance, calling upon the visual, auditory, and muscular sensations related to your movement. At the deepest levels of concentrating, you can fool your body into thinking that you are actually skiing.

During the lesson, you can incorporate skiing imagery in the following situations.

At the top of a run. After providing students with feedback, ask them to close their eyes and rehearse how they want to ski just before their run. Have them focus their imagery on the technical or mental cues that you want them to work on. Tell them to put themselves in a balanced body position with their hands forward and to move their bodies just as if they were skiing.

Combining the imagined sensations with the actual physical sensations generated while moving in place will enhance the value of ski imagery. Skiing imagery at the top of a run has several benefits. It encourages students to be aware of the sensations of skiing; it narrows their focus; and it gives students a positive and successful image to begin their run—all of which can improve their confidence and reduce their over-intensity.

At the end of a run. If students have just had a great run, the most important thing you can do is to help them remember it. If they repeat the run with skiing imagery, they are more likely to retain these images for the next run.

In contrast, if students just had a poor run, the most important thing you can do is to help them *erase* that imagery. This entails having students "edit" the run and imagine themselves skiing well, which will allow them to purge bad feelings from their minds and muscles and replace them with positive feelings and images.

On the lift. Again, you can always make good use of lift time by encouraging skiing imagery. Remind students of what they are working on, and have them close their eyes and imagine how they want to ski the next run. If the students' feet are dangling off the chair, they can move them with their imagery to experience that combination of imagined and real physical sensations.

One concern skiers often express when they start using skiing imagery is that they keep making mistakes in their head. Reassure your students that this is normal and will decrease with time.

To help students have only positive images, share this analogy with them: Tell them that when they make a mistake in their imagery, they can rewind the "video," and "edit" it with good skiing. If they have trouble editing their imagery when they imagine themselves skiing at full speed, they can slow the video down. Then, as students are able to imagine themselves skiing well in slow motion, they can progressively speed up the video to normal speed.

Skiing imagery is a skill that students can develop with time. Many students initially indicate that their images are not that clear, but let them know that with a little practice, the images will come into focus. Also, remember that the emphasis in good skiing imagery is on feeling the imagery as well as imagining it. Be sure that students concentrate on *feeling* the physical sensations when they are actually skiing.

Retaining Learning

To help students retain or anchor learning, you must (1) provide adequate practice time in the appropriate environment; (2) provide individualized feedback that is specific to the task and performance; and (3) check for understanding to make sure that students have assimilated the learning.

Practice

Whether students are beginning, intermediate, or advanced skiers, they will need plenty of time to develop new skills. Once students are comfortable with the new skill or movement, you can distribute practice time at intervals throughout the day.

Practice time can provide students with lateral learning opportunities in which they take new skills into new situations. Too often students venture onto tough terrain after the lesson and forget everything they have learned because their experience has been limited to a perfectly groomed slope.

Initiate learning on non-challenging terrain, but eventually allow students to practice new skills in situations and conditions they will encounter on the mountain. After introducing a new skill or movement, set up practice situations that will help students anchor learning and allow you to closely monitor practice time.

It is important to provide feedback and reinforcement to make sure the students are performing the new skill or movement correctly. In this way, you are controlling the learning environment and guiding the students every step of the way.

When students have learned a new skill or movement, they should first practice the maneuver on smooth, groomed terrain so they can focus on what has been introduced without being distracted by the challenges of the slope. Many repetitions in this neutral environment are important—do not make the mistake of destroying the learning progress by moving the group to a new skill or to challenging terrain too quickly.

Beginning students usually are allowed ample practice time, and you would do well to promote a similar atmosphere of patience with all students. For example, beginners learn to make wedge and wedge-christie turns in the low-pressure, practice environment of the beginner's slope. When it is time to venture onto the green slopes of the mountain, they take their existing skills and apply them to this new situation. It is not necessary to layer any new skills on top of what they have learned. The instructor simply allows practice time in a new environment and provides feedback about the student's application of the newly learned skill.

Similarly, even advanced skiers need smooth terrain to learn new movements before applying them to challenging situations. Many slalom racers or bump skiers perfect their short-turn techniques on groomed snow. This allows their movement patterns, timing, and reactions to become automatic. Once advanced skiers are comfortable with a particular skill or movement pattern, however, they can then apply it to a variety of situations. The challenge then becomes *where* to ski rather than *how* to ski.

Relating Practice to Ability

You will need to vary the intensity of your students' practice based on their ability level. To determine the practice content, identify which of the three stages of learning your students are in: the verbal-cognitive stage; the motor stage; or the autonomous stage.

The **verbal-cognitive stage** is characterized by talking, thinking, and acquiring simple skills. When working with students at this stage, try to stem practice from the relatively simple movements they are learning, guiding students to perform a roughly correct version of them. Seek to make instruction and demonstrations easy, and use interesting motivational techniques. At this stage, it is often enough to simply demonstrate a skill and say "do this." Explanation can be used to fine-tune skill, and frequent feedback about knowledge and performance in skiing is beneficial.

Students in the next stage of learning, the **motor stage,** are learning to improve their movement patterns. Strategies that lead to long-term retention of learning are paramount. Mental training is a highly effective method of learning at this stage. This consists of imagining successful action, as in skiing imagery. It is also helpful to show students how to detect movement errors on their own, which will be useful to them in their free-skiing time.

At this level, feedback is still effective but should occur less frequently than in the verbal-cognitive stage. Too much feedback can encourage over-dependence on you. As with the verbal stage, you should encourage fundamental movement patterns. Variable practice, that is, practicing a skill with many different variations, is recommended (e.g., when students practice a single skill on various types of terrain).

The **autonomous stage,** or advanced stage, of learning refers to information processing and the subsequent **automaticity** of action, that is, the state in which the skier processes a great deal of complex information quickly and effortlessly, and automatically delivers the appropriate response.

Skiers at the autonomous stage exhibit well-developed movement patterns, and higher-level performance is the focus. Practice should include both physical and mental skills and is geared toward developing automaticity. When automaticity develops, skiing is "internalized," meaning that correct responses are generated subconsciously. This lends mastery and increased freedom for the skier to perform consistently at that level—this is how experts make skiing look easy.

Automaticity will develop relatively slowly, with great investment of practice. It has been estimated that a person can develop automaticity of a task only after at least 300 trials of that task under favorable conditions.

Feedback

One of the most effective ways to anchor your students' learning is to provide consistent, positive feedback and reinforcement, and to provide it at the proper place and time.

When students are given a task to perform, they typically ski with only that in mind. Be sure to always limit your feedback to the task at hand. Otherwise you will confuse the students by giving them too many things to think about, and risk tempering their feelings of accomplishment by giving them a negative "yes, but..." comment.

For example, if you ask the students to ski to a stopping point and focus on flexion and extension movements, be sure to follow up with feedback relevant to the task. Never say, "Nice flexion and extension, but your pole timing was way off." This "yes, but..." comment only detracts from the original focus and feedback.

Be careful not to dispense general or "global" feedback in group lessons, such as: "Some of us aren't using the pole properly. Let's try it again." This kind of feedback makes every student wonder if he or she performed the task correctly.

Specific, individualized feedback would consist of: "Mary and Ted, that was exactly right. John, try planting the pole a little bit softer next time. You were stabbing the snow so hard it made your arm jerk! Fred, why don't you follow me and try to swing your pole in the rhythm of my turn? Your timing was a little bit off. Okay, everyone, let's try it again!"

Individualized feedback must be sensitive and focused. If you have developed true partnership with students, then it should be easy to provide them with honest, individual feedback.

If there is no partnership and rapport, then students might view feedback as an attack. Rather than single out a student as an uncoordinated skier, provide sensitive and diplomatic feedback to guide performance toward success.

Finally, students know when they have a good run and a bad

run, and you should not insult their intelligence by saying "that's good" when performance is poor. Insincere praise will only take away from the power of positive feedback when it is deserved.

Honestly acknowledge when a student makes errors and provide feedback to help improve performance. Comments should be sincere and constructive, for example: "George, you didn't look as though you were able to concentrate on that turn. There were just too many people on the slope when you took off. I think you have a clear spot now. Why don't you try it again? Remember, keep your upper body facing down the hill."

Trust and shared responsibility for the learning process in a lesson will allow your students to be more accepting of your feedback. Once your students believe that you care about their learning experience, they will accept your feedback and try harder to make the changes you request.

Giving Feedback

Here are some specific guidelines to providing feedback.

1. *Target the behavior.* Be careful not to confuse the behavior with the person.
2. *Be specific.* Try not to obscure feedback by adding on general feedback unrelated to what is being learned at the time.
3. *Target behavior the student can change.* If the goal is unattainable, then feedback will be irrelevant. Work on realistic goals, and give feedback on progress and success.

4. *Use "I" statements and opinions.* Take responsibility for the feedback, in other words, your feedback is your opinion.

   A statement starting with "I noticed..." is more objective than one starting with "You did..."
5. *Provide a reason for the feedback.* Let the student know why the feedback is important to his or her progress.
6. *Do not belabor points.* If the student does not understand your observations, change your presentation.
7. *Offer incentives.* Make sure the student understands the rewards in store after the change in behavior. Emphasize that the effort will pay off eventually.
8. *Beware of eliciting strong emotions.* If the student rejects your suggestion or displays hostility, try a different approach and show sensitivity to the students' concerns.
9. *Show empathy.* Let the student know that you realize how hard it can be to change behavior. Offer support.
10. *Wait for the appropriate time.* Give feedback when the student is likely to be receptive to it. Ideas will not be well-received by a student who is too tired, cold, or frustrated to hear them—wait for a better time.
11. *Recognize any change in behavior.* Reward changes immediately. Reinforce the new patterns and provide opportunity to anchor the new behavior.

Checking for Understanding

You must check for understanding continually to determine whether students have anchored their learning and to ensure that the lesson is creating the intended results. This process will help you decide whether to change the pace or your presentation style to keep students motivated and involved.

You can check for understanding by looking at students' progress, asking for information, listening to them describe what they are doing, and providing periodic recaps of the lesson material.

If a student is having trouble learning a new skill, there are a number of ways to handle the problem. You can change how you present information to find out if using a different teaching style geared to a different learning preference will help. You also can cycle back through the Teaching Model to determine whether the goal needs to be changed. As a last resort, you can ask the student if there is a problem that is inhibiting the learning. Students need to take some of the responsibility for learning—it is not always your fault if they do not understand the concepts or skills.

Encourage students to describe their experiences and interpretations, which will allow you to check the students' understanding and gauge success. What students say may surprise you. Revisit key points of a lesson throughout the day to help students keep the purpose and results of every activity clear in their minds.

Closure

Closure is a necessary element of a successful lesson that happens throughout each phase of the lesson—not only at the end of the day. Bringing closure to every learning activity helps anchor learning, even if the closure consists of only a brief wrap-up after an activity. It is a great way to check for understanding and "clean the slate" for the next activity or learning segment.

The end-of-day closure involves more than just finishing the lesson. This is the time to review and summarize the original goal of the lesson and how the students worked toward the goal. Always encourage students to share their thoughts and feelings about the activities they explored along the way. By verbalizing their perceptions of the high and low points of the day, students help anchor their learning.

Closure for the whole lesson has a few more elements than closure for an activity learning segment. End-of-day closure is a time to provide "homework" and guide students in their independent practice. You can give students tips about how to work on skiing (without your constant input and suggestions) in ways that refer the students back to the lesson.

For example, you could say "Mary, you made some great progress toward parallel skiing today. If you're out on your own tomorrow, be sure to practice skiing with a little more speed when the slopes are smooth and flat. That's where you had a real breakthrough in your skiing today. When the terrain gets harder, don't feel bad if the wedge christie returns. Just keep gaining confidence on the easier slopes, and that will transfer to the harder slopes later on."

You can "soft-sell" students into another lesson during closure, also. Once the lesson has been summarized, students will need guidance for their next step in the learning process. Students do not need to be pushed into another day of lessons. Just giving them a taste of the fun adventures that will take place in the next lesson can be enough to bring them back.

Here is an example of how to soft-sell another lesson: "We really got that parallel turn off to a good start today. At your next lesson you'll be ready to continue to practice the parallel turn on smooth slopes and start to learn how to change it and apply it to different situations on the mountain." You can personally invite students back for another lesson without pressuring them into something they might not want to do. Most people react favorably to suggestions and invitations.

Not all students need another lesson right away, and you should guide the student's next lesson purchase with honest feedback. For example, you might tell a student who skis intermediate terrain adequately: "John, it's great you're going to spend a few days practicing and then skiing with your family. I hope you have a really good time. Maybe when you return next season, you should try a lesson in the bumps. You're ready to get out there and start pushing yourself in some harder terrain. I think a specialty lesson would be just perfect! Here's my card. Give me a call when you come back and I'll help you find just the right class."

Closure is a process that works best when students can give complete focus to the events of the day without distractions. Many instructors make the mistake of trying to bring closure to a lesson at the bottom of the hill on the last run. At this point, most students already have their mind on other things, such as picking up their children or getting to the parking lot.

It is best to start bringing the lesson to a close one or two runs before reaching the bottom. You might stop at the top of one run and review the goal of the day. Then, after the class skis for a distance, you could spend the next rest-stop reviewing the activities and listening to students' experiences. At the top of the next and last run, you could give individual "homework," and at a stop toward the bottom of the hill, soft-sell the students on their next lesson purchase. By the time the group reaches the bottom, they need only share their goodbyes.

One of the most important benefits, to you, of summarizing the lesson is that it can help you gain insight into your teaching skills, based on what students say. It is better to get feedback from the students than to make assumptions about the success of a lesson. You may have felt one activity went well, only to learn that many of the students had trouble with it or did not understand what they were supposed to do.

By allowing students to honestly share their insights about the lesson, you can hear the students' perceptions about their triumphs and mistakes. This candid dialogue can provide you with important clues on how to strengthen your teaching approach so you can structure fun, successful lessons for ski area guests.

The Skiing Model

criteria. Fundamental to the PSIA instructional approach, the Skiing Model addresses the technical and mechanical aspects of skiing.

The following overview of the Skiing Model will prepare you for a more specific look at its individual components later in this chapter. Remember that your own approach to teaching is tempered by your style and personality as well as by student needs. Regardless of your approach, however, you can organize your teaching by basing it on the proven, timeless elements of PSIA's Skiing Model.

The Skiing Model is made up of the following components:

- The four fundamental skills of skiing—balancing, rotary, edge-control, and pressure-control movements.

- Common features of the fundamental skills at all levels.
- The Center Line, a model for appropriate movement patterns for a variety of circumstances. (The model consists of four reference maneuvers—wedge, wedge-christie, parallel, and dynamic-parallel turns.)
- Progressions, those sequences of skiing movements oriented toward educational objectives or goals, connecting from least complicated to more difficult.

PSIA instructors refer to the components of the Skiing Model to identify the proficiency level of skiers as they progress through the phases of beginning, intermediate, and advanced skiing (levels 1 through 9). Further, by comparing

As you are sure to know (or will soon discover), much is required of you as a ski teacher. Not only must you understand all the nuances of proficient skiing, but you must be able to describe them to others. You must have the ability to assess student levels and skiing development clearly and quickly, and you must conduct the multifaceted process of effective lesson planning time and again.

Further, you must continually develop and refine your own skiing skills so you can provide an example of proficient skiing and relay your own perspectives to the students you teach.

The Skiing Model—one of the three main components of the American Teaching System—is designed to help you meet these

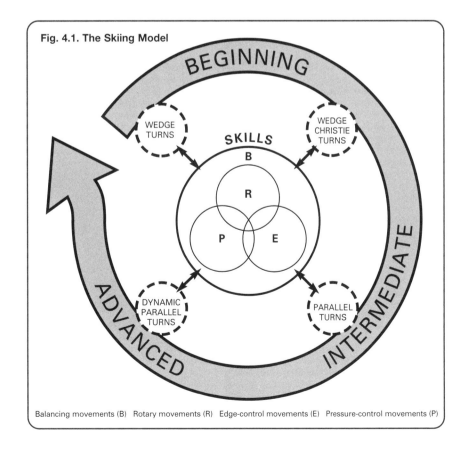

Fig. 4.1. The Skiing Model

Balancing movements (B) Rotary movements (R) Edge-control movements (E) Pressure-control movements (P)

the elements of the Skiing Model with what you observe in a student's skiing, you can determine how to go about helping the student improve his or her skills.

Figure 4.1 represents the concept that students develop the skills to perform various types of turns corresponding to the beginning, intermediate, or advanced phases of skiing. As the instructor, you guide this process by taking students through a series of **progressions**, moving from easier to more difficult performance.

As the figure shows, the Skiing Model's core consists of four **fundamental skills** that are common to all skiing: balancing movements, rotary movements, edge-control movements, and pressure-control movements. The double-headed arrows between the fundamental skills and the Center Line turns represent the dual functions of understanding and improving movement.

When students perform turns, you evaluate them based on the four core skills. If you identify a skill focus that can enhance the student's skiing (i.e., improved edge sensitivity), you can have the student concentrate on this area. The four **Center Line reference maneuvers**—wedge, wedge-christie, parallel, and dynamic-parallel turns—radiate from the central skills core.

Note: As you read through this chapter, you may find some unfamiliar ski terminology and movement principles. Please refer to the appropriate section of this chapter or the glossary for explanation about concepts that are new to you.

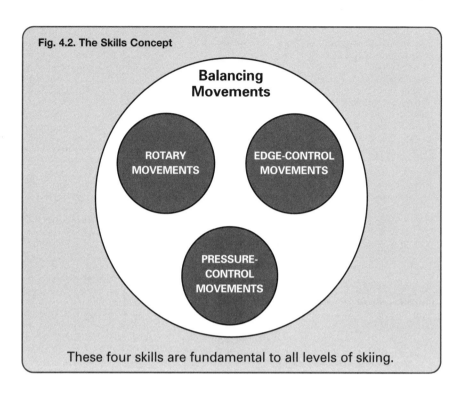

Fig. 4.2. The Skills Concept

Balancing Movements

ROTARY MOVEMENTS

EDGE-CONTROL MOVEMENTS

PRESSURE-CONTROL MOVEMENTS

These four skills are fundamental to all levels of skiing.

Ski instructors use terms in a variety of ways, so always state what you mean by a term and ask others to do the same. This text emphasizes the primary, current usages for terms; however, in some cases less-preferred or older usages are noted. Always remember that while the use of ski terminology is an effective way to communicate with other instructors, you may need to translate these terms in a non-technical way for students.

The Skills Concept

A **skill** is the ability to bring about results with maximum certainty, minimum energy, or minimum time. A skill is also a specific movement sequence to accompany a given task or group of tasks.

Golfing, swimming, playing soccer, and skiing all require component skills that can be isolated, analyzed, and developed in order to produce an overall performance. Your job as a ski instructor or coach is to recognize which skiing skills need improvement and understand how to create situations in which skiers can learn to apply their skills in the most efficient way.

The **skills concept** consists of four fundamental skiing skills (fig. 4.2). These four areas represent broad categories within which there are many specific applications of movement. The function of the PSIA skills concept is to help you recognize the component movement patterns of skiing so you can help students adjust and integrate these patterns into a cohesive whole. Furthermore, the skills concept serves as a versatile technical tool because it helps you understand and analyze these component skills as well as identify which of them needs attention and improvement.

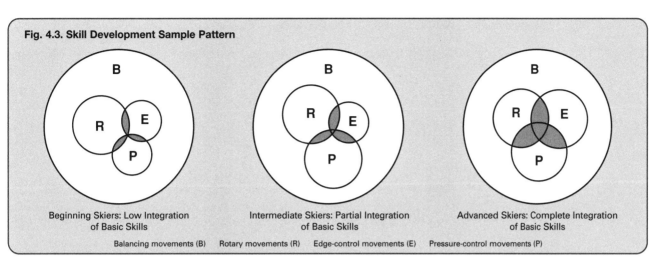

Fig. 4.3. Skill Development Sample Pattern

Beginning Skiers: Low Integration of Basic Skills

Intermediate Skiers: Partial Integration of Basic Skills

Advanced Skiers: Complete Integration of Basic Skills

Balancing movements (B)   Rotary movements (R)   Edge-control movements (E)   Pressure-control movements (P)

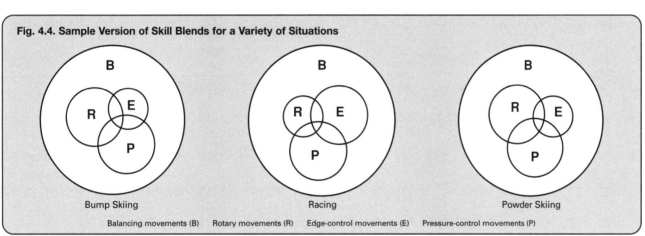

Fig. 4.4. Sample Version of Skill Blends for a Variety of Situations

Bump Skiing

Racing

Powder Skiing

Balancing movements (B)   Rotary movements (R)   Edge-control movements (E)   Pressure-control movements (P)

Skill Development

The difference between an accomplished skier and a novice skier is that the higher-level skier has fully developed skiing skills and knows how and when to call upon these skills depending on the situation. The novice skier, on the other hand, is only beginning to learn what the skills are, and has yet to learn how to link the appropriate skills effectively and seamlessly depending on internal and external variables.

Advanced skiers apply well-developed skills with different levels of intensity while they are responding to variations in terrain, conditions, or maneuvers. They can easily alter the skill blend required for bump skiing when making a transition to racing or powder skiing, for example, and they do not have to focus on the individual skills required for this activity. They respond to each situation with the appropriate movements in a fluid, subtle manner.

In contrast, most beginning skiers generate movements with indiscriminate intensity as they seek to gain a sense of comfort and control. They are likely to make exaggerated movements to achieve results on skis, with balancing movements that consist of bending at the waist, waving the arms, or assuming a wide stance. The rotary movements of novice skiers mostly involve large muscle groups, such as hip rotation or upper-body rotation. Although these movements help some people gain a sense of control on skis, they impede the controlled, graceful motions required in skiing.

Somewhere between the advanced and beginning skier is the intermediate, who is on the brink of moving to a higher proficiency level but who occasionally reverts to lower-level maneuvers when challenged.

Figure 4.3 illustrates the degree or level of a person's **skill development**, depending on whether the individual is a beginning, intermediate, or advanced skier. As the diagram shows, beginning skiers focus on the essential skills of balancing, rotary, edge-control, and pressure-control movements; intermediate skiers work on developing integration of these movements; and advanced skiers routinely blend these skills in different degrees. Similarly, figure 4.4 illustrates skill blending as applied to various situations.

It is important to realize that you may altogether frustrate a novice skier's ability to turn if you focus on helping the individual eliminate a gross movement without ensuring that he or she understands how to use a more subtle movement. It is far more effective to add to or refine a desirable movement—thereby rendering the old gross movement unnecessary —than simply to eliminate an inefficient movement.

Your goal is not only to help students develop well-rounded, basic skills but to teach them to integrate and apply their skills in different ways to enhance their overall enjoyment of the sport. This integration is an important element of the lesson and requires that you have a clear understanding of the specific mechanical movements within each of the skill categories.

Skills and Mechanics

Each of the fundamental skills can be broken down into specific movements. These movements are described here to help you understand, analyze, and evaluate what

movements skiers make, how skiers accomplish movements, and what the results are. The goal is to create a targeted lesson that addresses exactly which skills are lacking, which are well-developed, and which require further development.

1. Balancing Movements

Skiing is a sport that requires dynamic balancing movements. **Balance** in skiing refers to the movements you make to control forces and maintain desired alignment. Balance is never static or stationary while skiing—it is balance in motion. Each turn is a new adventure, and a constant adjustment of balance is required.

Balancing movements are generally divided into two categories: (1) fore/aft balance and (2) lateral (side-to-side) balance. Fore/aft balance is determined by where on your foot you feel the most pressure. A centered position, in which pressure is felt on the entire foot, is desired in most skiing situations. Accomplished skiers continually make small adjustments (balancing movements) to maintain this centered stance.

Lateral, or side-to-side, balance is affected by the width of the skier's stance, the shape and size of the turn, the speed of the turn, the snow conditions, and the skier's skill level. Lateral balance changes continually throughout the turn. To achieve balance the skier uses lateral movements, aligning the long bones of the legs with the external forces of the turn. The skier usually maintains balance by moving the center of mass toward the inside of

the turn. This would also cause the center of mass to take a shorter path than that of the skis (fig. 4.5).

The lateral movement of a World-Cup downhill racer would be greater than that shown in figure 4.5, whereas the lateral movement of someone maintaining good balance while making low-speed turns on groomed terrain would be less. Beginning skiers may obtain a secure feeling through a wide wedge, which produces a wide base of support.

It is difficult for skiers to maintain proper lateral balance if they have too narrow a stance or underdeveloped edging skills relative to the type of turns they are making. These skiers will especially notice the effect of inadequate lateral balance in icy conditions and moguls. Whether a skier is making wedge turns or skiing bumps, balancing movements ultimately affect all other skills.

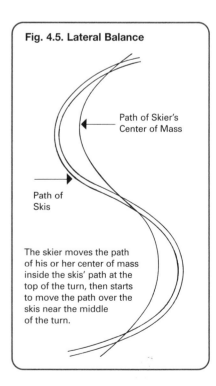

Fig. 4.5. Lateral Balance

Path of Skier's Center of Mass

Path of Skis

The skier moves the path of his or her center of mass inside the skis' path at the top of the turn, then starts to move the path over the skis near the middle of the turn.

2. Rotary Movements

All skiers use some kind of rotary movement to help them change direction. These movements increase, limit, or decrease the rotational forces on the skis. However, each skier may use quite distinct body movements to achieve a turn, and these distinctions often produce different results for different skiers.

For example, two skiers at the wedge-christie stage may be making the same kind of turn, but their rotary movements may be entirely different. One skier may start to turn by rotating the shoulders and hips while opening the skis into a wedge. This kind of rotary movement may result in late matching and excessive skidding. The other skier may stem the uphill ski into a wedge, push off the downhill ski, and match quickly. This kind of rotary movement may result in a sharp turn that goes from start to finish with no middle.

These two skiers, each making a wedge-christie turn and each using rotary movements, have a completely different outcome depending on how their bodies apply rotary movement. Instructors need to be able to clearly distinguish between different types of rotary movement in order to analyze and prescribe movement accurately.

Rotary movement should facilitate the turning capability of the ski. However, many skiers have undeveloped pressure-control and edge-control skills, and they depend upon rotary movements as a primary means of turning.

Inefficient rotary movement affects all other aspects of their skiing. Too much or too little rotary movement produces haphazard turning power, which can affect stance and balance, edging capabilities, and pressure control.

To understand these cause-and-effect relationships you must understand the primary rotary movements in skiing, described as follows.

a. *Rotation.* The use of internal or external forces to rotate all or a part of the body (fig. 4.6). Sometimes this can produce rotation of the ski directly, such as in leg rotation. Other times one part of the body begins to rotate until it hits its physiological limit, at which time that rotation is passed on to the next body segment. Upper-body rotation, produced either muscularly or by external forces (such as a pole plant), is such a rotation. In this case the upper body rotates until it is restricted by either a tightening of the muscles in the side and abdomen or by their complete extension. At that point the rotation is passed on to the hips, legs, feet, and, ultimately, the ski.

b. *Counter-rotation.* The use of muscular force to rotate one part of the body (such as the torso) in one direction and another part of the body (such as the legs) in the opposite direction (fig. 4.7). This type of movement requires that anchoring external forces (such as edged skis or a pole plant) be minimized. Hop turns without a pole plant (and without a

wind-up before hopping) are an example of a turn in which counter-rotation is evident.

c. *Blocking and anticipation.* **Blocking** is the use of internal (i.e., muscles) and external (i.e., pole plant) forces to stop rotation of the upper body. Managing large rotary movements of the upper body is a hallmark of proficient skiing.

The skier may stabilize the upper body by contracting the abdominal muscles or by planting the pole. The blocking movement of the pole plant allows the skis to travel into a twisted relationship with the body near the end of the turn (i.e., the skis continue to turn even though the upper body has been blocked from doing so).

At this point the skier is in an anticipated stance. When the edges are released, the body seeks to realign itself from the twisting (fig. 4.8). This natural realignment produces a rotary force and the turning movement is called **anticipation and release.**

d. *Rotary push-off.* The use of internal muscular force to push off the feet, which causes rotation. Hop turns about the tips of the skis require exaggerated rotary push-off. Stemming one ski and using the other ski to push from is a more subtle example (fig. 4.9).

It is important to note that skiers often use these primary rotary movements in combination, starting the turn with one movement and completing it with another.

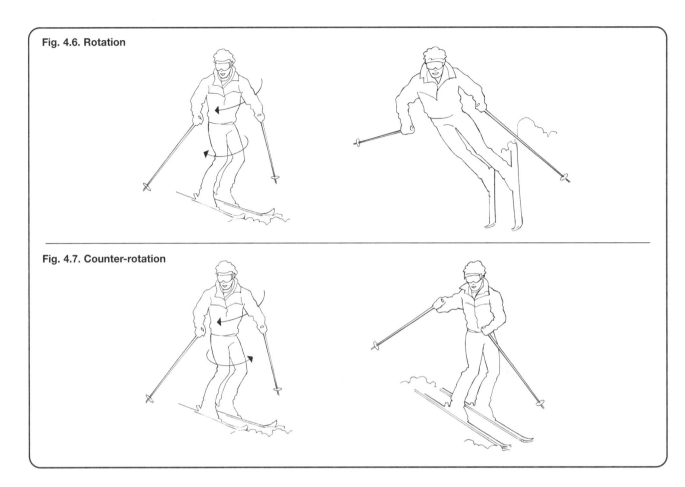

Fig. 4.6. Rotation

Fig. 4.7. Counter-rotation

Lower-level skiers may experience difficulty with turn initiation and completion, owing to crude rotary skill usage. An unskilled parallel skier may start the turn with a rotary push-off movement; however, if the push-off is done from an inadequate edge angle, the rotary movement may be insufficient to develop the turn. The skier may have to add an upper-body rotation to bring the skis around. The rotation pulls the skier onto the inside ski toward the end of the turn, creating an inefficient edge angle to shape and control the turn. The process repeats with each subsequent turn.

Note: Keep in mind that the verbiage used to describe rotary movement varies widely. Over the years, some terms have evolved new meanings, whereas others are commonly associated with several different meanings, especially those that involve parts of the body rotating in opposite directions. For example, many instructors refer to blocking as a countering, while others consider counter-rotation as countering. When discussing these concepts, it is wise to determine how an instructor or trainer uses these words in order to avoid confusion about meaning.

3. Pressure-Control Movements

The force of a skier's weight while standing on skis is distributed over the bottom of the skis as pressure. If a moving ski is on edge, applying pressure to it causes it to bend into an arc, thus causing it to turn. Therefore, the amount of pressure on the ski affects the amount to which the ski contributes to the turn.

The amount of pressure applied to the ski depends on the forces acting on the ski at the ski-snow interface. Pressure-control movements are those that affect the forces at this interface by increasing, maintaining, or releasing pressure.

As in rotary movements, the amount of pressure appropriate to a given turn depends on the terrain, snow conditions, and the skier's intention and desired outcome. A combination of skier

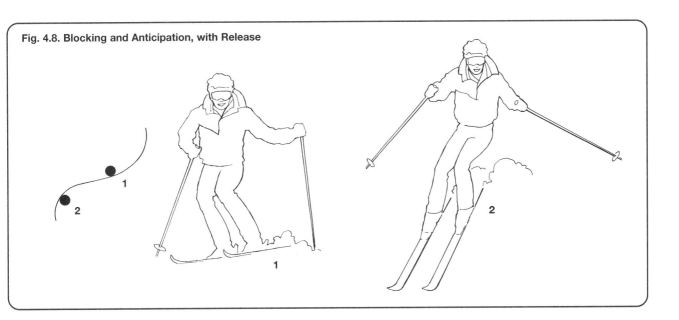

Fig. 4.8. Blocking and Anticipation, with Release

movements, ski characteristics, turn shape, and terrain and snow conditions dictates the pressure along the ski at any instant.

The primary pressure-control movements (figs. 4.10–4.12) are described as follows.

a. *Leverage*. Movement that creates pressure on the forward or the aft part of the ski. The skier can create forward pressure by moving the body over the front of the ski or by drawing the feet back under the body (fig. 4.10). Simultaneous flexion of the ankle and knee can also produce forward leverage through the front of the boot. Similarly, the skier can create pressure on the aft part of the ski by moving the body back or by moving the feet forward.

b. *Extension*. The movement of the leg from a bent position to one that is straighter (fig. 4.11). Although extension generally refers to increasing the angle between adjacent limbs, in pressure-control movements this

term normally refers to the straightening movement of the leg. As extension begins, it creates pressure on the ski, and as it is slowed, it reduces pressure on the ski.

c. *Flexion*. The movement of the leg from a relatively straight position to one that is more bent (fig. 4.11). In general, flexion refers to movements that decrease angles at a joint.

Fig. 4.9. Rotary Push-off

If flexion is performed quickly, it *reduces* pressure on the ski. Then, upon slowing or stopping, pressure *increases* on the ski. Slow flexion directed laterally increases edge angle and therefore pressure during a turn.

Note: Extension does not necessarily require that the skier move his or her body into a more upright position, nor does flexion require the skier to become more compact. Instead, one leg is often extending as the other is flexing, which produces a lateral motion of the center of mass rather than a vertical one. This creates a "long-leg, short-leg" appearance (fig. 4.12). Pressure is then transferred from the outside ski of the old turn to the outside ski of the new turn.

Extension and flexion also facilitate edge change, without which there would be no control of the direction of the pressure. The pressuring and edging movements in a ski turn are closely linked.

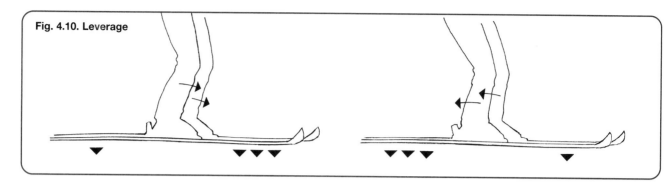

Fig. 4.10. Leverage

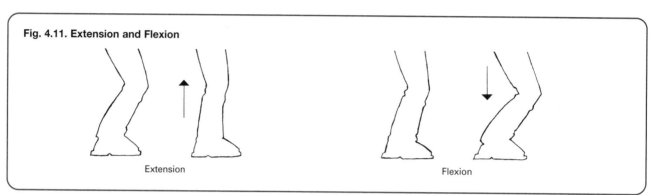

Fig. 4.11. Extension and Flexion

Extension

Flexion

4. Edge-Control Movements

As indicated in the discussion of pressure-control movements, pressure and edging are closely tied. In contrast to the notion that edges are solely for controlling speed, their purpose in modern skiing is to "bite" into the snow and ensure reliable ski-snow contact. Edging does produce forces that can slow or stop a skier, but over-reliance on these tools results in inefficient skiing. Conversely, the highly carved turn is very efficient and fast.

Edge angle is determined by the skier's stance and the steepness of the slope (fig. 4.13). Pressure-control movements may affect the amount of pressure (and force) at the ski-snow interface, but edge angle will determine the direction in which the force of the ski acts.

Edge-control movements can be thought of as those movements that either increase, decrease, or maintain edge angles. These important movements determine how a turn is started, controlled, and completed. The movements that

students use to effect edging can reveal much about their skiing, which can help you identify cause-and-effect relationships so you can target areas in need of improvement. Edge-control movements are described as follows.

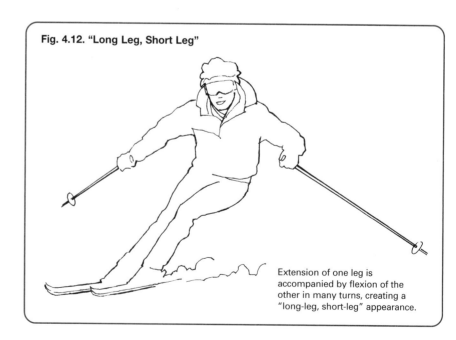

Fig. 4.12. "Long Leg, Short Leg"

Extension of one leg is accompanied by flexion of the other in many turns, creating a "long-leg, short-leg" appearance.

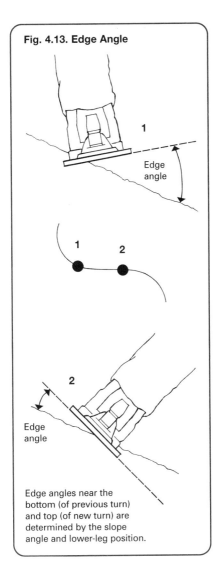

Fig. 4.13. Edge Angle

1

Edge angle

1   **2**

2

Edge angle

Edge angles near the bottom (of previous turn) and top (of new turn) are determined by the slope angle and lower-leg position.

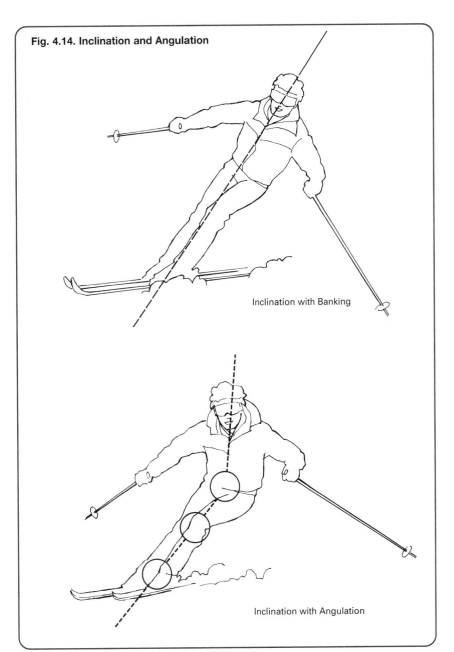

Fig. 4.14. Inclination and Angulation

Inclination with Banking

Inclination with Angulation

a. *Inclination.* The movement of the skier's body to the inside of the turn. When done at the turn initiation (sometimes referred to as "crossover"), inclination can create an edge change. When done throughout the turn, inclination increases the edge angle to the snow surface (fig. 4.14).

b. *Angulation.* The angles skiers create at their joints to control the degree of edge angle in the snow while remaining in balance laterally (fig. 4.14). The ankles, knees, hips, and spine are used to create angulation in skiing. The hip joint and lower spine support the largest edge angle and form the major source of angulation in modern skiing. The ankle can increase and decrease edge angle through eversion (turning the sole of the foot outward) and inversion (turning the sole of the foot inward).

Edge-control movements directly affect all the other skills. For example, large edge angles inhibit rotary movements, as demonstrated by children who ski in too wide a wedge. They may have difficulty learning to turn until they narrow their wedge, decrease their edge angle, and allow their skis to turn.

Conversely, the other skills directly affect the application of edge-control movements. Parallel skiers who use excessive upper-body rotation generally pull themselves onto the inside ski and inhibit their ability to angulate. Without angulation, their skis have inadequate edge angle, and the result is excessive skidding in the control phase of the turn.

Skills Blend

Although the fundamental skills are presented here as distinct groups, it is important to understand that they are all used to make a turn, and the movements described are all interrelated, hence the term **skills blend.**

For example, pressure-control movements affect edge-control movements and rotary movements. The skier enables edge change at the beginning of the turn by extending (a pressure-control movement) and reducing angles in the body. The accomplished skier blends these movements, depending on the situation. In a series of short-radius turns, the skier initiates turns by releasing the edges and applying subtle leg rotation to guide the skis into the turn and onto the new edges. The ski design helps the skier turn as he or she makes correct edge- and pressure-control movements and engages the skis' edges. At the same time, the bent skis store energy. Finishing the turn in an anticipated position, the skier is ready to release the energy stored in the ski to help initiate a new turn.

As this example demonstrates, the skills concept is profoundly valuable to ski instructors. It

reduces skiing into simple, understandable movements that all levels of skiers can see, feel, and understand. Isolation of the various skills allows you to assess students' needs and thereby plan skills development. The lesson can then proceed with a selected skill development that the students understand easily. This newly improved skill can be blended with the other skills, resulting in better overall performance.

In conclusion, good skiing is characterized by the application and blending of the skills to the ever-changing demands of skiing.

The Center Line

Ski teaching requires you to recognize the inefficient and the efficient movements people make when skiing, and then translate your impressions into a deliberate series of steps that will move students toward the fulfillment of their performance goals.

Movement analysis is the term used for this process of evaluation in skiing. It consists of (1) identifying and reinforcing good skill performance and (2) recognizing and targeting those skills that need more development.

High-quality movement analysis depends upon a clear model for comparison. PSIA provides precisely such a model in the Center Line, the American Teaching System's fundamental reference for movement analysis. The Center Line links the concepts of skill development and ski turns.

The four specific reference maneuvers of the Center Line are the

wedge, wedge-christie, parallel, and dynamic-parallel turns. Once you have a thorough understanding of the movements that make up these maneuvers, you can help students blend the fundamental skills into movement patterns that improve skiing performance.

Final forms, or "school figures," were once the norm for how skiers should ski. These were narrowly defined ways to move that all skiers were to emulate. In contrast, the Center Line principle is that skiers select movements appropriate to a variety of factors (e.g., body type, turn type, snow conditions, terrain, etc.) rather than try to ski in a specific position. This is an important point, because a Center Line turn is open to individual interpretation as long as it fits within the parameters of efficiency and function.

It may be helpful to think of the Center Line maneuvers as movement "zones" (fig. 4.15). The word **zone**, when used in the context of skiing, is a broad term used to describe the turn type and all its variations.

The Center Line zones are linked by movement patterns that build upon each other. The wedge turn is linked to the dynamic-parallel turn and all skiing in some way. The zones are not stand-alone figures for testing purposes, although the Center Line reference maneuvers give certification programs focus, discipline, and structure. They are movement "targets," allowing you to help students build upon and blend the four skills at each level.

Think of each zone as a floor,

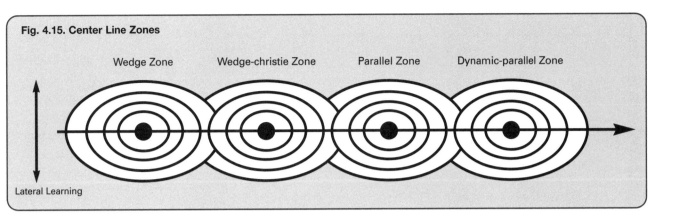

Fig. 4.15. Center Line Zones

Wedge Zone   Wedge-christie Zone   Parallel Zone   Dynamic-parallel Zone

Lateral Learning

or foundation, rather than a ceiling. Each supports the process of growth and diversity rather than contains or restricts your understanding. For example, the skills students learn in the wedge zone are refined rather than replaced as they progress through the wedge-christie and parallel zones.

The movement patterns and the skills within each zone act as springboards for lateral learning (exploration using skill blends other than those represented by the Center Line) and should be adapted to a variety of circumstances.

While providing your students with the latitude to learn within a skill zone, the Center Line reference also helps you stay on track in learning and teaching. As you experiment with new movements and distinctions, it is sometimes difficult to differentiate between that which is fundamental and that which is exaggerated. The four zones of the Center Line act as clarifying beacons for knowing how effectively a person is skiing.

The Center Line can help you anchor your focus and develop a fine eye for movement detail and precision. Each of the four Center Line zones serves as a clear "lens"

for viewing many types of skiing movements—they open your vision to a wide experience of learning and performance.

PSIA instructors continue to refine and update the Center Line to improve its clarity and its relevance to ski teaching as well as to enhance instructor skiing performance. The goal is to give ski teachers an effective blend of skiing skills to support their exploration of the great variety that skiing offers. Disciplined study and practice, within the structure of the Center Line, provides the freedom of movement to ski with creativity and expression.

The image of skiing has become more elegant, dynamic, and visually effective for demonstration as a result of the Center Line. This is what is referred to as functional skiing: it looks good because it works well.

Note: To promote clarity in skiing descriptions, this manual uses the following convention. In descriptions of Center Line maneuvers, the ski on the outside of the turn is referred to as the outside ski, and the ski on the inside of the turn is referred to as the inside ski (rather than uphill and downhill

ski, respectively). This usage supports the fact that Center Line turns are linked, with no traverses between them. The turn itself always has an "outside" and "inside" component. The glossary and later sections of this chapter cover more potentially new terminology in the Center Line descriptions.

Center Line Zones

The following sections describe skiing movements, and their effects, that are part of the Center Line zones. These movements are common features of all Center Line maneuvers.

1. *Movement:*
   At the end of the previous turn, the body and skis are in a countered relationship.
   Effect:
   The skier will seek to realign the legs and skis with the upper body upon releasing the edges of the skis.

2. *Movement:*
   At the end of the previous turn, the skier starts the new turn by extending the new outside leg. Note that the intended movement is lateral rather than vertical.

Photo 4.1. Wedge Turns

Effect:
a. Causes the center of mass to move from the center of the previous turn toward the center of the new turn.
b. Facilitates a change of edge angle in lower levels and an edge change at higher levels. Note that for all parallel turns, the release of the edge of the "old" outside ski is facilitated by this lateral movement.
c. Initiates a transfer of pressure from the old outside ski to the new outside ski. The increase of pressure to the outside ski (on its inside edge) causes the ski to bend, producing a majority of the turning force required.

3. *Movement:*
At the end of the previous turn, the skier swings the new inside pole forward and toward the center of the new turn.

Effect:
a. Aids in rhythm and movement of the body into the new turn.
b. Assists in stabilizing the upper body.

4. *Movement:*
The skier actively guides both skis into the new turn.
Effect:
In lower performance zones, this movement produces most of the skis' turning. In higher performance zones, this movement serves to assist and control the natural turning properties of the ski.

5. *Movement:*
The skier's center of mass continues to move toward the center of new turn.
Effect:
a. Permits a greater edge angle. The higher the degree of edge, the more the ski can bend.

b. Allows the pressure on the inside edge of the outside ski to become dominant.
c. Permits dynamic balance.

6. *Movement:*
The skier uses flexion of the ankles, knees, and hips.
Effect:
a. Assists in creating dynamic balance.
b. May be used to control forces in the turn.
   1) through absorption
   2) through control of edge angle
c. Flexing the knee and ankle of the outside leg at the end of one turn complements extension of the outside leg of the next turn to transfer pressure and change edge angle.

7. *Movement:*
At the end of the turn, the skier turns the skis and lower body slightly farther than the upper

Photo 4.2. Wedge Turns

the rotary movements of the feet and legs, and fine control of edge and pressure movements to maintain a constant speed and radius (photos 4.1, 4.2).

When making wedge turns, it is important to ski with quiet body movement, taking care not to restrict or freeze the smooth, flowing movements necessary to all skiing. The skier must seek a sense of rhythm, flow, and control from turn to turn, and emphasize a rounded, deliberate turn shape.

The specific movements of the wedge turn are described in the following section.

1. Start the turn from a previous turn so they are rhythmically linked. Extend the leg slightly. During the previous turn, there is slightly increased flexion of the ankle, knee, and hip to move the center of mass toward the inside of the turn. The extension at turn initiation decreases flexion, neutralizes the stance, and decreases the edge angle on the downhill/outside ski. This neutral stance and balancing movement facilitates the smooth and easy blending of other skills necessary to start the skis down the fall line.
2. Guide both skis actively. The forebody of both skis will be powerfully engaged in the direction change.
3. Gradually equalize pressure between the skis.
4. As the skis near the fall line, the forces in the turn increase pressure on the inside edge of the outside ski. The outside ski becomes the dominant ski in producing turn shape.

body to bring the body into a countered relationship.
Effect:
See Movement 1 (i.e., return to the beginning of the cycle).

The skier performs all of these movements from a functional stance that is determined by terrain, speed, and the skier's physique. Note that movements 1 and 7 are essentially the same

movement. This implies that turns are linked so as to maximize efficiency. The turn shape produced by these movements serves to control speed.

Wedge Turn

In the wedge turn, the skier conducts the fundamental skills of skiing in a slow manner. The skier making a wedge turn demonstrates

5. Throughout the turn, continue maintaining the center of mass in its orientation toward the inside of the turn, relative to the outside ski. You can do this by flexing the ankles, knees, and hips, while tipping the legs inward. This will help you maintain edge and pressure, which will considerably enhance the performance of your skis.

6. Turn the skis and lower body slightly more than the upper body to create a slightly countered relationship to the ski. As you continue through the turn, slightly advance your inside ski, knee, hip, shoulder, and hand.

7. Keep the width of the wedge relatively constant throughout the turn. Control turn speed with turn shape, rather than the size of the wedge.

The wedge turn is easy to analyze and study, and therefore serves as a groundwork for the further development of skiing and teaching.

Note: The term "wedge turn" has essentially replaced the term "snowplow turn," although many students may be more familiar with the latter term.

Guiding Student Performance —Wedge Turns

An awareness of the following key movement patterns will help you guide student performance in all skiing activities and levels.

Here are the Center Line movements of the wedge turn.

• Extend slightly while moving toward the new turn, releasing

Photo 4.3. Wedge-christie Turn

edges (reducing the downhill ski edge angle) to start the turn and flexing to continue turning the skis throughout the turn.

• Keep the flex in both legs comparable, with pressure on both feet about equal. The pressure distribution and the amount of flex in each leg throughout the turn (and from turn to turn) should vary only slightly.

• Use a twisting motion of your legs to actively turn the skis.

• Pressure the outside ski as it is increasingly edged so you can

take advantage of the natural turning properties of the ski.

• Maintain a slightly countered stance to help support balance, alignment, turning activity, and weight distribution toward the outside ski. This also helps in the beginning of the new turn.

Wedge-Christie Turn

The wedge christie uses the basic skills of the wedge turn at a slightly higher speed and performance level to link the wedge turn with

Photo 4.4. Wedge-christie Turn

the parallel turn. It consists of the movement patterns of the wedge turn during its initiation and those of the parallel turn during the arc and completion of the turn. The study and understanding of how the skier "matches" the skis into a parallel stance and opens them into a wedge is crucial to the blending of the fundamental skills and improved performance.

This turn has many variations (photos 4.3, 4.4). In the beginning stages of wedge-christie turns, the wedge is maintained until near the completion of the turn before matching. At the higher level, the skier develops only a very small opening with the skis that gets the skier to the inside edge of the new outside ski, followed by immediate matching. The turn is a round, skidded arc with a degree of carving that is less than the parallel turn.

The specific movements of the wedge-christie turn are described as follows. Note that the movement patterns of the wedge christie are quite similar to those of the wedge turn, described in the previous section.

1. Allow both skis to open from parallel into a narrow wedge with the help of extension and edge release. Begin slightly advancing the "new" inside foot and leg to help create a countered relationship between the upper and lower body.

2. At the same time, begin to swing the new inside pole basket forward, along with the wrist, elbow, and arm. The pole swing and its following touch help you maintain rhythm and

prompt you to move your body into the turn. Note that the movement of the old outside ski off its edge tends to fulfill the stabilizing function of the pole touch.

3. Before matching the skis, you should already be in such a balanced stance so that no gross movement adjustments will be necessary to match the skis and remain in the proper stance.

4. Use the pole touch as a timing trigger. Match the skis into a parallel stance by moving your body inside the turn, which will flatten the ski, and continue to advance the inside foot and leg.

These inside ski movements change the ski's edge engagement in the snow from the inside edge to the outside edge, placing both skis on corresponding edges—either both left edges or both right edges. This edge change of the inside ski facilitates the increased steering of the foot to a parallel relationship with the outside ski. The edges are no longer in opposition. Because of increased speed, edge angle, and pressure on the outside ski, the light inside ski is easily matched. Your inside ski may come off the snow to assist edge change in dynamic situations.

5. Before your outside ski crosses the fall line, complete the matching movements of your skis with the inside ski remaining active in matching the arc of the outside ski.

6. Progressively increase edging and pressure to control the amount of skid and to develop

a consistently round, skidded shape to the arc of the turn.

7. Keep your wrist and hand forward while you flex them to swing the pole shaft and basket back as you move past the point of pole touch.

8. As speed increases, produce more edging and pressure on the outside ski, and increase angulation in your ankles, knees, and hips.

Guiding Student Performance —Wedge-Christie Turns

The wedge-christie turn is the pivotal point between the wedge and parallel turns, providing the skier a smooth and easy transition into parallel turning.

Here are the Center Line movements of the wedge-christie turn.

• Control speed and turn shape by using corresponding edges.

• Move toward the center of the new turn by extending slightly and releasing edges while opening the wedge with both skis to initiate the turn. Actively turn both ski tips toward the new turn.

• Continuously "roll" the knees, and guide the inside leg, foot, and ski from the wedge opening to parallel matching and throughout the arc of the parallel portion of the turn.

• Incorporate pole use to enhance movement flow and turn linkage, timing, and rhythm.

• Facilitate turn shape and ski matching by increasing speed, edge angle, and pressure to the outside ski.

Parallel Turn

The parallel turn is a staple turn for advanced skiers. Once it is achieved, some variety of the parallel turn will be used in nearly all skiing. The successful transition from wedge-christie to parallel turns is dependent on the skier's ability to perform an early weight transfer.

Center Line parallel turns are shown in photos 4.5 and 4.6. The specific movements of the parallel turn are described as follows.

1. Near the end of the turn, use the wrist and elbow to swing the outside pole basket toward the new turn.

2. Stay slightly flexed throughout the turn completion, with pressure dominant on the outside ski.

3. A change in pressure dominance from the former outside ski to the new outside ski begins with an extension of the new outside leg. In comparison to the wedge christie development, this change of pressure dominance is earlier. Accompanying this extension movement is a simultaneous release of both skis' edges. The subsequent movement to the new corresponding edges allows the ski to provide a majority of the necessary turning force.

4. The extension movement toward the new turn, along with the pole swing, contributes to the pole touch in the snow, which should be to the side and slightly ahead of the boots. These movements, along with pressure transfer from edge to

Photo 4.5. Parallel Turns

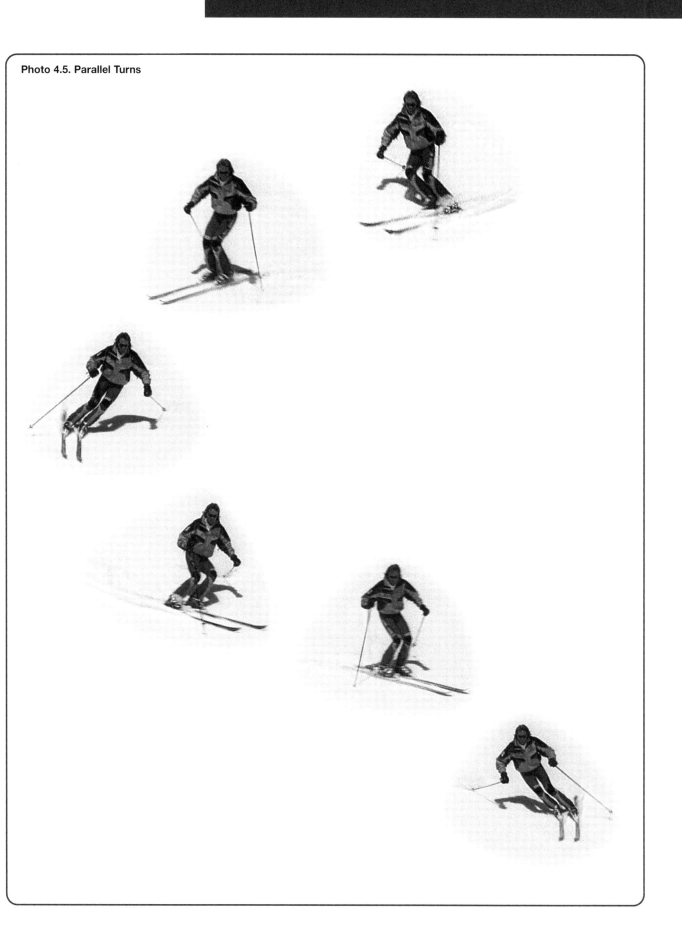

Photo 4.6. Parallel Turns

edge and rotary movement of the lower body, combine to produce the turn initiation.

5. During the initiation, continue to guide the inside ski actively, maintaining a parallel relationship with the outside ski and directing both legs and feet simultaneously along the arc of the intended turn.

6. Use mild, or shallow, edge angles to help you direct both skis into the new turn.

7. You will be skiing slightly faster than when skiing the wedge christie, although the arc of the turn will show a similar rounded skid.

8. Keep your skis parallel and your stance comfortable— neither a wide track stance nor

one with legs locked together is appropriate.

9. The outside leg and ski produce the greatest pressure and therefore control the arc of the turn, while the active steering of the inside leg complements the outside leg.

10. After initiating the turn, progressively turn the skis and increase pressure to the outside leg while flexing the inside leg. These movements combine to create optimal pressure and edge angles. The pressure on the outside leg is primarily distributed to the inside front area of leg, with pressure applied over the whole foot. This helps you create a rounded arc that is more or less carved, depending

on your needs, ability, and intended precision. Most of the needed turning action is provided by pressure and the resultant arc.

Guiding Student Performance —Parallel Turns

Students must be aware of the key movements described under parallel turns to progress to the more advanced levels of skiing. These movement patterns also enhance elegance, versatility, and efficiency.

Here are the Center Line movements of the parallel turn.

• Change pressure from the downhill to the uphill ski earlier by slightly extending your outside

Photo 4.7. Dynamic-parallel Turns

leg while moving toward the center of the new turn.

- Use the pole as a connecting link between turns, and during the preparation and initiation phases of a turn.
- Roll both skis off of their uphill edges and continue to roll them to the new edges during turn initiation. This coordinated edge change allows for a smooth turn initiation.
- Above the fall line, your hip movement toward the inside of the turn is dominant. Flex your ankles and knees later in the turn to maintain alignment and control pressure on the ski.
- These movements enable you to control both turn shape and speed.

Dynamic-Parallel Turn

The parallel turn is the basis for the dynamic-parallel turn. The fundamental skills are blended like the parallel turn, but increased speed, challenging changes of direction, and a high level of carving require a more dynamic refinement of movement patterns and an expanded understanding of all advanced skiing movements.

Center Line dynamic-parallel turns are shown in photos 4.7 and 4.8. The specific movements of the dynamic-parallel turn are described as follows.

1. At turn initiation the pressure transfer to the new outside ski is deliberate as you move *toward* the new turn. It is essential to recognize that this is principally a lateral movement toward the new turn as opposed to moving the hips up and over the new outside ski during the pressure change.

2. Actively commit the middle of the body (hip area) toward the next turn while rolling the skis onto the new edges. This commitment releases the edge grip from the previous turn. Therefore, it supports the rotary action (steering and continued guiding) in the feet and legs into and through the new turn. This movement of the body, releasing the old turn and committing to the new one, also contributes to carrying energy from one turn to the next.

Photo 4.8. Dynamic-parallel Turns

3. Conduct the pole swing movement and touch as described in the parallel turn.
4. The rotary movements of the inside ski work to complement the rotary movements of the outside ski rather than create a base of support. Once you have committed to the new turn, continue this movement pattern of the inside ski throughout the arc of the turn.
5. The speed—particularly of the center of mass—varies little from turn to turn.
6. The extension movement at the start of the turn creates an edge change. During (and often following) the edge change, the movements usually follow this sequence: (1) pressure transfer from ski to ski, (2) steering movement toward the new turn contributing to edge change, and (3) engaging the edges by applying pressure to edged skis. This all takes place long before the ski tips reach the fall line.
7. Intensity, duration, and timing of movements throughout the arc of the turn determine the size, shape, and speed of the turn, (e.g., short, medium, long, gliding, braking). Generally these variations are different strategies dictated by special situations.
8. The basic movement patterns of wedge turns are required in the dynamic parallel, even though the skis remain parallel and the speed, power, and intensity have increased.
9. The functional parallel stance is neither a wide track nor a stance with the skis and feet locked together. A few inches of separation is common.

Terrain steepness, turn shape, individual body type, and speed all contribute to the appropriate separation of the skis and legs. For example, the separation will increase as the inward tilt (inclination) of the skier increases due to faster speed and changes in turn shape. Steep terrain causes a similar effect.

10. Even though this turn is carved, it is not a railed or edge-locked turn. It requires you to apply the appropriate amount of edge and pressure to guide the skis on the desired path, thus allowing a variety of turn radii and turn shapes.

Guiding Student Performance —Dynamic-Parallel Turns

The following key movements guide students to develop more precision and crispness in their skiing and a more complete mountain mastery. They increase the student's skiing efficiency and improve movements so appropriate modifications can be naturally applied to various terrain, speed, and snow conditions. Here are the Center Line movements of the dynamic-parallel turn.

- At turn initiation, transfer pressure from the downhill/outside ski to the uphill/inside ski more deliberately, as your body moves more quickly toward the new turn.
- Use pole swing and touch actively to help carry the energy from turn to turn.

- Ski in a comfortable stance rather than one that is overly wide or with legs locked together.
- Increase the dynamics of the parallel-turn movements for faster speeds and a greater variety of turn shapes and snow conditions.
- Increase the use of edge angles and pressure to control the turn shape.

The Center Line concept provides a basis for efficient skiing in all snow and terrain conditions. Note how the skiers maintain balance and control while applying skiing skills in a variety of conditions, such as bumps, powder, and crud snow (photos 4.9–4.13).

Movement Principles

All instructors, whether experienced or new to the profession, benefit from understanding the physical and technical aspects of skiing as well as movement principles that govern how the skier's body, ski equipment, and snow surface interact. These factors determine how skiers manage forces in skiing and the resultant movement.

Modern skiing techniques have evolved from time-proven methods, influenced by changes in equipment design, innovations in slope grooming, and an increased understanding of the human body's capabilities. Today's skis are high-technology tools that produce most of the necessary turning forces if pressure and torque are applied to an edged ski.

Terrain and snow conditions

Photo 4.9. Bumps

Photo 4.10. Bumps

affect the way that skis respond. Anyone who has skied both powder and hardpack knows that skis respond quite differently to these two conditions. An advanced skier negotiating a steep chute is constantly making decisions based on the feedback from both skis and terrain. But even a beginning skier responds to the skis and terrain, analyzing the movements involved in the task at hand. Although ski technique changes, movement principles remain the same.

An understanding of anatomy (the body's structure) links the concepts of mechanics to human motion. Movement principles and body structure determine both the possibilities and limitations in movement. (See chapter 7, Anatomy and Conditioning, for a discussion of the structural support of the body—the skeleton, the muscles, and the joints.)

By relating basic mechanical ideas to the Skiing Model, you can achieve a better understanding of movement principles as they pertain to skiing. This step is important because an understanding of mechanics alone—without application to skiing—is of little value to you as an instructor. The application of these mechanical concepts to skiing lays the foundation for the careful evaluations of skiers based on observations of their skiing. Too many instructors are able to determine *what* is ineffective or inefficient in an individual's skiing but miss *why* it is that way.

Photo 4.11. Extension and Flexion (in Bumps)

Photo 4.12. Powder

Photo 4.13. Crud

Movement analysis is the instructor's primary tool for providing the "why."

This discussion, however, is not complete. Extensive literature on movement principles is available through other sources (see Suggested Reading). Movement principles are also discussed in the study guides corresponding to this manual.

Note: The concept of skiing mechanics forms the basis for much of the common terminology used in skiing. Terms such as balance, force, pressure, rotation, and efficiency all have precise definitions in mechanics, and an understanding of them prevents misunderstandings that occur when using inexact language.

Mechanical Concepts

Before examining movement principles, consider the following basic concepts of mechanics and anatomy.

In the realm of mechanics, **force** is the property that produces a change in motion (speed and/or direction). Forces may be internal or external to the human body. The primary sources of internal forces are those produced by muscular contraction and relaxation. Common examples of external forces are gravity and the forces produced at the ski-snow contact point.

An important concept in skiing is the additive properties of forces. In skiing, these forces consist of

the effects of gravity, the ski-snow interaction force, and so forth, which together produce the net force to change speed and direction, and therefore enable turning. All of the individual forces acting on a body may be combined to determine the net force on it. One must also realize that even though several forces might act on a body, if their net value is zero no change in motion will be produced.

Closely related to force is **pressure,** which is simply a force distributed over an area. A common example of pressure in skiing is the pressure that is applied to the length of your skis when you stand on them. The force is located primarily at the center of the ski, but it produces the pressure distribution along the length of the ski. (The exact distribution depends on the ski's design.) Controlling the pressure distribution while skiing is a requisite skill for all accomplished skiers.

The areas of rotary movements and rotation are often fraught with controversy. The usage of these terms is discussed here to provide you with a frame of reference.

Rotary movements in skiing refer to the body or body segments moving in an arc about an axis. There are three axes around which rotary movement occurs (fig. 4.16). In skiing, discussion often focuses on angular motion about the vertical axis of the body, although rotation about the other two axes is possible. (Many skiers have flipped over their ski tips, demonstrating rotation about the frontal axis!)

In mechanics, **rotation** refers to the angular motion of a body about

Fig. 4.16. Axes of Rotation

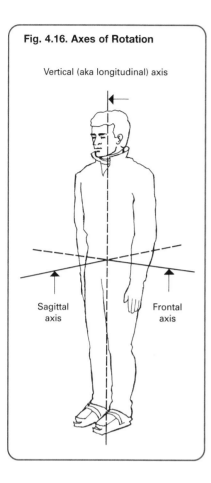

Vertical (aka longitudinal) axis

Sagittal axis

Frontal axis

an axis. In kinesiology (i.e., human movement science), the actions of joints that result in rotary movement are called rotation.

Efficiency is another term that is widely used in skiing today. Making an efficient turn does not mean doing it "the easiest way." **Movement efficiency** is technically defined as the ratio between the amount of input energy and the amount of movement produced. (Movement here refers to intended movement rather than extraneous movement.) Thus, a movement that is accomplished with more energy than necessary is considered to have low efficiency, whereas the same movement produced with less energy has a higher efficiency.

When instructors describe a

skier's turns as efficient, they mean that the skier expends minimum energy to produce the turn under a given set of conditions. Typically, advanced skiers make much more efficient movements and therefore might ski all day using less energy than that expended by a beginner in a two-hour class lesson. However, all skiers make inefficient turns at times (sometimes out of necessity and sometimes by choice), as anyone who has made hop turns can attest.

Balance

Although you may know intuitively what balance is, you may not be able to clearly define this concept for your students.

Balance in biomechanics refers to the process of controlling forces to produce a desired motion. In skiing, balance most often refers to **dynamic balance** (balance in motion) as opposed to **static balance** (balance in the absence of motion). For example, the position you assume to balance while standing or straight-running is much different from that required for balanced skiing during a turn.

Figure 4.17 shows a skier effectively balanced on skis, with body angles in the appropriate position relative to the skis for a given speed and radius of turn.

When you are properly aligned, your body can efficiently use forces produced in the turn. In contrast, if you are inappropriately aligned, you must make continual adjustments to stay upright. The optimal position is not one that is achieved and then held; rather, it

Fig. 4.17. Balance

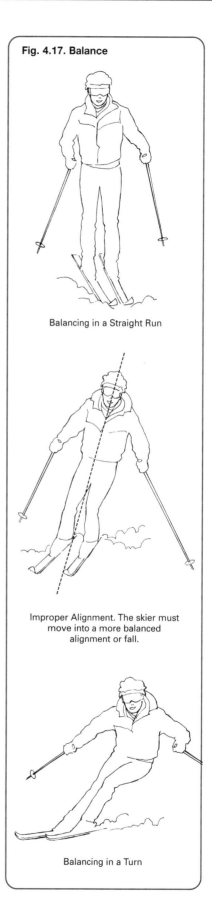

Balancing in a Straight Run

Improper Alignment. The skier must move into a more balanced alignment or fall.

Balancing in a Turn

changes continuously throughout the turn.

What is optimal alignment, exactly? To understand this, you must first grasp the concept of **center of mass.** Think of your body as made of up of many small elements (of mass). The average location of these elemental masses is the center of mass. It is located in the navel area when you are standing erect with your arms at your sides. The position of the center of mass is generally somewhat lower for women than for men.

Alignment

From the skier's perspective as well as from a mechanical viewpoint, proper **alignment** refers to the positioning of the body so that the forces passing through it produce the intended movement.

If you are standing on your skis without moving, gravity is acting on you, but there is no apparent change in motion. This is because force just equal to the gravitational force is produced at the ski-snow contact point, referred to as the **ski-snow interaction force**. Thus the net force is zero, and no movement is produced.

In a wide stance, your body can move laterally to another location where you can maintain static balance. The criterion for maintaining this position is that your center of mass must not stray too far from the base of support (i.e., the feet). In more technical terms, the ski-snow interaction forces must act along a line that passes close to your center of mass so you can maintain alignment

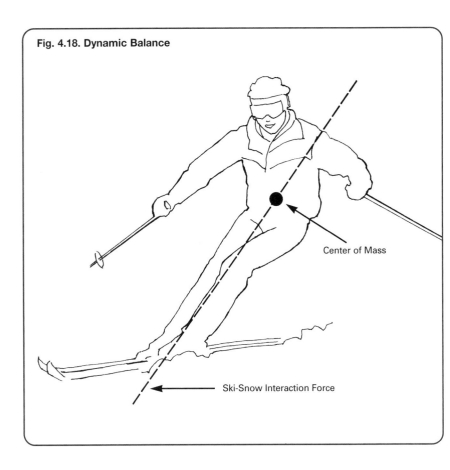

Fig. 4.18. Dynamic Balance

Center of Mass

Ski-Snow Interaction Force

(i.e., remain standing).

When your body is statically balanced, gravitational force transfers through the vertebral column, pelvis, hip joints, femurs, knee joints, tibias, ankle joints, and feet, and through the skis.

Considering the body as a whole, the base of support is the feet, and a wider stance produces a more stable base. However, with respect to how forces are transferred through the body by muscular movement, each joint surface may be considered as an independent base of support. If the joint surface contact area is maximized through proper alignment, the joint is more stable and has the ability to translate forces with less ligamentous and muscular support. With an efficiently aligned joint, pressure is

evenly distributed, and the joint is less subject to trauma from rotational or compressive forces. Thus, the ligaments and joint cartilage retain greater integrity.

In a ski turn, more complex and constantly changing forces act on the body, with positive net forces (as indicated by the body's constant variations in speed and direction). The issue of alignment becomes even more critical. Dynamic balance allows you to maintain proper alignment with maximum efficiency through movement of the body fore or aft as well as laterally.

Turns require a change in motion and a positive net force. As shown in figure 4.18, the skier has moved the ski onto the edge, directing the ski-snow interaction force toward the center of the turn. This unbalanced force produces a change of motion that causes the skier to turn.

As in the static case, efficient alignment occurs when the ski-snow interaction forces act along a line that passes near the center of mass. The exact location of the imaginary line with respect to the center of mass depends on the desired turn shape. If the line of these ski-snow interaction forces wanders too far from the center of mass, you will have to make a correction.

For example, if you move too far inside a turn, your skis will slide from under your body unless you shorten the turn radius. (More force in the turn direction produces greater change of motion.) Similarly, if your body is not far enough inside the turn, the resulting turn radius will be longer than desired.

Center Line Efficiency

The Center Line maneuvers represent an efficient combination of movements that produce and control forces used in turning. You achieve balance throughout the turn by using skeletal support while allowing your muscles to provide small adjustment movements. The fore/aft balance point is centered so that you feel pressure on your entire foot, and you achieve lateral balance by continuously varying the position of the center of mass throughout the turn to maintain alignment.

In an effective ski turn, you blend skills to position your body so that it balances chiefly on the skeleton, leaving the muscles free for minor corrections and preparation for the next move. In well-blended turns, you control speed by the shape of your turns rather than with inefficient braking and skidding, which tend to interrupt the smooth flow of the center of mass.

An appropriate blend of skills produces efficient turns with your body remaining properly aligned throughout the turn. Such turns will have an uninterrupted movement of the center of mass down the slope, and will exhibit a rhythm and flow that is obvious to even a casual observer.

In contrast, jerky skiing motions or a rigid appearance of the upper body are both signs of inefficient skiing that leads to fatigue. Jerky motions indicate that the body is continually expending energy to correct balance, which can be due to improper alignment or over-edging, for example. Similarly, keeping the body rigid also requires significant muscular effort.

Development Phases and Performance Targets

Generally, students feel they are either **beginning, intermediate,** or **advanced** skiers, since they lack the background to determine where they fit within the nine different performance levels PSIA has identified (see sidebar). **Expert** is a term that people often confuse with the term advanced; however, it refers to more than skiing performance. The word expert also implies the knowledge and the experience typical of an authority or master.

Whereas some skiers in the upper level of ability are truly experts, the following structure of student development is based on beginning, intermediate, and advanced categories, or phases. The structure serves as a basic guideline for performance and as a quick reference for movement classification (fig. 4.19).

It is critical that students experience improvement and acknowledgement whether they are working within a single phase or developing into the next phase.

The beginning phase is characterized by rapid learning and improved performance. It is also the phase in which skiers are presented with the greatest amount of new information.

Skiers in the intermediate phase can enjoy the freedom of adapting to changes in terrain, snow, turning, and speed. Students feel good about these levels of achievement though they may have their sights set on enhanced performance. The word intermediate suggests success in skiing combined with aspiration to move on to a more advanced level.

Skiers achieve advanced-phase skiing when they display competence with the challenging turns and conditions of upper-level skiing. Nevertheless, they may display advanced skills on moderate terrain and smooth conditions, but their ability to apply these skills to difficult or ungroomed snow conditions, challenging terrain, or a variety of speeds and turn shapes may border more on intermediate.

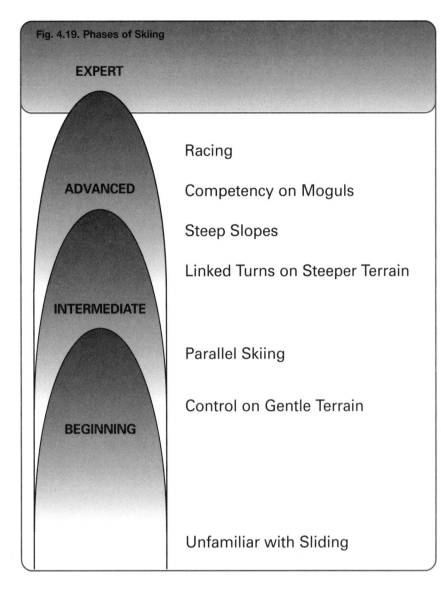

Fig. 4.19. Phases of Skiing

EXPERT

ADVANCED

Racing

Competency on Moguls

Steep Slopes

Linked Turns on Steeper Terrain

INTERMEDIATE

Parallel Skiing

Control on Gentle Terrain

BEGINNING

Unfamiliar with Sliding

These three general phases are not permanent destinations for most skiers. Skiers pass through them depending on terrain and conditions, frequency of practice, quality of instruction, and their enjoyment of and commitment to skiing.

PSIA Skier Levels

The terms beginning, intermediate, and advanced are efficient for identifying students based on their general ability level. However, ski schools may elect to identify skiers by more specific skiing levels or benchmarks—the nine PSIA skier levels mentioned previously to devise a more in-depth needs assessment.

A ski school may or may not choose to openly identify these levels to students. Nevertheless, it is helpful for you to be aware of the skills and their progressional blending at distinct levels or benchmarks. Furthermore, you can stimulate learning by setting attainable and exciting goals and performance targets with each level.

Clearly, there is some overlap between the levels. For example, a skier who exhibits the highest performance level of a wedge-christie turn is essentially performing at the level of a basic parallel turn. This overlapping of skill levels reinforces the concept of the Center Line movements as zones rather than fixed movement patterns.

You can expect students to display varying abilities in the performance of a particular turn. Your objective is to identify and refine a student's underlying skills and movement patterns, knowing that skiers display varying abilities in the performance of a particular turn. You can then use this information to determine the terrain and snow conditions students are most likely able to ski. In most cases, the performance of these key movements is the basis for how students view their own skiing performance and for how instructors organize lesson plans.

PSIA has devised key skiing activities, described below, that can help you determine the performance level of a skier (1 through 9). Also included here are brief descriptions of what these students typically experience during the lesson. This information provides a "big picture" of the lesson. You will need to refer to the study guides that accompany this manual for lesson patterns and specific detail on lesson delivery.

Phase One—Beginning

In this phase, students range from those who are being introduced to skiing to those who have the ability to make strong wedge turns on all green terrain and the easiest blue terrain. As the instructor, you can be a source of information that increases the student's sense of comfort and belonging in the sport. The main objective at this or phase is to help students discover the excitement of skiing.

Level 1

Student: First time on skis.

Technical Content: Walking, straight gliding, and gliding wedge; introduction to wedge turn

Key Skiing Activities:
- Conduct orientation to equipment and environment.
- Introduce standing, walking, sliding, and climbing on skis.
- Have students perform straight running on parallel skis.
- Use a variety of wedge activities:
  - Step/brush to wedge
  - Flat wedge push
  - Wedge change-up (i.e., wedge to a straight run and back to wedge)
  - Gliding or easy wedge
  - Braking or speed-control wedge
  - Wedge traverse
  - Easy (mild) wedge turns

Lesson content helps the student
- discover the excitement of skiing;
- develop a sense of comfort and belonging in the sport of skiing;
- experience freedom of movement, travel, and propulsion;
- feel and understand basic posture and how equipment helps performance, movement control, and balance; and
- develop confidence from being able to glide, stop, and make very basic changes in direction with the stability of a wedge stance.

Level 2

Student: Has spent a few hours on the slopes and can ski in a cautious wedge stance on easiest terrain; can link basic wedge turns.

Technical Content: Wedge turns that are progressively more round and rhythmic

Key Skiing Activities:
- Review wedge activities.
- Refine wedge movements, balance, and stance.
- Flex and settle to finish turns; extend and release to start turns.
- Use feet to execute active turning.
- Ski with the increasing pressure as the turn develops.
- Engage edge/sidecut to create an arc.

Lesson content helps the student
- build confidence through improved speed control and stopping skills;
- experience the excitement and benefit of the lift ride and expanded terrain, when ready;
- acquire the new feeling of skidding skis when guiding the ski tips simultaneously;
- gain awareness that ankle and knee flex change the skis' turning response; and

- have the freedom to change direction and master descent on easy terrain.

Level 3

Student: Skis with a solid wedge turns on easier green trails.

Technical Content: Wedge turn exploration and improvement; introduction to wedge-christie turns

Key Skiing Activities:
- Perform wedge turns with active foot and leg turning and pressure/edge change.
- Link wedge turns with no interrupting traverse.
- Vary wedge turn radii from short to medium to long.
- Slightly increase speed of wedge turn to enable an easier transition to wedge christie.
- Introduce wedge christie.

Lesson content helps the student
- improve speed and direction control;
- make quicker turn completions, with increased confidence on steeper terrain;
- begin to feel the rhythm of skiing;
- achieve leg relaxation through parallel matching; and
- have access to more skiing terrain options.

Phase Two— Intermediate

Skiers in this phase are matching to parallel at the end of a wedge turn, making parallel turns on blue terrain, and beginning to learn the skills needed to ski black terrain. The main objective at this phase is to help students expand the possibilities for fun and performance.

Level 4

Student: Skis on all green trails confidently with wedge turns or beginning wedge-christie turns (starts turns with a wedge and matches in the fall line).

Technical Content: Wedge-christie turns, with progressively earlier matching

Key Skiing Activities:
- Extend parallel skidding activity.
- Begin wedge to parallel matching after the fall line.
- Expand turn shape and rhythm changes—long to short, slow to quick.
- Enhance edge/pressure (sidecut and flex) awareness.
- Develop strong stance and alignment characteristics for higher-level balancing movements (inside ski ahead, slightly countered relationship, etc.).
- Increase speed on easier terrain.

Lesson content helps the student
- experience a new and exciting feeling of control through skidding on corresponding edges;
- explore skiing sensations through more elegance and style;
- have greater awareness of inside leg and foot turning power, and increased outside ski pressure;
- develop confidence at higher speed, with more immediate control of turn shape and speed; and

- have greater opportunity to explore various terrain.

Level 5

Student: Skis wedge-christie turns on easier blue runs (using a wedge or step to enter the turn, then matching the skis in a wide stance).

Technical Content: Wedge-christie turn exploration and improvement; introduction to parallel turns

Key Skiing Activities:
- Enhance wedge opening with pole swing, use touch to trigger parallel matching.
- Use pole touch for rhythm and timing.
- Develop a narrower wedge opening with both skis, earlier parallel matching, and longer parallel christie. This is accomplished through
  - increased speed, edge angle, outside ski pressure, body angles,
  - gradual application of edging and pressure to shape turn,
  - parallel or little wedge to start turns on mild terrain, and
  - exploration of terrain changes —knolls, rolls, and bumps.
- Increase awareness of inside leg and foot turning power; increase outside ski edge/pressure.
- Use practice, mileage, and repetition to reinforce narrower support base and quicker activity.
- Introduce parallel turn.

Lesson content helps the student

- reduce the wedge and add pole use;
- exhibit more continuous and flowing movements, from the extension and edge release (wedge or parallel) through the wedge-christie finish;
- refine large movements;
- ski with greater outside ski pressure and a lighter inside ski;
- flex while matching through the turn to control turn shape and speed;
- gain confidence and knowledge on steeper terrain and in varied snow to enhance experimentation; and
- explore more of the mountain.

Level 6

Student: Skis beginning parallel turns on green terrain and advanced wedge-christie turns on blue terrain.

Technical Content: Parallel turns with simultaneous edge change on green and blue terrain; introduction to bumps and easy black terrain

Key Skiing Activities:

- Start the turn with the skis parallel.
- Use poles earlier to form a continuous link from turn completion through initiation.
- Develop smooth, flowing turns and rhythm changes.
- Increase sense of "carving" to complement "skidding."

Lesson content helps the student

- gain the confidence to "let go"

and move the entire body toward the new turn;

- feel the elegance and continuity in skiing;
- develop greater sensitivity to the simultaneous turning of the skis, especially the inside ski to start the turn;
- achieve earlier pressure change to the outside ski, which complements inside ski guiding activity;
- find control from the parallel arc of the turn rather than rely on the wedge; and
- accommodate terrain changes with greater ease and fun, using a variety of short to long turns.

Phase Three—Advanced

In this phase, parallel skiers develop new sensations, style, elegance, precision, and all-terrain mastery. This phase includes skiers who consistently ski parallel turns and are seeking turn refinement and solid performance under a variety of terrain and snow conditions. A continued excitement for learning and a passion for excellence are the hallmarks of advanced skiers. The main objective at this phase is to help students make their best even better.

Level 7

Student: Skis in a comfortable, open-stance parallel (stance about hip-width) on all blue and less-challenging, groomed, black terrain. The student also skis in very easy blue bumps, maintaining rhythm and speed control.

Technical Content: Exploration

and improvement of parallel turn; introduction to dynamic-parallel turn; exploration and improvement of skills in bumps, gates, steeper terrain, and variable snow

Key Skiing Activities

- Develop style, elegance, and precision in medium-radius turns to develop form and function.
- Practice short-radius turns in the fall line, for speed control on steeper terrain.
- Experiment with pole use varieties use as a blocking and sensory instrument.
- Refine skiing tactics—*where* to ski to enhance *how* to ski.
- Increase lateral body angles—ankles, knees, and hip/spine throughout the turn.
- Continue developing an upper- and lower-body "countered" relationship, creating efficient angles.
- Emphasize carving turns.

Lesson content helps the student

- experience enhanced lateral movement as well as more sophisticated fore/aft movement;
- develop narrower stance to facilitate turning;
- use more distinct pressure differences—less between turns and more during turns;
- use poles as a more natural part of the dynamics and elegance of different turn types;
- feel and understand his or her own skiing, plus learn by observing skiing skills in others;
- have more movement of the body to the inside of the turn as turning forces increase; and
- link turns seamlessly.

Level 8

Student: Skis short and long dynamic-parallel turns on green, blue, and easier black terrain, while skiing more open-stance parallel turns on harder and double-black slopes. Student can ski in the fall line in blue and less-challenging black bumps with few stops and good speed control but hesitates in steep bumps. Skis with confidence in light powder but still has trouble in heavy, wet, or crusted snow.

Technical Content: Dynamic parallel turns in all snow conditions and on all slopes

Key Skiing Activities:
- Introduce medium to long dynamic-parallel turns.
- Develop more refinement in carved turns.
- Adjust and control turn shape and speed.
- Apply earlier and greater outside ski pressure with increased edge angle.
- Introduce further inward movement of the body.
- Apply skiing to steeper terrain.
- Ski at higher speeds, where appropriate.
- Expand versatility in varied terrain and snow conditions.

Lesson content helps the student
- engage in active, energetic skiing;
- appreciate the need for good physical conditioning as runs are longer, pressure changes are more dramatic, and the reaction time for varying terrain is shorter;
- enhance turn dynamics through positive attitude;
- use active balancing activities from turn to turn; and
- modify basic ski technique for varying conditions—more equal pressuring for powder, and more flexion, extension, and active absorption for bumps.

Level 9

Student: Is proficient in all kinds of skiing at dynamic speeds.

Technical Content: Exploration and improvement of dynamic skiing in all environments; refinement of timing, intensity and variety of tactics; strengthening of weaker skills

Key Skiing Activities
- Introduce long and short dynamic-parallel turns on steep terrain.
- Improve carving versatility and accuracy.
- Form strategies for skiing in a manner that is light and playful or aggressive and quick.
- Expand line selections in bumps, mastery in powder and crud conditions, and speed in a race course.
- Develop greater awareness and understanding of the mountain.
- Develop skills and knowledge to positively and powerfully influence the performance of others.

Lesson content helps the student
- turn the skis at will, encompassing everything from a quick, under-the-foot pivot to progressive, smooth, rolling carved turns;
- apply unique solutions to a skiing situation, with knowledge of key skiing movements and the ability to apply them (i.e., lateral learning);
- develop increased respect for the skiing and mountain environment;
- experience the joys and sensations of skiing on all terrain and at a variety of speeds; and
- maintain a strong desire to continue learning and improving performance (the "carrot" of obtaining expert status is now in sight).

Skiing Activities

The following list contains on-ski activities for students in the various skill levels. You will find them useful as you explain, demonstrate, review, and evaluate skiing. The skills concept can help you identify and analyze the components of these movements, which reflect key breakthrough areas that you should help students develop along with Center Line maneuvers.

Beginning Phase
- Traverse
- Braking wedge to a stop
- Wedge change-up
- Sidestep
- Herringbone

Intermediate Phase
- Hockey stop
- Sideslip (edge lock and edge release)
- Uphill wedge christie
- Pole plant and swing
- Skating

Advanced Phase

- Hop turn with up-unweighting
- Braking short turn with edge set
- Absorption turn for bumps and soft snow
- Step turn (parallel, diverging, and converging)
- Advanced sideslip (e.g., falling leaf)

Study Guides

The study guides that correspond with this manual contain detailed discussion and step-by-step sample progressions for teaching students in the various skill development levels described in this chapter. The following list indicates where this material is located in each study guide.

   The study guides not only provide you with information about how to teach students in the various development levels, but they are designed to help you prepare for certification as a Level I, Level II, or Level III instructor.

Cross-referencing by Skier Level

- Beginning-phase skier, skier levels 1 through 3, *Level I Study Guide*
- Intermediate-phase skier, skier levels 4 through 6, *Level II Study Guide*
- Advanced-phase skier, skier levels 7 through 9, *Level III Study Guide*

Cross-referencing by Center Line Movement Zones

- Wedge turn, *Level I Study Guide,* steps 7 through 11
- Wedge-christie turn, *Level I Study Guide,* steps 12 through 13, and *Level II Study Guide,* skier levels 4 through 5
- Parallel turn, *Level II Study Guide,* skier levels 5 through 6
- Dynamic-parallel turn, *Level III Study Guide,* short turns, medium turns, and turn applications

Cross-Referencing by Skills (located under Technical Aspects of Skill Development subheadings in the study guides)

- Balancing movements, *Level I Study Guide,* steps 1 through 13; *Level II Study Guide,* skier levels 4 through 6; *Level III Study Guide,* short and medium turns
- Rotary movements, *Level I Study Guide,* steps 1 through 13; *Level II Study Guide,* skier levels 4 through 6; *Level III Study Guide,* short and medium turns
- Pressure-control movements, *Level I Study Guide,* steps 1 through 13; *Level II Study Guide,* skier levels 4 through 6; *Level III Study Guide,* short and medium turns
- Edge-control movements, *Level I Study Guide,* steps 1 through 13; *Level II Study Guide,* skier levels 4 through 6; *Level III Study Guide,* short and medium turns

Ski Equipment

If students are not using the right equipment for their physical characteristics and ability level, their path to optimal performance will be frustrating and difficult—for them *and* for you.

To help students make the right decisions about purchasing or modifying their gear, you need to know how to select equipment, understand the performance characteristics of equipment, and understand the options and as well as the ramifications of modifying equipment.

Your students will benefit from your input and they will appreciate being able to make informed decisions about their equipment as a result of your commitment to stay abreast of new product releases and technology trends.

Modern Ski Design

Trends in ski design are significantly affecting the manner in which and the speed with which people are learning to ski. This chapter discusses modern ski design and provides descriptions of the newer shaped skis and specialty powder (wide-bodied) skis (fig. 5.1).

Undoubtedly, some information in this chapter may soon be obsolete, as equipment manufacturers continue to discover ways to fine-tune these products. However, the basic tenets of good, sound teaching, which are set forth in the Teaching Model, will retain their applicability and integrity, regardless of the ski design being used.

Skiers use the skiing skills identified in the Teaching Model, although skill blends can be

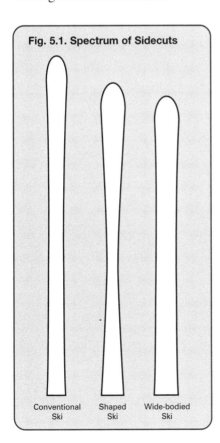

Fig. 5.1. Spectrum of Sidecuts

Conventional Ski   Shaped Ski   Wide-bodied Ski

dramatically different on certain types of equipment. Although these skills still make up the skier's movements, he or she will apply them in a different order or level of intensity, depending on the equipment being used.

The advantage of using these equipment innovations when teaching others to ski is that they allow students to feel movement changes far more readily than with conventional equipment. This can be particularly beneficial when students might otherwise overlook the subtleties of equipment performance, as when they are distracted by demanding terrain or snow conditions, for example.

From an immediate perspective, the significant changes in ski design over the last few years are affecting how people learn to ski; in the long term, these innovations promise to change the future of skiing.

Manufacturers are now offering equipment that merges recent developments in racing ski and snowboard design, such as different ski shapes and new construction technologies. The technology for the new shaped skis came from the World Cup skis, with specific applications of the designs adapted for recreational skiers. The technology for wide-bodied skis is the result of manufacturers' willingness to push the limits of ski design in an effort to achieve the kind of carving that is available to snowboarders.

By offering equipment that combines the benefits of ski racing and snowboarding technology, manufacturers have provided recreational skiers with an easier, more enjoyable way to learn to ski. These innovations are enabling many skiers to experience the actual sensation of carving for the first time. Further, skiers are finding that they can reach higher performance levels in all kinds of conditions more quickly than ever before.

These changes in skis may have as significant an effect on the skiing public in the near future as the short skis did in the 1970s. It is important to embrace these innovations openly, and to alter your way of teaching accordingly, with willingness and a positive attitude. Consider this new technology—and what it requires of you as a ski instructor—as an opportunity to improve your own expertise, and to offer the increasingly discriminating ski area guest with more reasons to take ski lessons.

Features of Modern Skis

Modern ski design consists of excellent features that allow for proficient skiing under a variety of conditions, even for beginning and intermediate skiers. Improved materials and techniques for ski construction have made continuous improvements in skis.

The following are some features of modern skis.

• *Ease of turning.* Skis currently available allow for easier turning, better edge grip, and tighter turning radii, largely because of better materials and better manufacturing techniques. A well-tuned, high-torsion, soft-flexing ski with adequate sidecut will

bend very easily into a clean, carving arc, even at reasonably slow speeds.

• *Edge grip.* Good edge grip keeps the ski from drifting out of the arc, which enables a secure, balanced stance. Manufacturers have learned to balance and control the torsional stability. Too much torsional rigidity (i.e., resistance to twist along a ski's longitudinal axis) makes it hard to turn. Too little will not allow the edges to grip well. Also, proper tuning has an obvious effect on edge grip.

• *Turning radius.* A ski's sidecut largely determines the speed and size of turning radius. **Sidecut** refers to the way skis are shaped, so that when viewing skis flat on the snow from above, they display greater width at the tips and tails than in the middle. Deeper sidecuts, which are the current trend, have given skis the capability to carve nearly perfect arcs in the snow.

Manufacturers are producing skis in a variety of sidecuts, most of them radically deeper than previous designs.

Shaped Skis

Skis in this category are known by several terms, including shaped, super sidecut, deep sidecut, and parabolic, among others. They are almost as wide at the tip and tail as the fat skis, and they are as narrow or narrower at the waist than conventional skis.

Because of the radical sidecut, these skis start to carve a turn immediately after they are tipped

on edge, with minimal or no rotary motion. It is almost as if the ski does the turning! You do not have to force the turn, which allows you to carve a controlled, round turn on packed and hard-packed snow, ice, powder, and crud conditions.

Although this technology is new to recreational skiing, racing skis have been made with quite deep sidecuts for several years. Whereas racing has always focused on carving, manufacturers have up until now been hesitant to provide such carving abilities to intermediate skiers. These skis make it possible to connect parallel turns without any slipping between edge changes—so the skier carves rather than skids turns, even at very slow speeds or with lesser edge angles.

Skiers must respond to the design change with changing skill blends. For example, the rotary skill takes on a different application when applied to the shaped ski. Tipping the skis to an edge creates complementary leg rotation. Initiating rotary leg movements to start the turn is unnecessary and ineffective because this movement creates torque that pivots the skis. The rotary movement exists because leg turning follows as the turn develops. The ski-snow angles and the arc that the sidecut forms dictate leg turning to keep up with turn shaping.

This ability to carve is a wonderful advantage to intermediate skiers, because they can now sense what carving is without having to risk high speeds to experience it. Many skiers tend to rely too heavily on rotary skills at the expense of edging and pressure. With deep sidecuts, you feel the stable turning of the sidecut immediately and quickly become comfortable with the feeling of pressure to the edge. The sidecut tends to "hug" the snow in the turn, giving a very positive signal that the ski will continue to turn easily and that it will be easy to maintain control.

Conversely, if your leg initiates turning or twisting before the ski has engaged, the turns will result in skidding. Skidding on shaped skis is disconcerting at best. Skidding or other movements that create any torque make the skis unstable. Leg steering is a relatively powerful force and, if used, will overpower the skis and the sidecut design features. The skis' strength comes from the amount of edge contact with the snow when they are tipped. If you apply a rotary force to initiate the turn, you will not appreciate the true benefits of these skis.

Shaped skis are designed to perform with the complete sidecut engaged in the snow. Tipping the skis from a straight run will create an effective first-time experience for skiers. The skis create adequate turning and rotation of the legs to complement the edge angle. When you engage the skis, the design promotes a carved arc, and this radius brings your legs into rotation to keep up with the arc the ski is defining. If you rotate your legs to change direction, the skis will skid because they are shorter and have less mass.

Because the edges maintain such good carving contact with the snow, the skis are more stable at

shorter lengths than conventional skis, for advanced skiers and intermediates alike. There is as much edge contact when a 190-centimeter shaped ski is tipped to carve as on a 204-centimeter conventional ski, because the entire length is engaged and cutting into the snow. Furthermore, the skis tend to ski well in most conditions. The wide tip provides buoyancy in powder, while the deep sidecut allows carving on packed snow.

Many extreme designs are being applied and used—from radical sidecuts at one end of the scale to mild sidecuts at the other end. Although there is no question that deeper sidecuts in racing and recreational skis improve turning, it may be that the most radical designs will give way to more moderate ones, just as tennis-racquet heads went from oversized to midsized in the 1970s and 1980s. In fact, several more moderate designs that are currently available are developing a strong following.

Regardless of where the sidecut developments will lead, it looks as though conventional sidecuts no longer have a stronghold. Carved turns for all skiers are now available, and they are here to stay.

Specialty Powder (Wide-Bodied) Skis

The specialty powder skis work exceptionally well in all types of loose, unpacked snow, and some even work well on snow-packed slopes. They are all wider than conventional skis, hence they are often referred to as wide-bodied, or fat, skis.

Wide-bodied skis are designed to improve a person's ability to ski powder—they make powder skiing easier, more fun, and more accessible to a broader range of skiers. Their main advantage is that they are easier to turn and are more stable in the snow. This has a tremendous effect on improving confidence, balance, and stance. Skiers usually describe the feeling of skiing on wide-bodied skis as a light or floating sensation. Wide-bodied skis enable people to quickly learn the more efficient, rhythmic flexion and extension movements typical of great powder skiing.

Technically, these skis respond well to deflection from the snow when they are tipped to an angle in powder or crud conditions. Because they are wide and short they offer a strong platform when tipped. Snow builds under the base and gets compressed, making it easy for the ski to be directed into the arc. This feature gives them great buoyancy and deflection for turning.

Two types of specialty powder skis are available. The true fat skis are so wide that the bindings have to be mounted closer toward the inside edges so the skier can get enough leverage to edge the skis. These fat skis (also known as "fat boys") float the most, providing a stable, comfortable platform. Fat skis are very useful for intermediate powder skiers or for all powder skiers in very deep snow. They are available in lengths of 150 to 190 centimeters. Skiers usually choose them about 20 centimeters shorter than their normal skis for ease of turning; they can be skied shorter because the greater width compensates for length in providing stability. By now, these skis are a classic style likely to remain in production for a long time.

The next generation of wide skis (following the fats) are known as wide skis with sidecut. They are slightly narrower and longer than the "fats," although still not as long as conventional skis, and are center-mounted. These skis are excellent in powder but do not float as much as the fat skis. However, they are quite good on packed slopes so that they remain skiable when the powder gets skied out.

Ski Tuning

All types of skis, whether conventional or shaped, have to be tuned according to factory specifications and to individual taste and body alignment.

Hand tuning skis is a skill that requires instruction, time, practice, and proper tools. Many ski shops have excellent tuning facilities, and many instructors choose to have the experts do it, knowing that tuning considerations are critical to top ski performance. Proper edge beveling, edge sharpening, and ski base structuring (i.e., texturing the base of the skis) all have an enormous role in ease of turning, edge grip, and tightness of the turning arc.

Boots

The search for the correct ski boot may be long and difficult, but the effort is worth it. Although each person has a unique foot and leg structure, generally there are one or more styles of boots on the market that perfectly satisfy his or her needs.

The most important aspect of ski boot choice is the fit. In ski boot fitting, racers often try to jam their feet into boot shells that are too small, while most recreational skiers tend to buy them too big. The rule of thumb on fitting is that you should be able to fit one-and-one-half to two (loose) finger widths between the heel and the back of the shell when you are standing in the shell with your toes against the front of the boot, without the boot liner in place. Once the shell sizing is complete, most of the other features and characteristics can be modified, if necessary.

Ski boots should allow you to be in a proper, balanced stance while moving. You achieve a dynamically balanced stance when you can stand and move your body weight back and forth, from heel to toe, without waving your arms, bending over, or lifting your toes or heels. A ski boot should allow you to achieve this same balance while moving down the mountain. While trying boots in the shop, you should be able to lightly touch the tongue of the boot with your shins while in a balanced position over the ball of your foot (without having to drop your hips). You should also be able to straighten your leg without painful pressure on your calf.

Changes in snow, terrain, and speed will constantly challenge this balanced stance. Both the front and back of the boot must offer enough resistance to help keep you over your feet, yet be flexible enough to allow your ankles, knees, and hips adequate range of motion.

In the shop, you can distinctly feel the difference in overall stiffness in boots, although boots are usually slightly softer in indoor warmth. It is important to select the boot stiffness appropriate to your skiing ability level and style. Many instructors buy boots that are too stiff, offering a performance level rarely needed in the daily job of teaching. Students, on the other hand, tend to buy whatever the shop has available in their size. Therefore, you may want to discuss boot selection with your students, or even accompany them into the shop and help them select the appropriate boots for their needs.

Boot Categories

There are numerous ski boot styles available with various features and price tags, but they fall under five general categories:

- *"Convenience" boots.* These are boots with easy entry, walking comfort, and lots of padding. They are often quite comfortable but may not be very effective in translating foot movements to skiing or in supporting balance. These boots are targeted to beginner skiers.
- *Boots for intermediate skiers.* These have become increasingly good performers, allowing skiers to develop in good boots without having to jump from rentals to racing boots.
- *Women's boots.* These are improving each year as equipment

manufacturers and boot fitters increasingly base design on the anatomical features of women's lower legs and feet. Women's boots are no longer just lower-performance versions of men's boots with feminine cosmetics.

- *Boots for advanced skiers and racers.* Manufacturers are finally offering boots that combine good fit and comfort with performance. They are designed for advanced skiers and racers, but many advanced intermediate skiers also do well in them.

- *Rotary or edge boots.* Boots in this category either primarily enhance leg and foot rotation or they enhance edging. Rotary boots have cuffs that tend to bend forward and in the direction of the turn, while the edge boots tend to have more lateral rigidity for quick, powerful edge engagement. The boots that work well for the great majority of skiers share the primary characteristic of the Skiing Model—a seamless blend of rotary and edge/pressure capabilities.

Bindings

Bindings began with humble origins as leather thongs that held boots to skis. Today's bindings are expected not only to hold the boot to the ski but to release at a point just before any injury might occur. For many years, this seemed to be an adequate performance feature for bindings, but new technologies allow bindings to offer much more. The binding is assuming the responsibilities of flex control and vibration reduction in skis.

A modern binding can now be a safety device plus a performance-enhancer on par with skis and boots.

Binding companies are designing absorption systems placed between the toe piece and heel piece to detune or dampen skis. The benefit is smoother, more stable ski performance. The downside could be reduction of the skier's responsiveness because he or she is not getting the full "uncensored" effect of ski-snow contact.

Although these systems are relatively new, and almost unproven for recreational skiers, they satisfy the zeal of ski and boot manufacturers to enhance the skiing experience by controlling vibration and shock to the body.

Poles

Ski poles are an integral part of ski equipment. The proper length and grip design can have a profound influence on successful pole use and movements by helping you maintain a proper stance and control upper-body movements.

Thanks to the introduction of modern materials, many pole companies are producing lighter shafts that you can swing without much effort. The materials are carbon fiber or a carbon fiber-aluminum mix.

A useful initial way to select pole length is to invert a pole and grip the shaft under the basket. Your forearm should be at a 90-degree angle to the pole shaft, and your grip should allow freedom and ample range of motion of the wrist.

Although many handle designs

are available, the traditional plain-handled grip with adjustable wrist strap that has been on the market for many years is still the most popular design.

Proper and Improper Alignment

Ski teaching is based on the instructor's ability for recognizing or analyzing a student's movement and tailoring his or her lesson accordingly. This involves evaluating their alignment.

Great skiers have such a perfect skill blend that they show no discernable movement to begin turns; rather, they flow beautifully from turn to turn. The secret is in the feet and ankles—subtle, delicate movements direct and guide the ski into a turn.

Very little force or energy is needed to tip the ski to an edge. By simply rolling the foot and ankle to the inside, you push the ankle against the inside wall of the ski boot, and you can feel the ski edge starting to slice the snow (fig. 5.2). A balancing act follows as you make slight adjustments to edge and guide with the foot as the turn progresses. Increased ankle pressure to the side wall of the boot produces more edging.

Correct alignment efficiently transfers energy and power to the ski. If you do not have proper edging and rotary (turning) capabilities, you must compensate for improper alignment situations. Alignment defines your skiing movements because it influences the relationship between rotary and edging movements.

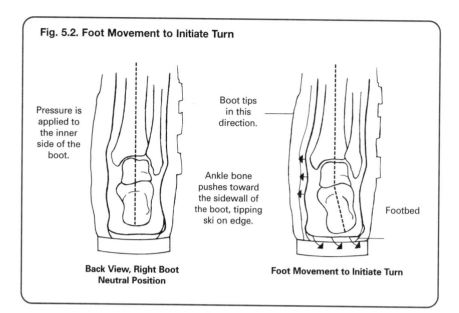

Fig. 5.2. Foot Movement to Initiate Turn

Pressure is applied to the inner side of the boot.

Boot tips in this direction.

Ankle bone pushes toward the sidewall of the boot, tipping ski on edge.

Footbed

Back View, Right Boot Neutral Position

Foot Movement to Initiate Turn

Problems from Improper Alignment

A properly aligned skier has balanced and symmetrical movement. Many skiers, due to their particular skeletal structure, are not able to ski in proper alignment without adjustments to their ski equipment. Some skiers are under-edged (not enough edge angle), while others are over-edged (too much edge angle). And some skiers are under-edged on one leg while being over-edged on the other.

The body has the ability to overcome even severe alignment problems by compensating for them in various ways: with an overly rotated upper body; an extremely countered position; severe leaning or tipping movements; overly pronounced rotary push-off; or an A-framed leg position that is the result of sideways heel pushing.

Even if you compensate for incorrect alignment, you can never be a completely effective skier because your stance and balance will always be compromised. Incorrect alignment limits you in the following ways.

- Your potential to improve is restricted because your balance is limited and you make poor use of ski design.
- You develop "bad habits" that may never be eliminated through practice or instruction.
- You are unable to ski smoothly or consistently when trying to link turns.
- You are unable to ski well in certain snow conditions. The skis will not hold on ice if under-edged and will catch on grippy snow when over-edged.
- Your compensatory movements and stance contribute to inappropriate use of and load on joints, and they may aggravate lower-back and knee problems.

Under-Edged Skiers

Under-edged skiers are over-flexed and levered forward in the boot

(fig. 5.3). In a basic traverse, they cannot ski with both skis at the same angle to the snow surface. Anatomically, the under-edged skier's feet, ankles, and legs are in a position that brings the knees to together (often touching) while leaving the feet up to 6 inches apart. This creates an A-framed or knock-kneed stance.

When the skier stands in ski boots on a flat surface, the same situation is apparent—the knees are touching, but the ski boots are apart and flat to the surface. While a certain amount of pronation is beneficial to transfer pressure and therefore enhance a balanced stance, too much pronation results in forces being misdirected to the arch rather than the inside of the boot.

Skiers with a strong athletic sense and movement awareness will compensate for under-edging: they will try to decrease rotary torque by reducing femur rotation. The movement involved requires counter-rotation (countering) of the hips early in the turn. When the hips are countered, the downhill leg can be straightened, which also decreases rotary forces and helps achieve edge angle through body inclination. The fine-tuning, motor-control capabilities of the foot and ankle are restricted, and the ability to vary turn shape is greatly diminished.

Over-Edged Skiers

Over-edged skiers (fig. 5.4) have just as much difficulty as under-edged skiers in making the ski work as a tool. The skis feel grabby and edge-high. Many skiers who are over-edged have learned that extreme beveling of the edges improves performance. Although beveling may help reduce the severity of these sensations, it cannot cure the problem.

Because over-edged skiers cannot perform the desired lower-body guiding, steering, and edging activities generated by the foot and ankle, they employ other methods of turning. These skiers have an extremely difficult time making short-radius turns and controlling pressure.

At turn initiation, to adapt, the skier starts inclining toward the mountain. As the ski starts to react to increased pressure on the edge, the skier gradually brings the upper body more square to the skis while progressing through the turn.

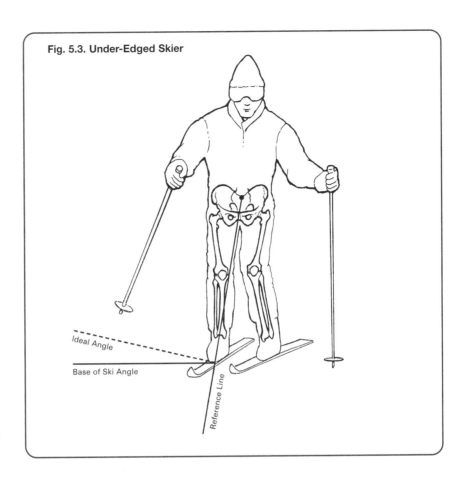

Fig. 5.3. Under-Edged Skier

Ideal Angle

Base of Ski Angle

Reference Line

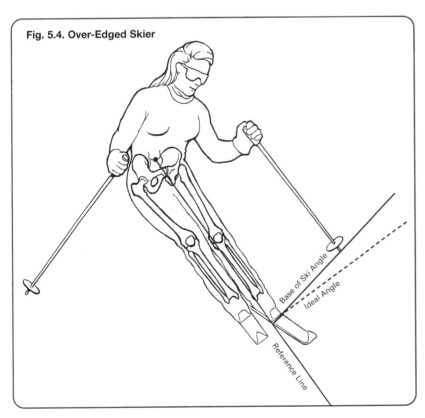

Fig. 5.4. Over-Edged Skier

Base of Ski Angle

Ideal Angle

Reference Line

This creates a seemingly controlled steering and guiding ability. The inside arm drops and moves behind the body during turn completion. This method is very subtle and is a way to control pressure as well as help the turning. Instructors refer to this student as an upper-body skier.

Improving Alignment with Equipment

The ability to learn proper movements on skis depends on the body's ability to work with the equipment correctly. If your students are not making technically effective movements while skiing, do not automatically assume that they have not learned the right movements. Consider the possibility that their problems are related to a biomechanical influence such as improper alignment.

As an instructor, you are involved with helping students solve their skiing problems, whether they arise from learned behavior or anatomical characteristics. The ski instructor is the logical choice for this role. Identifying the problem is the first step. To be effective, you must also be able to work with students and ski equipment technicians to help translate your observations into better skiing.

Some ski areas offer a comprehensive approach to helping skiers achieve proper alignment, and everyone from the recreational to the professional skier can benefit from such a program. The process begins with off-snow (static) and on-snow (dynamic) evaluations to identify whether alignment problems exist. Then the skier is assisted in obtaining properly designed custom insoles and selecting the appropriate boots, based on individual needs. Finally, alignment is again assessed to determine whether the skier needs further equipment modifications.

Although this approach can be greatly beneficial, the process is relatively new, not widely available, and demands trained, experienced technicians. Check in your region to see if these services are available.

The process starts with checking the ski boots. In addition to selecting a boot with appropriate features based on performance characteristics, every skier must have a qualified technician check and adjust the following: heel-to-toe height difference (ramp angle), the forward lean, and the cuff alignment to maintain a comfortable, dynamic balance. Boot selection and adjustment are critical to the success of this process because boots have design features that support skiing actions.

No two skiers are alike, so it is important to take time not only to select the proper boot but to have it customized. Once the proper boot has been selected and all the built-in adjustments are made, proper alignment modifications can vastly increase boot performance. This usually cannot be done with the cuff adjustment alone.

The standard (and quite successful) alignment system includes properly designed footbeds and under-the-boot wedges (cants). One of the critical parts of any alignment procedure is determining the center of mass of the knee at the joint line. Consequently, technicians must be familiar with the anatomy of the leg. The corrective process involves assessment and measurements, including an evaluation for orthotics, cuff adjustment, and checking alignment of the leg in the boot.

Subtle, appropriate movements of the foot and ankle enable efficient ski performance with minimal energy expenditure. An aligned foot contributes to proper skeletal positioning. If special insoles are selected, focus on a properly made footbed that does not restrict foot movement but promotes control. Insoles that are over-corrected and too rigid may lock the foot into a certain position.

After equipment modifications have been made, the most important, final step is helping the student identify, understand, and learn to apply the new skiing sensations created by changes in his or her equipment. Ideally, the student skis with you directly after an alignment correction so you can help the person identify and cope with the new sensations of properly aligned skiing.

An on-snow evaluation should include a program of movements that gives the student an immediate understanding of how his or her equipment either contributes to proper movements or detracts from progress. The process is simple and produces immediate results. You can watch students ski these maneuvers and determine what part of the body is creating the turn forces and balancing movements. For example, the student can traverse the slope while maintaining a straight line. He or she can also start in a traverse, release the edges to flatten the skis, and re-engage the edges back to a traverse. These maneuvers reveal whether movements start at the feet or higher up in the body. An efficiently aligned skier initiates ski movement with the feet.

After possibly years of skiing with and accommodating improper alignment, a lengthy adjustment period may be required to become familiar with the new feel of skiing. The improvement will often be immediate and obvious to the athletic individual, while others will require encouragement and additional time to become comfortable and discover new skiing opportunities.

The Promise of Technology

New technology promises to reshape and revitalize skiing. At the same time, instructors must not see technology as a remedy for all problems people have with learning to ski.

Think about it: How many skiers feel let down because they invested in some expensive new technology in skis, boots, bindings, or poles, only to find it was just a hype, did not really work as expected, or was outdated by the following year? This is one reason our students are very skeptical about new products and question how long the items will remain state-of-the-art.

Sometimes new technologies revitalize a sport, so instructors must strike a balance between abandoning the old and embracing the new. By staying current in technological advances, yet remaining flexible, you will be able to work with many different types of equipment, just as you work with many kinds of students.

chapter

6

Quest for Skiing Excellence

There are four components of skiing excellence: physical, technical, tactical, and psychological. These four components determine your present proficiency level as a skier and ultimately predict your potential for skiing excellence.

These components can be thought of in terms of a pyramid (fig. 6.1). The base or bottom layer of the pyramid represents your **physical skills,** or level of fitness. Your physical fitness determines your overall strength in the other components of the pyramid. As with most any other sport, if you are in good physical condition you'll be in better control of your skiing.

This base of physical skills supports the next layer, **technical skills.** Your technical expertise refers to your level of skiing skill

and versatility—the ability to ski with certain skills blends and make particular movements on skis. A well-rounded technical base of skiing makes it possible for you to respond to the many situations you encounter on the slopes.

Your **tactical skills** compose the next layer of the pyramid. These qualities consist of your ability to read and interpret variations in terrain, speed, or snow conditions, and to apply the appropriate strategies accordingly. Your ability to make the right tactical decisions enables you to perform your best in any given situation, whether you are choosing the best line in a bump field, negotiating a steep chute, or selecting a path through a race course.

The top layer of the pyramid represents your **psychological skills** and encompasses your attitudes and beliefs about learning and performing. Your attributes in this area help you perform under pressure and get through the inevitable ups and downs of learning and performance. Developed psychological skills help shape your attitude and enable you to function effectively under all conditions.

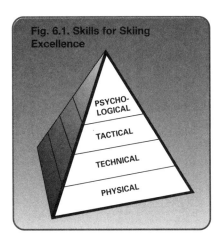

Fig. 6.1. Skills for Skiing Excellence

Physical Skills

Expert skiing requires highly developed fitness—a weak link in this area can decrease your total skiing performance.

Think about all the situations you encounter on the mountain and what they require of you. To make a skillful high-speed, long-radius turn you must have the strength to stay in balance on your outside leg and withstand pressures that can greatly exceed your own body weight. To ski moguls skillfully you must have the agility to make balanced foot-to-foot weight transfers with quickness and endurance. And to ski powder you must be able to extend and retract your legs repeatedly while accurately guiding them through a turn.

Fitness developed off-slope transfers to performance on-slope. No matter what your age or proficiency aspiration, you can take a giant step toward your skiing goals by improving your physical fitness. If you can make rapid foot-to-foot movements in a gym, you will most likely be able to do them on a steep, unforgiving mogul field. If you can leg-press close to your own body weight, you probably have the strength to make a high-speed turn on the snow. And if you can do exercises in which you bring your knees close to your chest repeatedly, you can probably make relatively sustained powder turns.

The following factors determine your level of fitness and therefore your ability to meet the demands of skiing.

Strength. The combination of power and endurance, and the ability of the muscles to exert force.

Power. The ability to generate a large force in a short time.

Endurance: The ability to perform sustained muscular effort at a given level.

Flexibility. The range of motion of the joints (such as the hips) or related series of joints (such as the spine).

Body composition. The proportion of fat weight to lean weight (e.g., bone, muscle, and tissue).

Aerobic capacity. The body's capacity to utilize oxygen. High aerobic capacity enables sustained activity.

Anaerobic capacity. The body's ability to produce work without processing oxygen. Anaerobic capacity is used during high-intensity, short-duration activities.

Skill. The capability to bring about a result with maximum certainty, minimum energy, or minimum time.

Although it takes a good aerobic base to ski all day, skiing also places high anaerobic demands on the body. Fitness tests done on elite skiers indicate they have *very high* levels of technical skill, strength, muscular endurance, and power; *moderate* amounts of flexibility; and *relatively high* cardiorespiratory ability.

Many athletes follow cycles of training designed to help them maintain a fitness base all year, and their training "peaks" at certain times of the year, corresponding with their competitive season.

For example, athletes on the U.S. Ski Team are in a cycle of general physical preparation during May, June, and July. During

this early season training, the athletes primarily focus on building endurance and strength. About 40 percent of training consists of aerobic and endurance-oriented exercises (biking, hiking, and running), 40 percent consists of strength training (weights and gymnastics), and 20 percent is devoted to anaerobic work (e.g., sprints, bounding—running with high-stepping strides—and pleiometrics—fitness routines requiring powerful, explosive movements such as jumping).

The ski team members focus on more ski-specific physical training during the months of August, September, and October. During this time, these athletes spend only 20 percent of their training time on endurance, with 40 percent on strength training and 40 percent on anaerobic training.

How does your pre-season training compare with the ski team's routine? How much of your time is spent on aerobic or endurance training versus strength, power, and anaerobic training?

You can meet the challenges of alpine skiing more effectively if you increase your power through activities such as lifting weights or sprinting, jumping, and bounding. And, you can build your aerobic endurance with biking, running, and in-line skating. If you do aerobic workouts regularly, consider structuring one or two of your weekly sessions to build your anaerobic base. These sessions can be shorter and higher-intensity than your aerobic workouts.

To get the most for your effort, seek help from a knowledgeable fitness professional *before* you embark on a training program. Based on your current level of fitness, this person can help you determine an appropriate and safe workout schedule, and also teach you about proper technique, such as the correct way to lift weights.

Technical Skills

Most everyone wants to ski with style and flair, but you must have a solid base of technical skills before you can begin to truly express yourself on skis.

The signature of true expertise is versatility: the blending of many movements in a smooth,

coordinated way in response to the situation at hand. Whether your goal is a performance outcome (e.g., getting down a double-black-diamond slope) or purely an expressive one (e.g., skiing with elegance and grace), you must first obtain basic technical skills so you can respond to situations in the manner you desire. (Exercises that incorporate these skills are described later in the chapter.)

Here are the fundamental technical skills of skiing and the ways in which you apply them in your skiing.

Balancing movements. You maintain dynamic lateral and fore/aft balance by pushing and pulling your feet. The ankles' range of motion to move your feet from side to side and fore and aft. You hold your arms in a comfortable position.

Rotary movements. In skiing, you use your legs to rotate and turn your skis.

Pressure-control movements. You control and transfer the pressure that builds on and against your skis by using foot-to-foot movements and by flexing and extending your legs.

Edge-control movements. You control the skis' edges by tipping your skis on and off their edges, using your feet, legs, hips, and trunk.

To synthesize all of these skiing fundamentals in an effective manner, you must focus on three key areas: balance, stance, and movement.

Balance refers specifically to balance in motion. Stance refers to

the positioning of the skier. *Movements* refer to the movements the skier uses to create the turn—the types of pressuring, edging, and rotary skills the skier uses for specific situations.

Balance

In balancing on your skis you make constant adjustments in your position to compensate for changes in terrain, snow conditions, speed, turn rhythm, and turn radius. Further, you balance on and against a carving ski during a turn as well as adjust to speed changes while in transition from one turn to the next.

Learning to perceive and compensate for the forces that develop in a turn is a primary aspect of learning to balance. Compensating expertly means you establish the needed inward lean before you can feel such forces. You literally let your body fall into space before your skis come around and catch you.

Balance demands a constant stream of modifications and adjustments, but the movement takes place within the parameters of a balanced area or zone. You know you are in balance when you can have a positive and selective effect on the application of your skiing movements and skills and when you can maintain an effective stance. Aspiring skiers often move in and out of the zone of balance, but great skiers move *within* the zone.

In skiing, you work your upper body in a way that complements your lower body and allows you to maintain a natural and athletic stance. You need not hold on tightly or clutch too heavily because to do so would arrest the pattern, freeze the movement, and check the endlessly changing flow of motion.

Skiing has a pattern like a dance, and because of this it is built on some of the same rules as dance. You cannot dance well unless you are completely in time with the music and in balance, neither leaning back on the last step nor pressing too far ahead on the next one. Instead, you are poised directly on the present step. Perfect poise and balance on the beat give good dancing and good skiing their sense of ease.

With skiing, however, you must be prepared to alter your balance and rhythm to respond to the variations in the "music," that is, the changing terrain and conditions. This requires *anticipating* changes in speed and terrain and making the appropriate adjustments—leading and committing with the center of mass, staying ahead, and getting to the front and to the middle of the ski, not on the heels. To ski well is to hover over the terrain, as if suspended by some hidden force. It may be thought of as a force of faith in your own ability.

Stance

Stance, the orientation of the body with the skis, is a key skill in any level of skiing. Proper stance is the cornerstone of muscular and skeletal efficiency.

Skiing requires ongoing alterations in stance. You constantly align and shape your body to

match your intended outcome, whether it is strong, functional, efficient, elegant, or aggressive skiing. Your torso and legs constantly move independently of each other without locking up into a position of facing down the hill.

Maintain a "strong" body on the inside of the turn, that is, the half of the body on the same side as the inside ski. You achieve this strong body when you focus on the inside-half of the body being ahead rather than the outside-half being behind. If, at the end of a turn, you settle back onto the outside ski, it has the effect of extending the inside ski forward, effectively "weakening" the inside turn-side.

Use your pole swing to start the new turn rather than to move out of the "back seat." Moving the inside-half of the body ahead into the new turn prepares you for what lies ahead.

To withstand the forces generated during turning, your stance should have an efficient blend of muscular and skeletal alignment. This alignment helps you maximize the potential of the equipment, balancing you perfectly on the whole foot to work the whole ski.

Skeletal alignment is perhaps the most essential aspect of stance, but, unfortunately, solutions to alignment problems are not always as simple or obvious as they may seem. Equipment modifications are not the only way to correct alignment. Furthermore, radical canting occasionally creates new stresses in the knees and new technical disadvantages that replace old

ones. Many alignment problems can be resolved effectively through proper stretching and strength training.

During skiing, your waist or torso area should be upright and strong. If you bend too much at the waist you will form a "hinge," that is, pressure on the outside ski will increase if you hit a bump or rut, causing you to collapse at the waist and lose your ability to maintain the desired turn.

Do not rely on the boots' rigidity to hold you up—keep a functional amount of tension in the legs. Establish constant contact with your boot cuffs, and maintain hard contact between the bottoms of your feet and the insoles. If your boots force you too far forward or too straight up, adjust the boot shell to create a good neutral stance. If the shaft angles of your boots are the same in both feet, the inside ski adds significantly to the power and arc of the turn.

Upper-body discipline, that is, hand positions and pole usage, also forms movement patterns critical to good skiing. Your arm and hand positions contribute to balanced and comfortable stance. You must learn to use poles in a way that stabilizes and balances the torso— sometimes planting poles, sometimes just swinging them. At certain times you use a checking/ planting movement of your poles to finish the previous turn; other times you use a swing-and-release movement to develop the new turn.

Variations in equipment design will cause subtle variations in movement as well, but fundamental movement patterns and the principles of stance remain surprisingly constant in skiing. An effective stance lets you create the desired skiing movements and deal with the dynamic forces you encounter, regardless of the type of equipment you use.

Movements

Movement patterns enable the components of edge release, pressure redistribution, and edge reengagement in a turn. These patterns consist of changes in timing and style—anticipating or responding to changes in speed and forces. The result is deliberate and accurate skiing where the skis and legs move away from center and back to center, linking fluid, round turns down the slope.

Fundamental Exercises

The hallmark of skiing mastery is versatility: being able to ski a spectrum of turn shapes and sizes, at different speeds, and on different pitches. It also means being prepared to respond to the unexpected: being able to hop, leap, jump, step, and skate on your skis.

An expert skier has the ability to take a series of incredibly complicated movements and create a seamless and seemingly effortless continuum of motion. Let go of the idea that each and every turn will look and feel the same—it simply will not happen. Explore the mountain with your skis rather than try to make each and every turn the same.

The following exercises will help you form a solid base for skiing versatility.

Hockey stops. Run your skis straight down the fall line, gain some speed, and then pivot your skis across the hill and into a sideslip. Engage your ski edges and come to a crisp stop. Make sure you bring your skis all the way across the hill, while you keep your mid and upper body targeted down the fall line. The objective is to ski both sides equally well and to turn your skis with your legs and feet.

Sideslips. Start with your skis pointed across the hill. Flatten your skis by extending and moving your legs away from the hill and rolling your skis off their edges. Slip sideways down the fall line for a distance, then re-engage the edges and come to a stop. Roll both skis onto a high edge by flexing and moving your thighs, knees, and lower legs inward. Try to sideslip with variations in speed, hill steepness, and edging intensities.

Balanced traverse. Ski across the hill with both uphill edges engaged. Stand in balance, with the majority of your weight on the downhill ski. Keep the uphill side of your body and your skis slightly ahead. The objective is to leave a clean track with your skis without slipping sideways.

Uphill christies. Point your skis straight down the fall line. Gain some speed, turn across the hill, and come to a smooth stop. The objective is to edge and turn your skis at the same time, thus making a rounded turn.

Skating. Skate straight down the fall line of a slope with a comfortable pitch. Ideally, you will stay in balance while moving from foot to foot to ski with extension off a well-edged ski.

Stem turns. Perform a classic stem christie: From a solid platform on your downhill ski, stem your uphill ski away from your body, up the hill and into the new turn. Commit your weight to the stemmed ski.

Hop turns. Make short turns with a hopped initiation. Finish a short turn and jump up high enough to clear your skis off the snow. Land in the fall line and steer your skis through the rest of the turn. On the next turn, try to jump and aim your skis down the hill, land, and *finish* the turn as well. With this exercise, learn to ski a spectrum of long to short hop turns.

Check turns. On a steep slope, start by hopping up, pivoting your skis all the way across the hill, and coming to a complete stop. The objective is to link these turns together, one after another. Try to inch your way down the slope by using a series of check turns.

Absorption turns. Start your turns by retracting your legs to your body rather than extending them. It feels a little backward but is a key movement pattern for bumps and powder. You should develop comfort with this movement in a variety of terrain and snow conditions.

One-ski skiing. Link short and long turns on one ski. Ideally, you should be able to turn equally well on either ski.

Step turns. Maintain the downhill ski as a platform and step the

uphill ski into a converging, diverging, or parallel position. From a medium-sized turn, step your inside ski up the hill. Set the ski on its edge, commit your weight to it, and steer it through the rest of the turn. Perform both converging and diverging steps. Do both long and short turns. Practice this to develop competency in a variety of step turns.

Carved parallel turns. Ski carved parallel turns that leave a smooth and round track in the snow. Change the rhythm—ski a couple of short turns, then long turns, and back to short turns again. Try to ski a spectrum from short to long turns.

Tactical Skills

When you ski, you move through many different environments on the mountain itself, from smooth,

groomed trails to cut-up, rough snow and moguls. To become an all-mountain, masterful skier you have to be able to respond to these ever-changing conditions.

It is important to select the right response at the right time. Although conscious decision-making is a tactical strategy, many responses become automatic as they are learned through miles and miles of skiing. This process of spontaneous reaction is referred to as **automaticity,** the intangible of skiing gained only through experience and mileage.

Moguls

Like snowflakes, no two moguls are alike. Moreover, the tactics and techniques you used in the bumps in the morning may not be suitable for them in the afternoon when mogul shapes or snow conditions

are likely to have changed.

You make tactical line choices to help control your speed and maintain ski-snow contact. Try to maintain your rhythm even when the line disappears. Learning to use the troughs, backs, sides, and tops of bumps allows you to turn where you wish so you can maintain a steady rhythm.

Many ski areas have runs with moguls on one side and groomed snow on the other. These situations offer a wonderful opportunity to learn about and practice mogul skiing because the groomed snow is a welcome break after you have wrestled over the rough side.

It is better to ski short sections well than longer sections when you are out of control. Bumps are honest and timely with feedback about your performance. If you are skiing moguls in an efficient, controlled manner, you will know it by the smooth and rhythmic feeling. Otherwise, you will feel as if you are on the back of a bucking bronco.

There are three basic lines of descent in skiing moguls: zipper line, round line, and long line.

Zipper Line

The zipper line is the most aggressive path of descent through moguls. This line is formed in the snow when people ski on the same path over and over again, creating a zipper-like staircase down the run. Skiing this line is a lot like being the bull-rider at the rodeo: it takes guts, commitment, and strength.

To ski the zipper line you have to stay centered over your feet and the downhill ski. Try to keep your shins in soft contact with the front of your boots at all times. If you lean back, you will tense up your leg muscles too much to hold yourself up rather than use them effectively as shock absorbers.

Keep your hips facing down the hill. Try not to let them get twisted around and pointed to the side or you will lose foot speed and edging ability. Skiers often make the mistake of folding at the waist to absorb moguls. Keep your body upright and absorb the bumps with your legs. This will put less stress on your lower back, muscles, and joints.

Your legs should absorb bumps with a pump-like action. Extend your legs and press the skis onto the backside of the bump to gain early ski-snow contact. Switch your weight to the new downhill ski as soon as possible and start the next turn. Keep your head level and use your eyes to look ahead, panning the upcoming terrain.

For a smooth run, you will need to "read" the bumps to gauge the correct speed for a given line. When you ski bumps at about the same speed as the skiers who made them, the ride becomes smoother. If you try to turn your skis too far across the fall line to control your speed, you will jam the tips of your skis into the sharp ruts and trip.

Round Line

The round line is an excellent option for skiing moguls. Unlike the zipper line, the round line allows you to ski at a speed that is most comfortable for you. This is useful when bumps are icy or if the terrain is steep and you want to ski slower.

The key to skiing this line is to maintain a constant rhythm, and to do this you must learn to ski the tops, sides, and troughs of moguls.

Instead of dropping into and riding the rut as you would in the zipper line, stay high and turn on the backside of the bumps. When your skis are up and out of the trough, you can turn farther across the hill without the risk of tripping and catching the tips or tails of your skis in a narrow rut or slot.

When you start your next turn, aim low toward the upcoming bump. Ski underneath the mogul and across the smooth, shallow part of the rut. By staying on the tops and sides, you are no longer forced to ski the speed dictated by the zipper line.

Long Line

The long line approach works best when the bumps are relatively smooth and small. It is also a great way to ski the bumps for the first time.

Ski a longer turn at a speed that is slower than you might normally ski. Try to maintain contact with the snow by actively flexing and extending your legs. As you roll over a bump, quickly tuck your legs underneath you. As you clear the top, start reaching and extending your legs to stay in contact with the snow.

Try to hop over the ruts now and then. As you ski over a mogul, try not to absorb it fully—let the bump loft you into the air. Aim and time your jump so that you land on the backside of the next mogul. Spot your landing, absorb the rut, and look for another take-off point. This is a wonderfully playful way to ski small and *unrhythmical* bumps. It may seem like choppy skiing, but when you time it right, it feels effortless.

Longer turns give you more time to start rotating your upper body in the direction of the old turn. Keep your center of mass aimed toward the next turn by reaching and swinging your pole downhill. If you maintain this upper-body discipline, you will find it easier to start the next turn.

Ice

Skiing ice demands razor-sharp skis and well-honed skills. On the days you can clearly see your reflection in the hard surface, your performance depends on how effectively you can get your skis to bite and grip.

Edge bite in these conditions means penetrating into the icy layer deep enough to make your skis hold. There are basically two ways to do this: with check turns and with sliced turns. Together these two extremes form a range—on any given icy day, you will probably use a combination of both.

Expert skiers can dance nimbly from one extreme to the other, always exploring the range of possibilities between the quick check turn and the smoother sliced turn.

Quest for Skiing Excellence

Check Turns

If speed control in icy conditions is your primary concern, you can set your body and skis up for a brief and intense edge set, or check, between turns. Start with your skis positioned across the fall line. Aim the center of your body down the hill. As you start the turn, plant

your downhill pole, and from this position extend enough to lift your skis off the surface and pivot them all the way around so that they point across the fall line in the opposite direction.

As you land, drive your thighs and lower legs toward the hill. This quick action immediately puts the skis on a higher edge and turns

them farther across the hill. A crisp edge-set results. Plant your pole firmly to stabilize your upper body and brace you against the decelerating forces of the check.

When you link these together, try to get off the old set of edges before the skis can break loose or "wash out." A checking edge should grip powerfully but briefly: get on the edges and off of them *fast*.

Watch your speed carefully. In icy and steep conditions, it is easy to get going very fast, very soon. Monitor each check turn to stay in control.

This speed-controlling turn is a very effective option when the run is very icy and narrow because you can creep down the steepest of slopes with a very short, staccato-like, speed-controlling rhythm.

Sliced Turns

The sliced turn is an effective way to ski in icy conditions when the slope is not very steep or when you want to maintain your speed. Because the shape of the turn is rounder and more carved, it allows you to keep your momentum flowing smoothly down the hill.

With check turns, your downhill speed flows straight down the mountain, but with sliced turns, you ski a slightly longer-radius turn and find a rhythm from side to side, following the path of your skis.

Feel for an earlier edge by tipping and turning your skis at the same time. As you move to the middle of the turn, extend your legs and reach out for a higher edge angle. At this point your outside ski should slice forward through the ice as your feet begin to arc back under you.

The holding power of a sliced turn comes from the ski moving forward through the arc of the turn—if the ski goes sideways you will probably have to check to finish the turn.

Powder and Crud

On your first run the snow was light, unbroken, and smooth. An hour later it is cut up, choppy, and thick. Skiing these conditions is challenging because just when you think you can anticipate the snow's texture, it changes. Again, the key is versatility—having many movement options at your disposal to help you deal with the diversity of natural snow conditions.

Learn to ski the ranges of extension and retraction. Extend to get up and out of thick snow and retract to stay in the deep and light snow. These two basic movement patterns form the ends of a spectrum of turning maneuvers that can be useful for either powder or crud conditions.

An aggressive extension off your legs when you turn will unweight your skis. If you extend hard and fast enough, you will actually hop up and out of the snow. The second option is to retract, or pull in, your legs and feet. If you retract quickly you can unweight your skis.

Try to keep your upper and lower body movements independent of each other, regardless of the snow conditions. Keep your poles, arms, shoulders, and trunk facing the fall line while using your legs to steer your turns. Very light snow will begin to compress under your skis. When you feel this pressure building, retract your feet and skis toward your center of mass.

As you retract your legs, feel your skis begin to unweight and glide toward the surface of the snow. When your ski tips peek out of the snow, start the new turn by rolling your skis off the "old" set of edges and onto the new set. Guide both skis simultaneously toward the new turn. As your center of mass moves downhill, extend your legs and steer your skis to the fall line. At this time, your skis will dive back into the snow. Continue to guide both ski tips through the arc of the turn.

Feel the subtle increase in pressure as the snow under your skis starts to compress. Keep guiding your legs and feet through the turn, followed by retraction. Start to swing your other pole and let your skis glide to the surface again.

Extension Turns

In thick, heavy snow, you have to extend your legs powerfully when starting your turns. You can then lift your skis up and out of the snow. Flex your legs at the end of the turn, and release your body up and out of the old turn with a smooth, powerful extension of the legs. Leap out of the snow from both feet. When you feel light, weightless, and your skis have cleared the snow, begin to turn both feet and both legs toward the fall line.

Unweighting can be a gift in soft, unruly snow. In some cases it is the only way to get the turn going. As you get better at it, or as the snow gets lighter and more forgiving, you can tone down the hop and give yourself a more subtle lift.

Retraction Turns

Retraction is a useful skiing tactic in dry, light, and very deep powder because it enables you to keep your skis in the snow instead of hopping up and out of it. Although keeping your skis in the snow requires more finesse and control, it is easier to sense the snow quality and judge the amount of steering power you will need for each turn.

In retracting, you pull your feet and legs toward your center of mass to unweight your skis. You absorb the energy from the skis instead of directing it up and into the new turn. As a result your skis glide up and down through the deep snow.

In the mid-phase or fall-line part of the turn, your skis are deep in the snow. As you complete the turn and retract your legs toward your body's center, your skis glide back up toward the surface. If you time it right, you will have minimal resistance to steering and you can initiate your turn with accuracy and precision.

Psychological Skills

Your psychological well-being enables you to deal with any fears, negative attitudes, and frustrations you may experience during your development as a skier. To enhance learning and performance, you need to keep these feelings in their proper perspective.

Psychological skills, at the top of the skills pyramid, are a very important link between the physical, technical, and tactical skills—all of which help you realize your ambitions in skiing.

Achieving a level of expertise is not an easy journey. This endeavor often starts out with great strides, frequent accomplishments, and an incredibly steep learning curve. As you continue to grow as a skier, however, new achievements become incrementally smaller and exponentially more difficult. Peaks and valleys emerge in learning, and performance and progress very often come to either a real or perceived plateau.

This experience can cause you to become complacent, content to slip sideways on the ice, or just escape to the lodge and drink hot chocolate when the snow gets too hard or too deep. You might even quit skiing altogether, becoming a spectator of a former passion.

You might be using some strategies to break out of the plateau. For instance, you might take a clinic or workshop, thinking that your experience at this type of event will provide you with all the answers. You might try, with determination, to apply helpful tips, such as "relax and breathe," and "keep your hands in front with your weight on the downhill ski." Or, you might buy the latest and greatest technology in ski equipment because you think this will make the difference.

Sometimes your method of dealing with the psychological ups and downs of skiing is haphazard or misaligned with your goals and does not bring you the desired results. The following sections contain some useful suggestions to help you keep these attitudes and feelings in proper perspective.

Personal Assessment

Think for a minute about what you want as a skier. Make sure your skiing aspirations are what you want for *yourself*. You may become disillusioned and disheartened with your accomplishment if you are doing it for someone else. It is important that this goal belongs to you, because personal ownership fuels desire.

Your goal should be attainable. Ask yourself these questions. Is your goal realistic for you? Do you have the physical, technical, and tactical skills necessary, or the potential to develop them? Can you build the foundation to make this aspiration a reality? Be honest with yourself and try to base your aspirations upon your potential for success.

The goal must be crystal clear. This is a vital element of setting goals. The more alive and succinct your goal is, the more likely you are to achieve it. Try briefly writing or describing the goal. Imagine yourself doing it successfully. If you enlist the help of others, you must be able to clearly communicate your goal to them.

Once you identify your greatest limiting factor—the missing piece of your success "puzzle"—work to overcome it until that liability becomes your greatest strength. After practicing something a few times, you might start to feel as if you have met your objective, but do not stop there. Keep in mind that sometimes you have to practice a skill relentlessly to master it.

Great achievers show high levels of persistence and accept responsibility for the result. When an idea to improve your skiing works, take the credit and do not call it luck. If your skiing does not improve, take the responsibility, and do not blame the situation *or* your equipment.

Finally, do not become overly obsessed with reaching your goal. The goal itself should not become so important that you view the process of attaining it as an obstacle. You may find that achieving goals is quite meaningful, but realize that the *process* itself is what will bring you long-lasting skills.

Find a Coach

If you are truly committed to achieving a level of excellence in skiing, seek out a coach. You do not need a full-time coach to continually oversee your development, but occasionally you will need an objective observer who can either alter or reinforce your efforts.

Feedback is critical! Imagine what it would be like to learn or perform without feedback—it would be like running a race and never finding out your finish time. Your intrinsic gauges (what you sense from the inside) and extrinsic gauges (the results of your actions) must be adjusted and regulated so they are pointing in the same direction. A coach can let you know if you are performing a movement the correct way and help you compare these internal sensations with external results.

When you find the right coach, you have to trust that person. Suspending your beliefs about skiing is probably the most difficult barrier to cross, particularly if you are adept at the sport. Initially, you must place belief before understanding. Realize that as your learning curve goes up, your performance curve may wane. If you let this interfere with your trust in your coach, you will likely begin to resist his or her observations and go right back to old habits.

Push Your Envelope

Risk-taking is an important element to achieving your personal best. By pushing yourself in an intelligent manner, you can develop your potential, and your skiing competency may surprise you.

Intelligent risk-taking means that you are keenly aware of the possible consequences of your actions: You know your personal limits, the limits of your equipment, and the how condition of the ski slope can affect your decisions.

When you try a new movement or practice a skill you may be inclined to focus inward and close off the outside environment. Try to resist this tendency, and be sure to choose runs that are uncrowded and relatively easy for you. Ski the trail a few times before you experiment, so you know it inside out.

As you gain comfort with a skill and decide to push it a little to test and stretch your limits, do it where you will not endanger

anyone. Be warmed up, physically and mentally. Pay attention and do not let your mind wander. Finally, when you get tired, be sure to quit or look for less-demanding terrain or snow conditions.

To support your dreams and aspirations as a skier, you must build a solid foundation of physical, technical, tactical, and psychological skills. If you fully develop these fundamental skills of skiing, then combine them with a spirit of adventure, you may find sources of finesse you never dreamed you had and strengths you never knew existed.

chapter

7

Anatomy and Conditioning

Skiing is not the kind of activity you can easily leap back into after months of being sedentary. Few, if any, sports allow such an abrupt return without levying some kind of toll on your body. As a professional skier, you need to maintain a fitness level throughout the year that will allow you to make the transition into the physical demands of the ski season both comfortably and safely. A well-planned conditioning routine will help you minimize the physical stresses of your profession, combat the fatigue of spending hours at a time on skis, and, consequently, reduce the potential for injury.

A well-rounded program of conditioning has many different facets. This chapter covers the basic concepts of body structure: the skeleton and the major muscles and joints involved in movement. This information is presented to give you an idea of how these structures contribute to a skier's alignment and balance.

Various elements of fitness are discussed, including motor control, aerobic and anaerobic capacity, muscular strength and endurance, and flexibility. A sample routine is provided to help you enhance flexibility. The chapter concludes with information on cross-training—how to best stay in condition for skiing by doing other selected conditioning activities, both during the ski season and off-season.

Anatomy

The primary goal in discussing anatomy is to help you understand how the muscles and skeleton function as a system to create balanced movement. This information is presented to increase your awareness of how the body works in the context of skiing, but it is simply an introduction. You are encouraged to learn more about this topic through coursework and reading.

The anatomical components discussed are the body's structural support—the skeleton, joints, and muscles—with a focus on the spine and lower extremities, since these areas are of primary importance in skiing. Remember, however, that *all* systems in the body interact at all times.

Your ability to achieve good alignment when skiing is affected by your natural skeletal alignment and by the balance of muscle flexibility and strength. If a muscle is too weak, it will be unable to maintain good positioning of the skeleton because other forces, such as gravity, will overcome it. If a muscle is too tight, it will pull the skeleton out of alignment, and weight-bearing on joint surfaces will be uneven.

Another factor affecting good alignment is your connective tissue, or fascia. This system supplies the flexible framework of the body. **Fascia** is a filmy membrane that encases all structures of the body, including bone, ligament, and muscle. If the fascia becomes restricted, such as with a surgical scar, it can limit the body's mobility and therefore change the skeletal alignment.

To achieve proper alignment with your skis, you must first have good internal alignment in your body. An evaluation by a health professional, such as an orthopedist or physical therapist, can provide you with the information you need to improve your alignment through exercise and treatment if needed.

Skeleton and Joints

This section discusses specific skeletal structures and the major joints (fig. 7.1). The skeleton and joints provide attachments for muscles, enabling the movements of skiing.

Spine. The **spinal column** is made up of individual segments called **vertebra**. There are four regions of the spine: (1) cervical (the neck), (2) thoracic (the middle back), (3) lumbar (the lower back), and (4) sacrum and coccyx (the tail

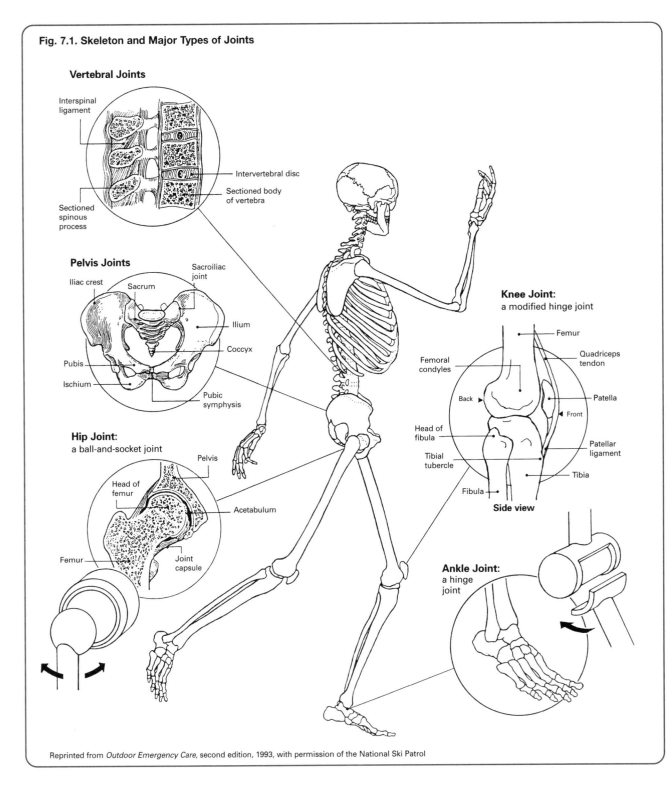

Fig. 7.1. Skeleton and Major Types of Joints

Vertebral Joints

Interspinal ligament

Intervertebral disc

Sectioned body of vertebra

Sectioned spinous process

Pelvis Joints

Iliac crest

Sacrum

Sacroiliac joint

Ilium

Coccyx

Pubis

Ischium

Pubic symphysis

Hip Joint:
a ball-and-socket joint

Pelvis

Head of femur

Acetabulum

Femur

Joint capsule

Knee Joint:
a modified hinge joint

Femur

Quadriceps tendon

Femoral condyles

Back

Front

Patella

Head of fibula

Patellar ligament

Tibial tubercle

Tibia

Fibula

Side view

Ankle Joint:
a hinge joint

Reprinted from *Outdoor Emergency Care*, second edition, 1993, with permission of the National Ski Patrol

bone), as shown in fig. 7.2.

Each region has a natural curve. The spine, when in proper alignment, is slightly curved **anteriorly** (toward the front of the body) in the cervical region, **posteriorly** (toward the back of the body) in the thoracic region, anteriorly in the lumbar region, and posteriorly in the sacral region.

The **spinal cord** travels through a space in the posterior aspect of each vertebra from the base of the skull to approximately the first lumbar segment. At this point, a group

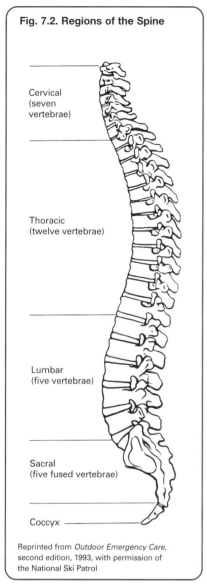

Fig. 7.2. Regions of the Spine

Cervical
(seven
vertebrae)

Thoracic
(twelve vertebrae)

Lumbar
(five vertebrae)

Sacral
(five fused vertebrae)

Coccyx

Reprinted from *Outdoor Emergency Care,*
second edition, 1993, with permission of
the National Ski Patrol

Pelvis. The spine rests on the pelvis where the sacrum joins with the ilium at the sacroiliac joints. The left and right sides of the pelvis join in the front of the body at the pubic symphysis. Movement occurs at all of these joints.

Hip Joint. The pelvis joins with the femur (the long bone of the thigh) at the hip joint (fig. 7.3). This joint is a **ball-and-socket joint** and is very stable. Like the shoulder, it moves in all directions, allowing bending and rotation. The muscles acting on the hip must be flexible and strong to achieve maximum function with minimum compensation from the back and other parts of the body.

Knee Joint. The knee joint is where the lower end of the femur joins with the tibia; the rounded ends of the femur rest on top of the relatively flat surface of the tibia (fig. 7.4). Between the femur and the tibial plateau is a piece of cartilage called the meniscus. It helps to stabilize the knee by providing shock absorption between the joint surfaces.

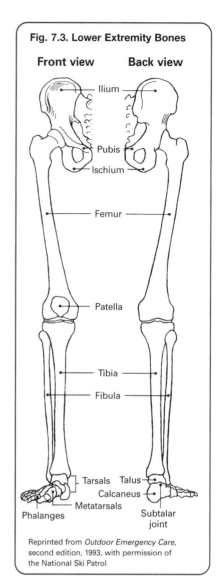

Fig. 7.3. Lower Extremity Bones

Front view   **Back view**

Ilium

Pubis

Ischium

Femur

Patella

Tibia

Fibula

Tarsals   Talus
Calcaneus
Metatarsals
Phalanges   Subtalar
                   joint

Reprinted from *Outdoor Emergency Care,*
second edition, 1993, with permission of
the National Ski Patrol

of individual nerves branch off of the spinal cord and pass through the posterior aspect of the vertebral column on their way to muscles and organs. This group of nerves resembles a horse's tail, hence the Latin name cauda equine.

Between each two vertebrae is the intervertebral disc. This disc has two components: a fibrous outer layer that gives the disc its structure, and an inner layer, a gel-like structure that serves as the primary shock absorber of the spine.

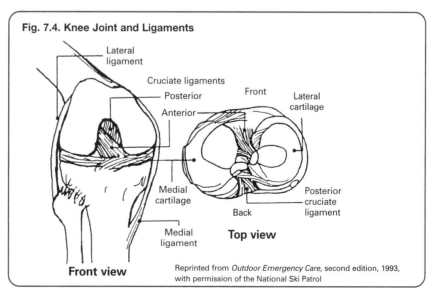

Fig. 7.4. Knee Joint and Ligaments

Lateral
ligament

Cruciate ligaments
Posterior   Front
Anterior   Lateral
                          cartilage

Medial
cartilage   Posterior
                          cruciate
Back   ligament

Medial
ligament   **Top view**

Front view

Reprinted from *Outdoor Emergency Care,* second edition, 1993,
with permission of the National Ski Patrol

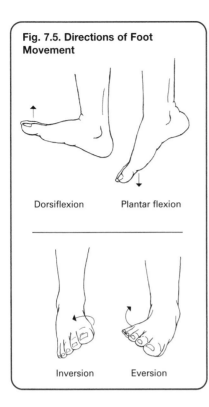

Fig. 7.5. Directions of Foot Movement

Dorsiflexion   Plantar flexion

Inversion   Eversion

Unlike the ball-and-socket joint of the hip, the knee is a modified **hinge joint** and is fairly unstable. Knee ligaments act as the primary stabilizers. The medial collateral ligament protects the inside of the knee and the lateral collateral ligament stabilizes the outside. The anterior cruciate ligament, or ACL, prevents the forward movement of the tibia on the femur, and the posterior cruciate ligament prevents it from moving backward.

The patella, or kneecap, joins with the femur in front of the knee. The patella is imbedded in the quadriceps tendon, and when the forces acting on it are balanced, it glides in a groove as the knee is bent and straightened. When the knee is bent, the quadriceps muscle is stretched, causing the patella to be pressed. When the knee is extended and the quadriceps is relaxed, the patella "floats."

Contracting the quadriceps when the knee is bent compresses the patella against the femur. During skiing, the knee is nearly always in a bent position, creating more compression at the patellofemoral joint.

Ankle Joint. The two bones of the lower leg, the tibia and fibula, make up the ankle joint as they join with the talus. The primary weight-bearing bone is the tibia, so the force of a person's weight is transferred to the foot via this bone.

The ankle is supported by ligaments and muscles. The ankle joint moves in four basic directions: **dorsiflexion** (moving the toes toward the front of the shin), **plantar flexion** (pointing the toes toward the floor), **inversion** (pointing the sole of the foot inward), and **eversion** (moving the sole of the foot outward).

These motions, illustrated in fig. 7.5, help you maintain your balance and are crucial to controlling the motions of boots and skis.

Foot. The foot joint of primary concern in skiing is the subtalar joint, made up of the talus in conjunction with the calcaneus. **Pronation** (flattening the arch) and **supination** (elevating the arch) are the motions associated with the subtalar joint. When the subtalar joint pronates, the tibia, because it is joined at the ankle with the talus, rotates medially (the shin turns inward toward the other leg). By the same token, the subtalar joint in supination causes a lateral (outward) rotation of the tibia. The foot pronates and supinates to help balance the body during skiing.

Muscles

This section discusses major muscles and muscle groups (fig. 7.6 and 7.7). Included are descriptions of the ways in which these muscle groups work in skiing, which will help you understand and correctly describe skiing movements and determine which exercises keep these muscles in top condition.

Trunk Extensors. Trunk extensors are the muscles that cause the spine to arch backward, increasing the lumbar curve. In skiing, the trunk extensors help you maintain your fore/aft balance. The muscles primarily responsible for extending the spine are the erector spinae.

Trunk Flexors. Trunk flexors enable the spine to bend into a rounded position. The primary trunk flexors are the rectus abdominus and the internal and external abdominal oblique muscles. You also use your trunk flexors to bend your spine, which helps you maintain fore/aft balance on skis. The obliques are involved in generating and controlling many rotary movements—your internal and external obliques work together to generate trunk rotation, involved in rotary movements of skiing. These muscles help to pull you into a more upright stance so you can avoid leaning back against your boots.

Hip Flexors. The hip flexors bring the thigh toward the abdomen. As with trunk flexors, hip flexors help you maintain fore/aft balance by pulling you forward over your skis. The primary hip flexors are the iliopsoas muscles, the rectus femoris, and the tensor fascia lata.

Fig. 7.6. Major Muscles—Front

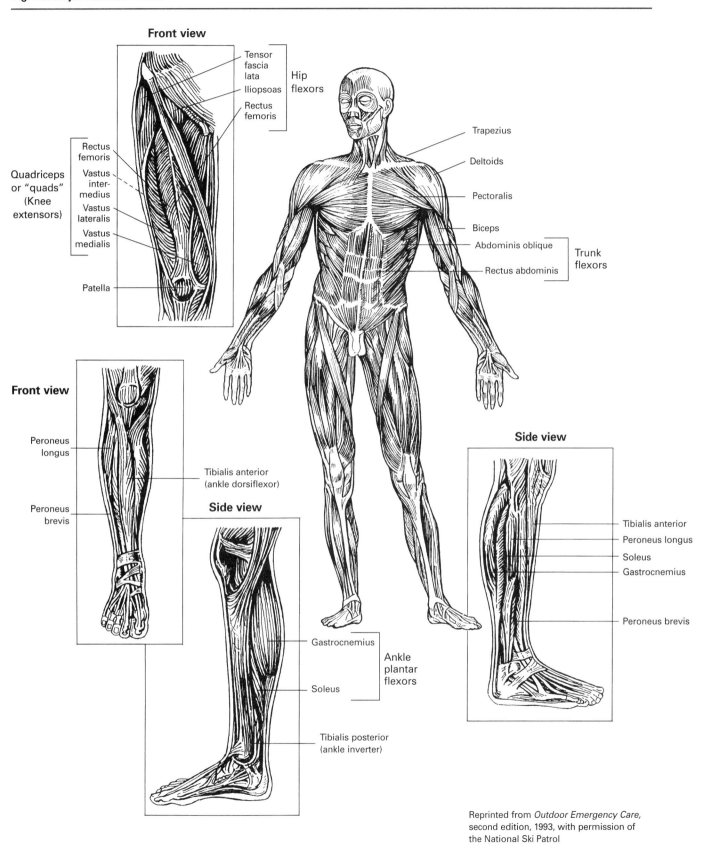

Front view

Tensor fascia lata
Iliopsoas
Rectus femoris

Hip flexors

Quadriceps or "quads" (Knee extensors)

Rectus femoris
Vastus inter-medius
Vastus lateralis
Vastus medialis

Patella

Trapezius

Deltoids

Pectoralis

Biceps

Abdominis oblique

Rectus abdominis

Trunk flexors

Front view

Peroneus longus

Peroneus brevis

Tibialis anterior (ankle dorsiflexor)

Side view

Gastrocnemius

Soleus

Tibialis posterior (ankle inverter)

Ankle plantar flexors

Side view

Tibialis anterior
Peroneus longus
Soleus
Gastrocnemius

Peroneus brevis

Reprinted from *Outdoor Emergency Care,* second edition, 1993, with permission of the National Ski Patrol

Fig. 7.7. Major Muscles—Back

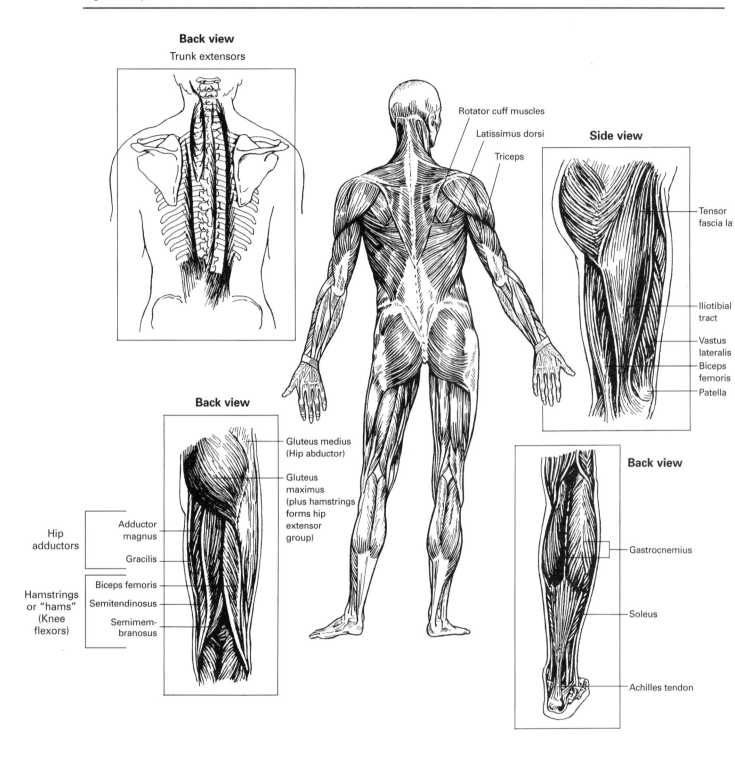

Back view
Trunk extensors

Rotator cuff muscles

Latissimus dorsi

Triceps

Side view

Tensor fascia la

Iliotibial tract

Vastus lateralis

Biceps femoris

Patella

Back view

Gluteus medius (Hip abductor)

Gluteus maximus (plus hamstrings forms hip extensor group)

Hip adductors
- Adductor magnus
- Gracilis

Hamstrings or "hams" (Knee flexors)
- Biceps femoris
- Semitendinosus
- Semimembranosus

Back view

Gastrocnemius

Soleus

Achilles tendon

Reprinted from *Outdoor Emergency Care,* second edition, 1993, with permission of the National Ski Patrol

Hip Extensors. The hip extensors enable you to move your thigh behind you. While you ski, your hip extensors, in active contraction, will lessen flexion in your legs. The gluteus maximus and hamstring muscles are the primary hip extensors.

Hip Rotators. The hip medial and lateral rotators are very important in balancing and supporting the other motions at the hip, and they help stabilize the femur in the hip socket. You incorporate hip rotator actions to maintain good alignment with your skis. Primary hip lateral rotators are the piriformis muscle, obturator internus and externus, and the gemellus superior and inferior. Hip medial rotators include the tensor fascia lata, and the gluteus minimus and medius. If you point your knees toward each other while standing, your hips will rotate medially. If you turn your knees outward, your hips will rotate laterally.

Hip Abductors. The hip abductors (outer thigh muscles) enable you to move the thigh away from the midline of the body. In combination with the hip adductors (inner thigh muscles), they play an important role in weight shifting to bring the center of mass into alignment with the supporting skeletal structure. When your feet are planted, your abductors act to tilt the pelvis to the side. The primary hip abductor is the gluteus medius.

Hip Adductors. The hip adductors (inner thigh muscles) are used to pull the legs together. You use them to stabilize your skis, keeping them on track and moving in the right direction. Balance in

strength and flexibility between the left and right adductors is very important to maintain good alignment with your skis.

Knee Extensors. The four extensors of the knee are known collectively as the quadriceps femoris, or quads. These muscles act as a unit to extend, or straighten, the knee. Along with the gluteus maximus and hamstrings, the quadriceps act to lessen leg flexion as you ski. The patella lies within the quadriceps tendon.

Knee Flexors. The primary knee flexor is the hamstring muscle group—three muscles that act together to bend the knee. The hamstrings also provide dynamic stability at the joint, helping the ACL prevent forward movement of the tibia on the femur. This is why it is so important for skiers to keep their hamstring muscles strong.

Ankle Dorsiflexors. The anterior tibialis is the primary dorsiflexor. This motion of lifting the top of the foot toward the shin helps you maintain fore/aft balance. The ankle dorsiflexors are most active during short turns and bump skiing.

Ankle Plantarflexors. The gastrocnemius and soleus muscles act together to point the foot down, away from the shin. You use these muscles when you stand on your toes or when you press the ball of your foot into your boot. It is important for skiers to have flexibility in the soleus, because this muscle will most limit forward motion of the shin over the ankle. The left and right soleus must be equally flexible so you can bend both knees equally.

Ankle Inverters. These muscles help elevate the arch and therefore transfer more weight to the outer border of the foot. The primary inverter is the posterior tibialis muscle. Ankle inversion helps you maintain good medial and lateral alignment.

Ankle Everters. The peroneus longus and brevis are the primary everters of the ankle. They act to flatten the arch, which places more pressure on the medial border of the foot. As with the ankle inverters, these muscles help you maintain good load distribution and medial and lateral alignment.

Fitness Concepts

This section contains a brief review of basic exercise components followed by a description of activities that stimulate conditioning and reinforce movement patterns that are specific to skiing.

Basic components of a conditioning program include activities that focus on

- motor control, such as coordination, balance, and agility,
- aerobic and anaerobic capacity,
- muscular strength and endurance, and
- muscle flexibility and joint mobility.

In addition to targeting the basic elements of conditioning, you can improve specific components of your performance with exercises that imitate the movement patterns of an activity. This is a basic principle of training known as **specificity.** First you have to understand the task, in this case, the specific attributes of skiing. In the simplest of terms, alpine skiing requires progressing down a snow-covered slope on skis in a controlled manner, using turning to change direction and control speed. Therefore, a fundamental objective of skiing is to maintain a balanced position under dynamic conditions.

Skiing is an excellent way to enhance body coordination, and it is better at developing strength than flexibility. A conditioning program to supplement skiing should include specific exercises for improving muscle flexibility and strength, additional cardiovascular conditioning, and coordination training while on the slope.

If you are not accustomed to exercise, check with your doctor before starting your exercise program. An evaluation by a health professional such as a physical therapist or exercise physiologist can provide you with the information you need to set up a personalized workout program.

You should analyze the activities you are involved in with respect to the following areas.

For example, does the activity develop aerobic capacity yet do little to develop muscle flexibility? Does it develop strength but provide limited opportunity to improve coordination?

Once you have identified the strengths and weaknesses of the activity, you will be better prepared to supplement it with other activities and exercises to create a well-rounded program.

Motor Control

The most important aspect of coordination in skiing is balance. To ski efficiently, you have to be able to align your center of mass with the forces acting on your skis. Before you can do this, however, you must experience the feeling of good alignment within your own body, that is, the sensation of transferring your weight through your joints to your base of support. The following simple exercises will help you integrate this sensation so you can recognize it and strive for it consistently while skiing.

These exercises are designed to get you thinking about alignment and balance, but the best way to develop coordination and agility is to practice your sport. While skiing, choose one aspect of your form to improve each day. For instance, you could start by focusing your attention on balance. Once you are consistently maintaining good alignment and balance, try to maintain that same good alignment on different terrain. There are many exercises to do on skis that will help you develop coordination, also. The *Alpine Handbook* (PSIA, 1996) lists ideas for these activities.

Weight Shifting—Lateral Movements

Stand in front of a full-length mirror with your feet shoulder-width apart and your hands on your hips. Keep your knees bent, as they are when you ski. Slowly shift your pelvis to the left, transferring most

of your weight to the left leg. Keep your hips level and your hands in place as you move. Do not bend your trunk to the side. Shift back to the center and then to the right in one smooth, continuous movement. Notice the sensation in your spine, hip joints, knee joints, ankles, and feet as you shift positions.

Gradually, shift more and more weight to each leg so that you can support yourself solely on that leg. Shift only as far as you need to maintain balance on the supporting leg. Feel and see how your body compensates when you move your center of mass too far to the side, beyond its base of support.

Once you have a good feel for transferring your weight, you can practice standing on one leg and maintaining good alignment. See how long you can stand without needing to put the other foot down. Challenge your body to make small movements to adjust, and close your eyes to make the exercise even more challenging. Practice this exercise with your knees bent, to emulate a regular skiing stance.

Weight Shifting—Fore/Aft Movements

Stand with your feet comfortably apart and your hands on your hips. Keep your knees bent, as they are when you ski. Slowly shift your pelvis forward over your toes, feeling the pressure in your foot move toward the ball of your foot. Shift your pelvis backward to transfer the weight to your heels. Bring your pelvis back to the center, so you can feel the weight evenly distributed along the entire surface of your foot. You can practice this with your eyes closed to increase the challenge.

Proper alignment occurs in the centered position. Your weight should be distributed evenly across the foot laterally, with no more pressure on the arch and big toe than on the outside edge of the foot.

Now translate these exercises to skiing. Try to generate the same or similar sensations in your lower body as you move through a turn. The same mechanics apply as you initiate the turn by moving your pelvis laterally in the appropriate direction.

Also, try to maintain a consistent amount of pressure through your joints as you transfer your weight from side to side. This encourages the most stable transition, requiring less intervention by the musculature and ligaments. Even as your pelvis is shifting from side to side, maintain an awareness of your fore/aft balance, continually making small adjustments to keep even pressure on your feet.

Aerobic Capacity

Aerobic conditioning provides a solid base for overall fitness. Aerobic exercises are those that are rhythmic and sustained, that use large muscles, and that elevate your heart rate and breathing rate. Examples are cross-country skiing, speed skating, in-line skating, running, biking, stair climbing, and swimming.

Research has indicated that elite alpine skiers have high aerobic capacities relative to the rest of the population. Tests indicate that alpine ski racers use up to 95 percent of their aerobic capacity during a giant slalom race. But you do not have to be a ski racer to effectively condition your heart. You can achieve similar results with exercise that is relatively long in duration and low in intensity, for example, running, cycling, and in-line skating.

The amount that your aerobic capacity is developed through skiing is highly variable. The conditioning effect depends on how efficiently you ski, the snow conditions (crud versus groomed snow, for example), and how long you ski between breaks, among other factors. For this reason, you may wish to supplement skiing with another activity that primarily increases aerobic capacity.

You should adhere to a few basic principles to develop good cardiovascular endurance. For your heart and lungs to work more efficiently, you should exercise at a level that challenges them but does not overwork them.

To build endurance, you need to exercise for a minimum of 20 to 30 minutes, three times per week. (Refer to the suggested reading section at the end of this book for more information on how to establish a workout of the appropriate intensity for you.)

Begin your aerobic workout with a few minutes of low-intensity aerobic exercise such as brisk walking, light calisthenics, or bicycling to elevate your body temperature. Next, perform a stretching regime, targeting the primary muscles used in your activity (e.g., for running, this would be the calves, quadriceps, and hamstrings).

Now you are ready to begin your aerobic workout. Take at least 5 minutes to gradually increase your exercise intensity. Maintain this level for at least 20 minutes, then gradually decrease to finish. Finish your session with more stretching—this is a good time to increase flexibility.

Anaerobic Capacity

Alpine skiing requires strength and power, both of which draw from your anaerobic as well as aerobic capacity. Anaerobic metabolism enables you to release energy without using oxygen, such as when you perform short bursts of high-intensity exercise.

In the absence of training, most people have a low anaerobic threshold—the point at which the requirement for anaerobic energy production is reached. You can raise your anaerobic threshold by training to increase your aerobic capacity. Another way to train anaerobic capacity is to intersperse short bursts of high-level activity when doing aerobic exercise, such as running or cycling.

Muscular Strength and Endurance

Peak muscular strength, the ability to generate maximal force, is important for resisting the large radial forces that occur when turning at fast speeds or in short-radius turns. Muscular endurance, the ability to maintain a certain level of muscle

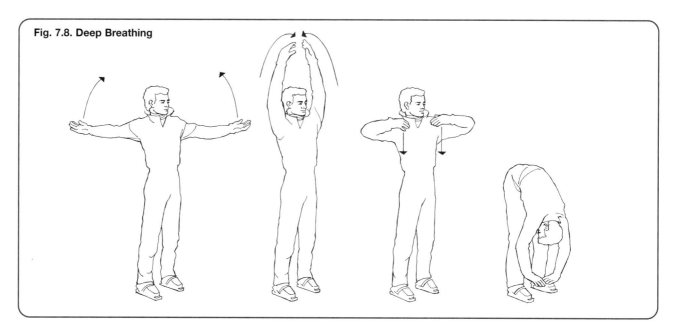

Fig. 7.8. Deep Breathing

force, is what you rely on to perform a series of turns and to maintain your stamina for an entire day of skiing—for the entire season, for that matter.

You can achieve strength and endurance through weight training and sustained, cross-training activities such as cycling, running, or in-line skating.

Flexibility

Flexibility is another important performance factor on which to focus your conditioning efforts. If you maintain flexibility, your muscles will be able to work effectively throughout their entire range of motion, which may also help protect you from injury.

For proper alignment while skiing or while performing any activity, your body needs to have a proper balance of muscle flexibility and strength, and joint and connective-tissue mobility and stability. You can achieve and maintain this balance through flexibility and

stretching exercises.

You can improve flexibility with a stretching program that emphasizes the major muscles involved in skiing (quadriceps, hamstrings, adductors, hip flexors, lower back, lower leg muscles, etc.). Initially, you may have to spend several minutes stretching each muscle group on a daily basis to make a significant improvement in your flexibility. But once you have accomplished an improved range of motion, you probably will not need to spend more than a minute per stretching session for each muscle group to maintain flexibility.

Many sports will not specifically help you reduce muscle imbalances—some may even perpetuate them. Weaker muscles are often compensated for by stronger muscles, and limited mobility in one part of the body may be balanced by excessive mobility in another. To change this pattern of compensation and achieve a truer balance in the body, you must isolate the

weak and inflexible muscles and exercise them regularly.

One way to condition your muscles is to perform dual-purpose exercises, that is, to strengthen one muscle group while stretching its opposing muscle or muscle group. For example, by extending your knee while in the sitting position, you are not only strengthening your quadriceps muscle but stretching the hamstrings as well (if you are careful not to let your spine flex during the movement). This exercise also helps you feel the relationship between opposing muscles and the effect that imbalances will have on the rest of your body (your low back, in this case).

It is important to perform exercises that are as close as possible to the way you move in real life, in this respect, those that imitate the movements you make in skiing. For instance, squats and leg presses are good ways to exercise the muscles you use in mogul skiing. The following exercises are developed with this principle in mind.

On-Snow, Warm-Up Exercise Regime

This section begins with a basic routine that's appropriate for skiers of all proficiency levels, followed by an enhanced routine for more advanced skiers.

The basic routine is performed with boots on and skis off, and the advanced routine is performed with both boots and skis on.

Use your discretion and common sense in selecting from these exercises. If you have a back or knee injury, some of these exercises may be inappropriate for you. Please consult your health professional before trying them.

Basic Routine

It is beneficial to begin an exercise program with a deep-breathing exercise to help you relax and focus on the task at hand.

Perform these exercises on even terrain with your ski boots on and skis off. Finish this sequence of exercises with a few more squats before you begin to ski. You may do more than the recommended number of repetitions.

Deep Breathing (fig. 7.8). Lift your arms out to the sides and then up over your head in a circular motion while taking a deep breath. Finish the inhale as your arms reach overhead. Exhale slowly as you press your arms down in front of your body, visualizing that you are pressing the air through your body, down into your legs, and out through the bottom of your feet.

Repeat three times, taking at least 10 seconds to inhale, and 10 seconds to exhale. Do not hold your breath between inhalation and exhalation.

Fig. 7.9. Basic Stretch with Rotation

Basic Stretch with Rotation (fig. 7.9). After the third exhalation, breathe in again while clasping your hands together and pressing the palms of your hands up toward the sky, reaching with your whole body. Exhale slowly as you twist to the right, and inhale as you return to the center. Exhale as you turn to the left, and inhale as you return to the center.

Repeat this two times on each side. (When twisting, *be careful to keep your hips pointing straight ahead* so that no rotational force affects your knees).

Neck Stretch (fig. 7.10). Relax your arms and let them hang loosely at your sides. Keep your shoulders back and down. Gently tip your head to the right side, then relax your neck to feel a gentle stretch. Gradually let your head move downward and forward so that the chin rests on the chest. Finish the movement by following the arc up and to the left side. Repeat this movement in the other direction. You should experience no discomfort with this exercise, only a comfortable stretch to the sides and back of the neck.

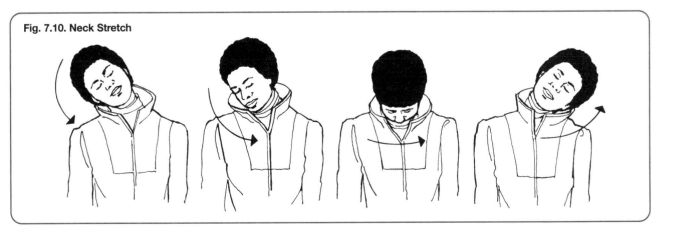

Fig. 7.10. Neck Stretch

Fig. 7.11. Basic Stretch with Side Bend

Fig. 7.12. Arm Circles

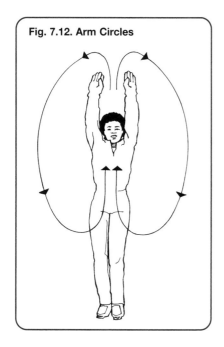

Fig. 7.13. Trunk Circles

Repeat this five times. Inhale as you move in one direction, exhale as you reverse the movement.

Basic Stretch with Side Bend (fig. 7.11). Inhale as you clasp your hands together again, pressing the palms upward as before. Exhale while reaching with both hands, slowly bending to the side to feel a stretch along the length of your body. Inhale as you return to the center. You do not need to bend far—simply elongate one side of your body, reaching up and over. Repeat this twice on each side.

Arm Circles (fig. 7.12). Circle both arms forward and then backward 15 times each. Reach out with your arms as if trying to lengthen them. Keep your neck relaxed and your stomach pulled up and in to support your back during this movement. Continue to breathe deeply and regularly.

Trunk Circles (fig. 7.13). Place your hands on your hips and, while keeping your lower body stationary, circle your upper body around to feel a gentle stretch in your back, sides, and abdomen. This movement should be very fluid and need not be large. Keep your circles small to start, and increase them as you feel your muscles getting looser.

Repeat this four times in each direction. Breathe in as you circle back and out as you circle forward.

Squats (fig. 7.14). Bring your ski poles in front of your body and inhale. Exhale as you squat down, bending your knees and hips while reaching your arms forward. Return to standing as you inhale. Squat only as is comfortable. Keep your feet in total contact with your ski boot and the ground, not allowing the heel to rise. Make sure that both of your knees bend over your toes. (When looking down, you should be able to see the big toe part of your boot between your knees).

Repeat this six times. Squat as far as you can comfortably, going deeper as your flexibility improves.

Hamstring Stretch (fig. 7.15). Place one foot in front of the other, resting on the heel of the front boot. Exhale as you lean forward, lifting your chest up and arching your back slightly. Feel a gentle stretch in the back of the thigh, in the hamstring muscle. Deep breathe two more times while

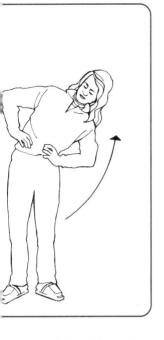

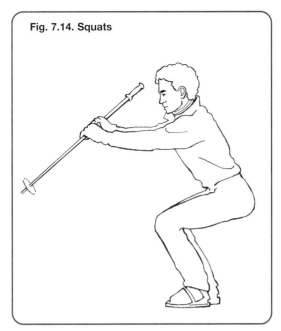

Fig. 7.14. Squats

Fig. 7.15. Hamstring Stretch

maintaining this position, relaxing into the stretch each time you exhale. Switch legs, then repeat.

Adductor Stretch (as shown in fig. 7.18, but without skis). Spread your feet apart into a wide stance. Bend one knee, shifting your weight so that the hip and knee are in line. Feel a stretch in the opposite inner thigh (adductor muscle). Breathe deeply two times, then repeat on the other side.

Abductor Stretch (fig. 7.16). Bring your legs together with your feet comfortably apart. Place your hands on your poles and slowly drop the right hip lower than the left. Feel a subtle stretch on the outside of the left hip. Try to keep the pelvis in good alignment, not letting it tilt forward or backward. Lift the left hip above the right and repeat five times, breathing in and out slowly with each movement. Repeat this five times on the other side.

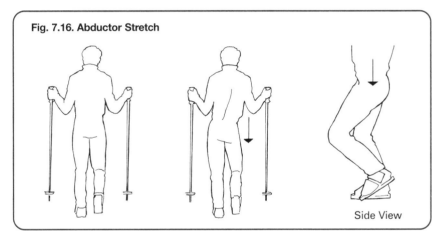

Fig. 7.16. Abductor Stretch

Side View

Quadriceps Stretch (fig. 7.17). Hold a ski pole in your right hand, planting it ahead of you and slightly to your right. With the left hand, reach back and grab the heel of your left boot, pulling it gently toward your buttocks to feel a stretch in the front of your left thigh. Try not to arch your back, instead squeeze your buttocks and pull in your abdominals to keep your back in a neutral position. Breathe deeply two times, maintaining the stretch. Repeat this on the other side.

Fig. 7.17. Quadriceps Stretch

Enhanced Routine

Advanced skiers may perform all the exercises in the enhanced routine on skis. Start by performing the first seven exercises (Deep Breathing through Squats) described in the basic routine. Then, add the following series to complete your warm-up. As with the basic routine, make sure you are on a level surface. Remember to finish this series of exercises with a few more squats before you begin to ski.

Adductor Stretch (fig. 7.18). Spread your feet apart into a wide stance. Bend your left knee. Feel a stretch in the right inner thigh (adductor muscle). The right leg will be straight and the inner edge of the right ski will be in the snow. Breathe deeply two times, then repeat the exercise on the other side, shifting your weight so that hip and knee are in line.

Hip Abductor Stretch (fig. 7.19). Plant your ski poles at 45 degrees to either side of you. Lift your right ski up and forward, keeping it in a straight line. Slowly cross the right ski over the left, setting it down next to and parallel to the left. (Your right foot will be crossed in front of your left.) Then slowly bend forward to feel a stretch in the back and side of your thigh. Hold for three deep breaths, relaxing into the stretch as you exhale. Keep your neck and spine relaxed. Repeat on the other side.

Quadriceps Stretch (fig. 7.20). Stand erect, planting your poles as

Fig. 7.18. Adductor Stretch

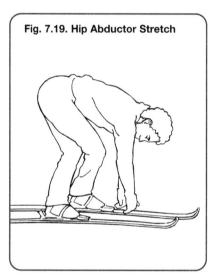

Fig. 7.19. Hip Abductor Stretch

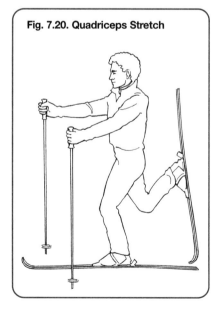

Fig. 7.20. Quadriceps Stretch

described above. Lift your right ski up and back behind you to rest the tip in the snow. Slowly lean back, bending your right knee until you feel a gentle stretch in the front of your thigh. Hold for three deep breaths, then relax. Repeat on the other side.

Hip Flexor Stretch (fig. 7.21). To get maximum benefit from this stretch, you may need to loosen your boots. Plant your poles as described above, then let your right leg slide back so that you end up in a lunge position. Feel a stretch in the front of your right hip and thigh and in your left buttock. Hold for three deep breaths, then repeat on the other side.

Cross-Training with Specificity for Skiing

Since most skiers do not have access to snow on a year-round basis, ongoing conditioning for skiing requires participation in other activities. To enhance various aspects of performance, many people **cross-train,** that is, partici-

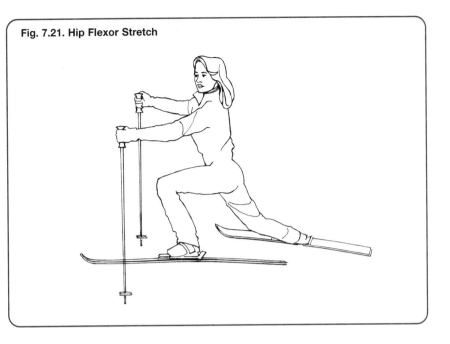

Fig. 7.21. Hip Flexor Stretch

pate in activities other than the primary sport in order to maintain or strengthen athletic proficiency. The general concept of cross-training is not new, although it has gained popularity in recent years. Sport-specific strength training is a centuries-old technique for improving performance.

Ultimately, you have to understand the physical requirements and fundamental skills of a sport to select training exercises that will provide you with the greatest transfer of proficiency and skills.

Features of Cross-Training Activities

Cross-training enables you to imitate the movements you make while skiing, providing an element of conditioning, practice, and focus to help you maintain your skiing proficiency level year-round. Cross-training exercises that most closely simulate skiing-specific movements are those that demand

dynamic balance with a fairly symmetrical stance, lateral movements with weight transfer, and flexion and extension of the ankles, knees, and hips to absorb and generate force. As with skiing, these movements need to be applied in situations that demand selection of appropriate line at varying speeds and over variable terrain.

A list of activities comparable to skiing include mountain biking, in-line skating, ice skating, horseback riding, motocross, jet skiing, and water skiing. All these activities contain critical components of the movements used in skiing and, with the exception of slalom water skiing, rely on a symmetrical stance.

Although it may not be practical for everyone to participate in these activities, they are discussed on the following pages to stimulate your thinking regarding specificity and how innovative types of dry-land training can mirror on-snow movement patterns.

Cross-Training Activities

Mountain biking will enhance your aerobic conditioning, muscular endurance, and strength, and will give you an opportunity to practice dynamic balance with movement patterns similar to skiing. By being self-powered, you increase your aerobic conditioning and muscular endurance. Riding uphill is physically challenging and builds your quadriceps and hamstring muscles, if you use toe-clips or clipless pedals and accentuate the pulling part of the pedal stroke.

Downhill mountain biking on dirt roads and single track is where you can practice dynamic balance at speed and cornering skills that are more specific to skiing. Fore/aft position is important to maintain the appropriate weight distribution over the front and back tires to control steering and limit skidding, and to keep the bike tracking cleanly in a turn.

Mountain biking offers other similarities to skiing, such as the need to maintain the trunk in a relatively upright position while leaning the bike (body) into the turn and using dominant pressure on the outside pedal (ski).

Additionally, simply riding a bike through a slalom course with emphasis on speed and line can also provide cross-over training for skiing movement patterns.

In-line skating probably provides the most specificity in terms of edging skills. Subtle lateral movements of the ankle (eversion and inversion) initiate changes in direction through pressure transfer, which translates directly up the leg to bring about more pronounced movements of knee and hip angulation and body inclination. As with mountain biking, the greatest similarity to skiing skills is with the downhill or slalom aspects of skating. However, if you use uphill skating for conditioning and downhill skating for skill development, you will have an efficient way to get a comprehensive workout.

The increased friction of in-line skating relative to skiing provides an important lesson. Too much rotary motion creates shear forces where the rollers contact the surface. These forces are counteracted by the friction of the surface on the rollers. In skiing, where friction between the snow and skis is substantially less, twisting forces of the upper body, legs, and feet can all result in skidding and chatter—a loss of precious time to the racer. The consequences of excessive rotary movements in skating can be more dramatic, with a rapid buildup of friction at the rollers, sending the skater sprawling. Hence, learning to travel a proper line on skates should translate into cleaner, carved skiing turns.

Ice skating is the winter equivalent of in-line skating but also can be done in the off-season if an indoor rink is available. Ice-skating provides you with valuable crossover skills for skiing and provides an excellent alternative form of training.

Horseback riding is another sport with skills and movements that have much in common with skiing. Riding a large, thundering animal over uneven terrain requires an active bilateral stance that is maintained with dynamic fore/aft and lateral movements. And choosing the proper line and correct timing for obstacles and jumps is as critical in riding as it is in skiing.

Motocross may be the activity most specific to downhill skiing overall because it demands dynamic weight transfer and balance at high speeds with large radial forces. Fore/aft and lateral movements are critical, along with substantial strength requirements, all while trying to negotiate the best line through a rolling bumpy course.

Riding **jet skis** or **wave runners** are two other motorized sports that have similar attributes to motocross. In addition to postural similarities, the element of vibration from a motor and riding across choppy water is similar to the chatter and oscillating movements that occur on the snow.

Water skiing uses the most similar tool—skis—and shares a few of snow skiing's basic principles. Like snow skiing, water skiing combines the movement patterns related to speed and rhythm with body inclination to link turns and pick a proper line (especially when negotiating a slalom course). Also, water skiing and snow skiing require the use of ski design.

Is there a connection between all these sports and success in skiing? As any coach, scout, or exercise scientist will tell you, that is a difficult question to answer. But do not let that deter you from experimenting with these activities, because intuition and experience often precede scientific confirmation. Certainly, mountain biking, skating, horseback riding, motocross, and water sports share many of the specific attributes required for snow skiing, and that is the key to selecting exercises for an appropriate cross-training program.

8

Safety Awareness

The dream image of skiing consists of floating effortlessly through untracked powder bathed in glorious sunshine—an ideal usually depicted in ski videos. The reality of skiing, however, involves moving downhill while avoiding other skiers, trees, and manmade and natural obstacles, in variable and often difficult weather conditions.

By its very nature, skiing is an inherently risky sport, and anyone who chooses to ski must accept this inherent risk. With risk, however, comes reward. The dream of achieving that perfect run is worth the risk for some skiers. As an instructor, your job is to help students realize their abilities and skiing dreams, while helping them understand the risks and responsibilities as well.

Skier Etiquette

You can elevate your enjoyment of skiing and help others have a positive experience by being alert, aware, and courteous on the mountain. To this end, the ski industry has adopted a "code" of behavior to guide skier conduct. This code, entitled Your Responsibility Code, is endorsed by the National Ski Areas Association, the Professional Ski Instructors of America, and the National Ski Patrol.

Surprisingly few skiers are aware of Your Responsibility Code, and even fewer can recite it. That is why it is important to reinforce this message whenever possible, so that your students, other skiers, and, indeed, the entire ski industry can benefit from more responsible conduct on the mountain.

Your Responsibility Code

1. Always stay in control, and be able to stop or avoid other people or objects.
2. People ahead of you have the right of way. It is your responsibility to avoid them.
3. You must not stop where you obstruct a trail or are not visible from above.
4. Whenever starting downhill or merging into a trail, look uphill and yield to others.
5. Always use devices to help prevent runaway equipment.
6. Observe all posted signs and warnings. Keep off closed trails and out of closed areas.
7. Prior to using any lift, you must have the knowledge and ability to load, ride, and unload safely.

Know the Code. It is your responsibility. This is a partial list. Be safety conscious.

If you have trouble remembering the entire code, the following mnemonic, or memory aid, can help you recall its components. It is easy to remember that skiing can cause cramps (spelled "crampps," in this case). Applied to Your Responsibility Code, the CRAMPPS mnemonic looks like this:

1. **Control.** Always stay in **control,** and be able to stop or avoid other people or objects.
2. **Right of Way.** People ahead of you have the **right of way**. It is your responsibility to avoid them.
3. **Above.** You must not stop where you obstruct a trail, or are not visible from **above.**
4. **Merging.** Whenever starting downhill or **merging** into a trail, look uphill and yield to others.
5. **Prevent.** Always use devices to help **prevent** runaway equipment.
6. **Posted.** Observe all **posted** signs and warnings. Keep off closed trails and out of closed areas.
7. **Safely.** Prior to using any lift, you must have the knowledge and ability to load, ride, and unload **safely.**

In addition, instructors can emphasize the safety message and demonstrate their safety awareness by

- advising students that skiing is inherently risky and that skiing responsibly reduces risk;

- reinforcing Your Responsibility Code throughout the lesson;
- conducting classes in appropriate areas and on suitable terrain;
- educating students about equipment, clothing, and ski fitness;
- being alert to changing weather and snow conditions; and
- encouraging the use of proper lift procedures.

Skiing and the Mountain Environment

Skiing allows you to experience the alpine environment in winter and its wide spectrum of climatic conditions. From the enchantment of warm, sunny days to the excitement of storm skiing—all of these conditions will challenge you to be knowledgeable and skillful enough to maintain comfort.

Some skiers find that adapting to changes in sun exposure, wind speeds, and temperatures is as difficult as mastering skiing itself. Because you have dealt with the challenges of the winter alpine environment as an instructor, you can share your experience with your students and help them learn to adapt to these demands.

It is important to accumulate knowledge about this unique environment on a regular basis so you can discuss ways in which it influences skiing. Weather, wildlife, geography, and geology are often easily observed from the chairlift, for example. In this respect you can expand students' horizons in ways that go beyond skiing itself.

Accidents and Injuries

As an instructor, you face the possibility of your students getting injured. Since you may be the first person in a position of authority at an accident scene, it is vitally important that you know what to do. *Policies and procedures vary among resorts, so you are primarily advised to follow the guidelines at your mountain.*

In general, if an injury occurs in your class, try to make the injured student as warm and comfortable as possible without removing equipment or moving the person. Reassure the student that the ski patrol will be summoned, and notify the ski patrol with specific information about the exact location of the injured party.

Improvements in ski equipment, particularly in the release capabilities of modern bindings, has led to a dramatic decline in the rate of skier accidents. Unfortunately, while the overall accident rate has fallen, the number of fatalities and serious injuries has risen. Most fatalities result from collisions, often with trees, and usually involve head injuries. A few skiers die every year in avalanches, almost always while skiing out of bounds. The best risk management method for controlling catastrophic and fatal injuries is to adhere to Your Responsibility Code.

Common non-catastrophic injuries include knee and thumb trauma. Among the most frequently reported injury in recent years has been the tearing of the anterior cruciate ligament (ACL) of the knee. (Refer to chapter 7 for a discussion of the ACL and associated structures). Strategies for the prevention and treatment of this injury are still in evolution. Many of these injuries require surgery, and better surgical repair procedures are continually being developed. And, increasingly, emphasis is being placed on early rehabilitation after ACL injuries.

You and the students you teach can reduce the chances of knee injury by being fit, strong, and flexible. The best way to maintain this level of fitness is to direct your training techniques toward increasing leg strength, which is key to consistently strong skiing performance. For more information on ski injuries, refer to the publications listed in the suggested reading section at the end of this manual.

"Skier's thumb" is another common injury usually sustained when the skier tries to break a fall with an outstretched hand while holding a ski pole (see fig. 8.1). As the thumb is bent backward, a tearing of the ulnar collateral ligament occurs. Unlike knee injuries, which frequently result in a visit to the orthopedic surgeon, thumb injuries are often ignored because the skier assumes it is just a simple sprain. Early intervention and medical attention are important for preventing a permanently weak thumb. Some people use poles with breakaway straps and thumb-protecting grips, and wear protective gloves (thumb guards) to reduce their chances of experiencing skier's thumb, although other people question the value of these features.

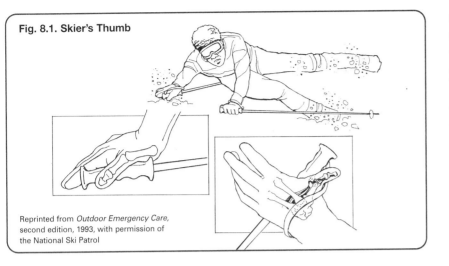

Fig. 8.1. Skier's Thumb

Reprinted from *Outdoor Emergency Care,*
second edition, 1993, with permission of
the National Ski Patrol

Sun Exposure

Chronic injuries to the skin and
eyes from the intense exposure to
the sun's ultraviolet (UV) rays at
high altitude merit comment. It is
imperative that skiers protect
themselves from sun-related injury
by wearing sunscreens, hats, goggles, and UV-reducing sunglasses.
Skin cancer, particularly malignant
melanoma, is caused by exposure
to the sun's UV rays. There is currently an epidemic of skin cancer
in the United States, and malignant
melanoma, in particular, is on the
rise. Skiers are at obvious risk in
the mountain environment because
high altitudes, thin atmosphere,
and a highly reflective snow
surface all markedly increase
exposure to UV radiation.

Local Cold Injuries

Temperatures in the winter environment can be extremely cold,
which can lead to a number of
problems for skiers. When human
tissues freeze, ice crystals actually
form, which leads to irreversible
blockage of small blood vessels.

Ironically, damaged frozen tissue is
similar to that produced by burns.

The mildest form of cold injury
is called "frostnip," which tends to
occur on body surfaces farthest
from the core: the ears, nose,
cheeks, hands, and feet. Frostnip is
characterized by pain and blanch-
ing (whiteness) of the skin. Skiers
may not be aware that the tip of
their nose or ears is beginning to
blanch. (Children, in particular,
must be watched very closely.)
Skiers should be immediately
advised to take steps to rewarm
that area of skin or they risk developing frostbite, a more dangerous
condition.

Frostbite and the so-called
"immersion foot" syndrome are
serious cold injuries in which the
extremity is kept cold and wet but
not frozen for long periods of time,
resulting in soft-tissue damage and
pain. With frostbite, actual freezing
of tissues occurs and can result in
destruction of vital tissues, including skin and muscle. It is important
to avoid overzealous rewarming or
further trauma. The affected person must avoid bearing weight or
walking upon a thawed, frostbitten

area, and also avoid refreezing the
area, which is very damaging. The
treatment of frostbite begins with
progressive rewarming of the
affected area and involves long-
term follow-up care, as it may take
three to six months for the extent
of tissue damage to be fully
realized.

Most cold injuries can be pre-
vented by wearing proper clothing
and seeking cold adaptation
through gradually longer exposure
to cold. As an instructor, you
should convey to your students the
importance of preparing for the
alpine environment by dressing in
layers of lightweight, absorbent,
breathable, wind- and waterproof
clothing, and wearing hats, neck
gators, face masks, and goggles. It
is entirely appropriate to discour-
age tobacco and alcohol consumption because they cause blood
vessels to constrict and impede
circulation. Additionally, alcohol
increases the risk of skiing accidents. You may need to take the
students for quick trips to the
lodge for hot beverages to raise
core body temperature and avoid
hypothermia and cold injuries.
Heat-generating activities such as
climbing uphill on skis may also
be useful.

Hypothermia

The alpine environment provides a
significant challenge to the heat-
regulating capabilities of humans.
However, you and your students
can maintain a normal body
temperature within a relatively
narrow range despite the extreme
conditions you may experience.

Heat is lost from the body in the following ways: by convection, which is heat loss due to air movement; by conduction, which is heat loss due to the body's contact with a cold surface; by radiation, which is heat loss to the environment from the head or extremities; and by evaporation, which is heat loss through perspiration.

The main mechanism that regulates heat loss is variation in blood flow to the body surface. The nervous system is capable of controlling constriction or dilation of blood vessels, producing dramatic reductions in surface blood flow, and shunting blood to internal organs. It is often helpful to think of the body as a central core that must be kept at a uniform temperature, surrounded by a dynamic insulating layer. This layer is the mediator of heat conservation and loss.

Integrating the various processes that control body temperature is a function of the hypothalamus, a part of the brain. The temperature-regulating mechanism is a feedback control system conceptually identical to a household thermostat. When the core temperature falls, sensors transmit signals to the hypothalamus, which then initiates a series of circulatory and metabolic responses directed at heat production and conservation.

Normal body temperature is somewhat variable. Some healthy persons may have body temperatures as low as 96.5°F. Deviations of body temperature of up to 5°F do not appreciably alter most body functions. However, if core temperature drops to 91°F or below,

confusion and loss of consciousness occur. At 86°F and below, potentially fatal heart rhythms occur.

Hypothermia is defined as a core temperature of 95°F or below and represents a medical emergency. Though a number of diseases may predispose one to hypothermia, alcohol consumption is a particular risk. Alcohol increases heat loss by dilating blood vessels and inhibiting heat-producing shivering. The earliest sign of impending hypothermia is shivering, so try to be alert to shivering among your students, and avoid excessive inactivity during the class. If some students get cold, have them do some exercises that generate muscle heat, such as walking uphill. When in doubt, have them take a quick break for a hot beverage.

High Altitude

The altitudes at which people ski present fascinating physiologic challenges. Primarily, the reduced oxygen levels above 6,000 feet cause a variety of biologic responses.

There are two recognized syndromes associated with high altitude: (1) chronic mountain sickness, or Monge's Disease, which affects permanent residents of high altitude and (2) acute mountain sickness (AMS), affecting the high-altitude visitor. Interestingly, if detected early, these abnormalities can be completely reversed by descending to sea level.

There are peculiar genetic factors involved in the susceptibility

to chronic mountain sickness. AMS, on the other hand, can affect anyone. Within 8 to 24 hours of travel to elevations above 6,000 feet, non-acclimatized individuals may experience fatigue, headache, insomnia and shortness of breath. At even higher elevations, swelling of the brain (cerebral edema) and lungs (pulmonary edema) can occur and may be life-threatening.

Rapid descent to lower elevation will reverse these dangerous processes before damage occurs if initiated early enough. Some may think they are merely fatigued or have had a bit too much to drink the night before. As an instructor, you should be alert to the signs of AMS—particularly if you work at a very high resort—and take steps to get the person off the mountain and to medical attention as quickly as possible. The physician may even recommend transportation of the person from the resort to much lower elevation, where the reversal of symptoms can be rapid and dramatic.

Experts have long recommended gradual ascent to high altitude, rest, and avoidance of alcohol as preventive measures against AMS. Recently some have advised the use of certain medications, including the diuretic acetazolamide (Diamox) or the corticosteroid dexamethasone (Decadron) for those particularly prone to AMS. However, these medications can have serious side effects and should not be taken without first consulting a physician.

For most people, prudent ascent, rest, and avoidance of alcohol are sufficient to minimize the effects of altitude. Fortunately, rapid adaptation to high altitude occurs, and by the second or third day of a ski trip, most skiers are happily riding the ski lifts.

Some areas have instituted large fines for violating ski area boundaries. Following Your Responsibility Code is, once again, the best prevention.

Avalanche

For most skiers, an approaching winter storm brings excitement and anticipation of powder skiing. For ski patrollers however, that same storm may mean avalanche mitigation work.

Reducing the risk of avalanche is no simple task. The patrollers who analyze snow conditions, assess avalanche risk, and then intentionally create slides before the snow can build up to dangerous levels are the unsung heros upon whom we all rely. Often taken for granted, the patrollers are out there, usually in miserable weather, for the benefit of everyone on the mountain.

Organized avalanche rescue is another patrol function. Since most avalanche victims die of suffocation, minimizing burial time is the key to a successful rescue. Patrollers decide the areas of highest search priority based on where the victim entered the slide path, where the victim disappeared, and the probable trajectory of the victim.

The best way to avoid being the victim of an avalanche is to ski in bounds. The ski patrol monitors snowpack and stabilizes avalanche hazard zones at ski areas by intentionally setting avalanches and by other means. In the memorable winter of 1992-93, there were 22 avalanche fatalities in the United States. All occurred out-of-bounds.

chapter

9

Introduction to Ski Area Ecology

With a few exceptions, ski areas generally have four things in common: (1) accumulations of snow, (2) hilly or mountainous terrain, (3) forest vegetation, and (4) heaviest use during winter. A skier is unlikely to contemplate much, other than the next turn, while sliding downhill. However, most of a skier's time is spent riding silently and smoothly at or above tree-top level on a chairlift, which affords an unsurpassed opportunity to observe and enjoy not only the splendid views but also the mountain ecosystem. The purpose of this chapter is to briefly introduce some of the features most easily seen during a ride up the mountain. By taking the time to become familiar with these features and providing insights to your student, you can help broaden their appreciation of

the natural environment as well as improve their skills as skiers.

Trees

Most ski areas in the United States are within an elevational range that is dominated by coniferous forests variously referred to as boreal (of the north), montane (of the mountains), or subalpine (below the tundra). The elevations at which these types of forests occur are highly variable depending on latitude (e.g., lower in Washington than New Mexico) and snow accumulation (e.g., lower on the Olympic Peninsula of Washington than in the nearby but drier Cascades). Most such ecosystems in the United States are dominated by pines, spruces, true firs, Douglas-firs, and hemlocks. These are described below.

Pines. This diverse group is generally characterized by clusters of two to five needles, conspicuous cones that hang downward, a rounded crown, and an overall open appearance. Most species have needles that are much longer than in the other groups of conifers and tend to be clumped toward the end of the twigs. Throughout most of the mountainous United States, pines are more dominant at lower elevations than the other conifers, although some species of pines occur at timberline. For pines and other trees at timberline or on exposed ridges, note that the limbs are often longer on the downwind side. Trees with this shape, referred to as "flag" trees, indicate persistent and strong winds that continually damage new tissue, resulting

in limited or no limb growth on the upwind side.

Pines may be divided into two groups. Soft (or "white") pines—such as the eastern and western white pine, the limber pine of the Central and Southern Rockies and Great Basin, and the whitebark pine of the Sierra Nevada and Northern Rockies—have long, limber limbs; long, slender cones; and grayish bark. Hard (or "yellow") pines generally have shorter limbs; more rounded cones; and rough, brown or reddish bark. The red pine and jack pine of the Upper Midwest and Northeast and the widespread lodgepole pine (fig. 9.1) of the West are good examples of hard pines likely to be seen at ski areas.

Many species of pines, especially lodgepole and jack pines, are among the first trees (along with aspen) to re-establish following a fire. Look at the plants near the ground (the "understory") beneath the mature pines. If the younger trees are another type of conifer (i.e., with more of a Christmas-tree appearance), you can conclude that the area is undergoing succession (the gradual replacement of one plant community by another) from a fire, insect outbreak, or other large-scale deforestation. In many cases, the prior disturbance may have occurred more than a century ago.

Spruces and True Firs. These classic "Christmas trees" have short, stiff needles that extend along most of the length of a twig. Most spruces have needles that are diamond-shaped or square in cross-section, while firs have needles that are flat and blunt at the tip. Firs generally also have limbs that are shorter than those of spruces (giving the effect of a tighter spire) and more distinctly layered. The most diagnostic difference is that the cones of firs grow upward, while those of spruces hang downward.

Common spruces at ski-area elevations include the red spruce in the East, Northeast, and Upper Midwest and the Engelmann spruce in mountains of the West, except California (fig. 9.2). Common firs include the balsam fir in the Northeast and Upper Midwest, Fraser fir in the Appalachians, subalpine fir throughout the Rockies and Cascades (fig. 9.3), red fir in the Sierras, and white fir in the southern Rockies, Great Basin, and Sierras. Several other species of spruce and fir are widespread in the mountains but limited to moist sites along streams, lake shores, or bogs instead of mountain slopes.

As mentioned in the discussion of pines, the vegetation of an area undergoes a slow process of succession following a disturbance such as fire. Throughout most of ski country, pines and aspen tend to dominate the post-disturbance forest initially because they are better adapted to the relatively dry conditions associated with a lack of shade and the poor soil resulting from removal of organic material by combustion or erosion. A high-elevation forest dominated by spruces and firs indicates a protracted period without major disturbance. This is called a climax community, in which the mature

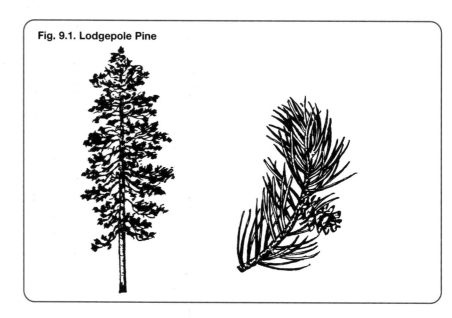

Fig. 9.1. Lodgepole Pine

Fig. 9.2. Englemann Spruce

Fig. 9.3. Subalpine Fir

trees and young trees are the same species. A climax forest is not replaced by another type unless loss of trees turns back the clock of succession.

Douglas-fir and Hemlocks. These similar conifers (the scientific name for Douglas-fir literally means false hemlock) share the pyramidal shape of spruces and true firs but differ in having a looser, more graceful appearance and softer needles. "Shaking hands" with a conifer quickly reveals whether it is one of the spruce/fir or Douglas-fir/hemlock groups; the latter are much friendlier to the touch.

In addition to having softer needles and a looser appearance, Douglas-firs can be differentiated from true firs by cones that hang downward and from spruces by cones that are shorter and rounder. Hemlocks differ from all these species by having small cones that hang from the very tips of the twigs. Eastern hemlocks, western hemlocks, and Douglas-firs are usually prevalent below the elevations of spruces and true firs, while the mountain hemlock is a high-elevation tree.

Quaking Aspen. This beautiful deciduous tree is common throughout the boreal, montane, and coastal coniferous forests. Aspen are often found along drainages and avalanche chutes, where moisture is greater, or on mountain slopes that have burned. Aspen are particularly interesting because most of the reproduction is by growth of new trees from the roots of older trees rather than by seeds. As a result, a large clump of aspen

may actually be the same plant (i.e., a clone). This is often evidenced by all of the trees in a clump having an identical growth form and, in the fall, identical leaf color. The ability of aspen to sprout from the roots is responsible for their rapid re-establishment following a fire. In most cases, aspen stands are temporary. The presence of young conifers beneath the aspen is an indication of the successional nature of the stands.

Aspen are an important component of the coniferous forest, for two reasons. First, the leafy foliage attracts a variety of insects and birds that are not adapted to feeding or nesting in conifers. Second, the soft wood is preferred by woodpeckers, which excavate cavities that they use for nesting initially but that later provide homes for a large number of other birds (including small owls) and small mammals. In the West, elk feed heavily on the tender sapwood of aspen in late winter, when the sap is rising and other food sources have been depleted. Use by elk is indicated by scarring on the trunks at heights of less than about 6 feet. A lucky observer might also see the claw marks of a young black bear on an aspen trunk or vertical rows of closely spaced holes (called "sapwells") drilled by a type of woodpecker known as a sapsucker.

Birds

Birds of northern or mountain environments have evolved two strategies for surviving winter: migrate to warmer climes or adapt to feeding on plant or animal

Fig. 9.4. Chickadee

material that is present throughout the winter. Obviously, species of the latter type are prevalent at ski areas. Some species specialize in feeding on insects or insect larvae that overwinter beneath the bark. The most conspicuous such group are the woodpeckers, most of which are black and white, climb along the trunk of trees, and have undulating flights. Smaller birds have weaker bills and therefore cannot bore as deeply beneath the bark as woodpeckers, but some species exploit insect prey that hide beneath bark flakes or among the needles and cones of conifers.

Winter songbirds that feed on insects on the trunk include nuthatches, which climb both up and down and are gray, black, and white, and also brown creepers, which are small, brown (no surprise), and climb only up. Chickadees—grayish, plump little birds whose call is their name—feed primarily on insects at ends of limbs (fig. 9.4). These active birds often hang upside down to reach prey on the undersides of the branches. Mixed flocks of all these species frequently move through a

Fig. 9.5. Pine Grosbeak

Fig. 9.6. Gray Jay

forest together for reasons that are the subject of much study. (Do they help each other find food or increase the chances of spotting and/or avoiding a predator?) Another group of insect-eaters, the kinglets, feed high in trees, usually as individuals. These tiny birds are olive-tan with white bars on their wings.

Small birds that feed primarily on plant material include juncos—grayish birds that have white outer tail feathers and often are seen hopping along the snow in search of seeds; pine siskins—streaked (tan and white) birds with slender bills, yellow on the wings, and a call that includes a buzzy trill that

ascends the scale; and crossbills—reddish or yellowish birds (depending on gender; the male is red) that travel in flocks and use their crossed bills to pry open cones and extract the seeds. Another bird of mountain forests, the pine grosbeak is larger and plumper than the red crossbill and has a smaller beak. The pastel rose coloration of the male and soft yellow-gray of the female make this perhaps the most beautiful of winter birds (fig. 9.5). Yet another group, the waxwings, are noted for their sleek, taupe plumage, delicate crests, and yellow-tipped tails, and by their preference for berries.

Larger birds in ski country are represented by several members of the crow family. Depending on your region, these may include the Steller's jay, with distinctive blue body, black head and crest, and raspy calls; gray jay (or "camp robber"), with soft gray plumage and soft whistles (fig. 9.6); Clark's nutcracker, with bold gray, black, and white plumage and raucous calls; black-billed magpie, with a distinctive long tail and black and white plumage; and common raven, a large, shaggy cousin of the crow, in nearly all mountainous regions. These intelligent birds are able to survive winter because of their ability to exploit a wide range of food sources. Many excellent field books are available to help you determine which of these species occur in your area.

Mammals

Most mammals do not migrate significant distances, but many species

avoid winter's extremes by either hibernating or remaining active beneath the snow. Other species are active above the snow all winter, although few mammals are observed while skiing. Fortunately, snow is an excellent material for holding tracks until they are obscured by wind or new snow.

Deer and elk may move from adjacent forests onto the edges of ski runs at night, particularly if shrubs have become established. Many shrubs are palatable and nutritious throughout the winter, and they are accessible as food because they protrude above the snow cover. Feeding on shrubs is called browsing, while feeding on grasses is called grazing. Even when the hoofprints of deer and elk are not distinct, the distance between the tracks (indicating long legs) and a generally straight line are characteristic of these species.

Tracks of coyotes, foxes, and bobcats differ from those of deer and elk by having the feet closer together. Additionally, tracks of predators often follow an irregular line (because the animal is searching for prey), and the smaller size of the animal allows it to travel beneath low branches. If the footprint is distinct, the presence of a pad and toes also rules out a hoofed animal. The track of a bobcat is round, while that of a coyote is oval, like a dog's track. Fox tracks are small and round, and the hair obscures the individual toes. Pairs of smaller tracks, with all four feet of similar size, may indicate a weasel or marten bounding through the snow.

Snowshoe hares and squirrels

(such as the widespread red squirrel or chickaree) have similar tracks, with large hind feet and small front feet. They differ, however, in that squirrels bound with front feet side by side, while rabbits and hares have their front feet offset. Of course, the snowshoe hares have especially large hind feet, as the name implies. Squirrels and hares are important winter prey for hawks, owls, coyotes, bobcats, and lynx.

A large rodent, the porcupine, is a less palatable prey than squirrels or rabbits, for obvious reasons. This species may rarely be seen asleep in a tree, but most often its presence is indicated by limbs or trunks that have been stripped of their bark as a porcupine feeds on the nutritious sapwood beneath.

Small rodents often survive primarily beneath uncompacted snow in the forest understory, where they feed on twigs, dried vegetation, seeds, and fruits. This environment is called the subnivean (below-the-snow) zone. A line of tiny tracks showing evidence of a tail or dragging belly indicates that a small critter—most commonly a vole (a mouse with a rounded snout, short tail, and tiny ears)—has braved the cold and predators to seek food.

Summer in Ski Country

Although this chapter has dealt with trees and winter wildlife use, ski areas (like all mountain ecosystems) are much more diverse and productive during summer. The abundant foliage, flowers, fruits,

and seeds produced during the short growing season support a myriad of small herbivores, ranging from insects to rabbits, that in turn support predatory species. A trip to a ski area in summer can be as rewarding in terms of the sights, sounds, and smells of nature as the slopes of snow were exhilarating during winter.

One additional piece of information: Many mountain ecosystems are delicate, and the short growing season provides a compressed period during which nature can heal any wounds. Ski areas once were refuges from human activity in summer. Now, however, increasing use by hikers and, especially, mountain bikers at many resorts poses a potential threat in terms of erosion, damage to vegetation, and disturbance of wildlife.

Please be respectful of nature and the creatures whose use of the mountains is limited to the short summer season. The easiest ways to accomplish this are to stay on designated trails, leave flowers and fruits as seed sources for the plants and food sources for wildlife, and respect posted closures of areas that support a special wildlife use or are being allowed to recover from disturbance.

appendix

Glossary

abdominal muscles. The muscles covering that part of the body between the chest and the pelvis and enclosing the stomach, intestines, liver, spleen, and pancreas.

abduct. To pull away from the midline.

abductors. The outer thigh muscles that act to separate the thighs.

ability. A stable, enduring trait that underlies skilled performance.

absorption. Flexion or retraction movements to help reduce the pressure buildup on skis that results from terrain variations or turn dynamics.

acute mountain sickness (AMS). A physical condition that may occur at altitudes above 7,500 feet. AMS is caused by lack of oxygen, which injures body cells directly because it interferes with oxygen-requiring chemical reactions. AMS also injures the body cells indirectly because of the changes it causes in the circulatory, respiratory, and nervous systems. Symptoms include fatigue, weakness, headache, loss of appetite, nausea, vomiting, and shortness of breath on exertion.

adaptive instruction. The teaching of individuals who are not able to use standard alpine, nordic, or snowboard equipment.

adduct. To draw toward the midline.

adductors. The inner thigh muscles that act to pull the legs together.

aerobic exercise. Continuous rhythmic exercise in which the large muscles of the body are used over an extended period, e.g., brisk walking, running, swimming, and cross-country skiing.

affective domain. The learning domain related to feelings, emotions, values, spirituality, and the appreciation of beauty, such as in art or wildlife. Learning a sport can create growth in the affective domain. *See also* **sensorimotor domain.**

aft. To the rear of the skis or snowboard.

agility. The capability to move quickly and easily.

alignment. The positioning of the body so that the forces derived from the interaction of the skis on the snow pass through the body's center of mass to produce the intended movement. The three categories of alignment as they relate to edging are: (1) balanced, in which the skier is properly aligned for optimum use of the ski edges, (2) under-edged, in which the skier produces insufficient edge angles, and (3) over-edged, in which the skier produces excessive edge angles. *See also* **canting, orthotic.**

American Teaching System (ATS). PSIA's education program that provides a guideline to the three basic tenets of teaching others to ski: the instructional aspects—the Teaching Model; the technical, or skill-related aspects—the Skiing Model; and the customer-relations, or guest-service, aspects—the Service Model.

anaerobic exercise. Exercise in which energy is released without the use of oxygen. The body releases this type of energy via a phosphate energy-delivery system that is later replenished by oxygen. Anaerobic activities that require short bursts of energy include weight lifting and sprinting.

anatomy. The human body and the science that deals with it.

anchoring. Techniques that teachers use to help students retain knowledge and skills, including

practice (mileage), positive reinforcement, and questioning.

angulation. The formation of angles between major adjacent and
supportive body segments through
movement in a diagonal or lateral
plane. The purpose of angulation is
to control the edge angles of the
skis on the snow. While skiers can
angulate from the ankles, knees,
hips, and spine, the hips produce
the greatest range of edge control.

anterior. Nearer to the front surface
of the body. *See also* **posterior.**

**anterior cruciate ligament
(ACL).** The knee ligament that
connects the femur (thigh bone)
with the tibia (shin bone) and prevents the forward movement of the
tibia on the femur. The posterior
cruciate ligament prevents backward movements of the tibia on
the femur.

anticipation. The act of preparing
for each turn by bringing the upper
and lower body into a twisted relationship. This is sometimes
referred to as a countered position.
To prepare for long-radius turns,
the skier turns the upper body in
the direction of the new turn. To
prepare for short-radius turns, the
skier turns the skis in the direction
of the new turn. *See also* **anticipation release,** and **rotation.**

anticipation release. Reducing the
twisted relationship between the
upper and lower body during turn
initiation. Muscles that were
stretched during anticipation are
rapidly contracted. This, coupled

with edge release, results in rapidly
turning the skis.

assessing. The process of evaluating student characteristics to determine how to structure individualized, effective lessons. The instructor collects important clues about
each student—emotional make-up,
expectations, learning preferences,
physical ability, and skiing experience—all of which indicate how
the student will receive information
and respond to learning. The
instructor assesses the student
throughout the lesson to ensure
synthesis and communication.

asymmetric snowboard. A snowboard that is not symmetric about
its long axis.

auditory learners. Learners who
process information verbally and
cognitively. These individuals respond well to verbal descriptions
of movements to be performed and
generally prefer to talk about their
experiences also.

autonomous stage. An advanced
stage of learning in which the
learner develops automaticity in
action and information processing.

axis. Convenient reference lines to
which anatomy or mechanical
movements are referred. The vertical axis of the body passes downward through the top of the head
and into the floor.

balance. The state of controlling the
forces generated by the ski-snow
interaction in order to remain poised
and properly aligned on skis.

balancing movements. Muscular
actions to maintain equilibrium, or
the desired alignment, on skis.
These movements are usually
divided into two categories:
(1) actions that affect fore and aft
balance and (2) actions that affect
lateral balance. Balancing movements are one of the four basic
skiing skills.

ball-and-socket joint. A joint in
which a knob-like part of one bone
fits into a socket of another, allowing rotation as well as flexion and
extension. The hip and shoulder
joints are ball-and-socket joints.

banking. In skiing, this refers to
leaning to the inside of the turn.

bevel. A way to prepare ski edges
that enhances turning and overall
ski performance. Beveling creates
a slight deviation from a 90-degree
edge angle that is placed on the
side and/or the bottom of the edge
to change the ski's performance.

bindings. Devices that attach the
skis or snowboard to the boots.

biomechanics. The study of the
mechanical principles affecting
movement of the living body. The
skier in motion is affected by the
forces exerted by muscles as well
as external forces on the skeletal
structure.

bi-ski. An adaptive device
designed for people who cannot
stand. The bi-ski consists of a seat
that is mounted on two short, fat
skis with extreme sidecut. The
skier maintains balance either with

hand-held outriggers or with outriggers fixed to the bi-ski.

blocking. Any movement or action that reduces or eliminates movement in a given direction. This term generally refers to reducing rotation of the upper body by blocking either internally (through contraction of the abdominal muscles) or externally (through use of the poles).

boot flexibility. The amount of resistance that the skier's boot provides to forward flexion.

braking. Any action that slows or stops forward movement.

braking wedge. Skiing with the skis in a convergent position with sufficient edge engagement to slow or stop the skier. *See also* **gliding wedge.**

brushing. Gently pressing the ski away from the body so the tail of the ski skims sideways across the snow. Brushing is often used as an exercise for beginning skiers who brush their skis into a wedge.

call-down. A class-handling method in which the instructor calls students one at a time to ski to a certain location. This allows the instructor to assess students individually and provide direct feedback.

camber. The arch that is formed when a ski or snowboard is placed on a flat surface, with the middle of the board higher than the tip and tail.

canting. The process of making lateral adjustments made to ski equipment to enhance optimal alignment and effective edging. This is typically accomplished by mounting plastic wedges underneath the binding to allow the skier to stand with the skis flat on the snow.

cardiovascular. The body system that involves the heart and blood vessels. The cardiovascular system is conditioned through aerobic exercise training.

carved turns. Turns in which the skis travel on edge with a minimum of lateral slipping or skidding. Pure carved turns display clean, long arcs in the snow. In most turns the amount of carving depends on the situation, the equipment, and the skier's ability and intent.

centered position. A position in which the skier is in balance on the skis without excessive lean to either side or fore and aft. There is no exact centering point. Speed, terrain, equipment, snow conditions, turn radius, hill steepness, and other factors influence the skier's centered position.

Center Line. PSIA's fundamental reference for movement analysis. It is a model for selecting appropriate movement patterns under a variety of circumstances. The Center Line reference turns are wedge, wedge-christie, parallel, and dynamic-parallel turns.

center of gravity. Essentially the same location as the skier's center of mass.

center of mass. The point at which the entire mass of the body may be considered to be concentrated. If the body is viewed as made up of many small elements of mass, the average location of these elemental masses is the center of mass.

checking for understanding. The process of determining whether students understand a task, exercise, or concept that has been presented to them. Methods to implement this important part of the Teaching Model include direct questioning, assessing performance, and observing whether the student can apply the material to a new situation.

check turns. Turns that have a brief and intense edge-set between them.

christie. A turn in which the skis skid on corresponding edges. *See also* **corresponding edges, opposing edges,** and **wedge christie.**

class handling. The ski instructor's interactions with the class. Aspects of class handling are based on the instructor's demeanor, how the instructor paces the lesson and organizes and presents material, and how the instructor motivates the students.

class organization. Ways in which the instructor delivers a lesson and moves a class from one location to another on the hill. Safety awareness, lesson content, snow conditions, and student characteristics are all factors that contribute to the way a class is organized.

closed question. A question that elicits a limited response. "Are your ski edges sharp?" is a closed question. *See also* **open question.**

closure. Bringing a learning segment to an end and helping students make sense of what they have learned. Closure occurs not only at the end of the day but throughout the lesson, before students turn their attention to new material or tasks.

cognitive domain. The learning domain related to thinking, analyzing, and speaking. *See also* **affective domain.**

command-style teaching. A teaching style in which the instructor tells the students what to do, directs them to do it (often one at a time), and gives feedback on their performance.

converging skis. Any ski position in which the tips are closer together than the tails. Skis converge when in a wedge or stem. *See also* **diverging skis.**

coordination. The harmonious functioning of muscles to execute movements.

corresponding edges. Like edges—both left edges or both right edges of the skis, as viewed by the skier. *See also* **opposing edges.**

counter-rotation. Twisting the torso in one direction and the legs in the opposite direction at the same time.

countering movements. Movements that place the upper and lower body in a twisted relationship, for example, allowing the feet to continue to turn while stabilizing the upper body with a pole plant. Skiers generally use countering movements to put the body into an anticipated position. *See also* **anticipation.**

Cross Country Ski Areas Association (CCSAA). An international trade association for nordic ski area owners and operators. CCSAA is dedicated to the enjoyment and promotion of cross-country skiing throughout North America.

cross lateral. Simultaneous movement of the opposite hand and foot in activities such as walking or walking on skis. The left hand moves forward while the right foot moves forward and vice versa.

cross over. Moving the body's center of mass forward and across the skis from the inside of one turn to the inside of the next turn.

cross under. Moving the feet and skis under the body's center of mass from the outside of one turn to the outside of the next turn.

customer service. Providing a service or product in a manner that places great value on customer satisfaction. Customer service touches

all aspects of ski area operations. The ski instructor is a conduit to customers' overall enjoyment of their mountain experience.

demonstration. Performing a skiing task or exercise while highlighting particular movements.

directional stance. The snowboarder's preferred stance, i.e., the foot he or she puts forward on the snowboard. Regular stance is when the left foot is in front; goofy stance is when the right foot is in front. *See also* **fakie.**

diverging skis. Any ski position in which the tails are closer together than the tips. The skis diverge when the skier does a herringbone, skates, or makes a diverging step turn. *See also* **converging skis.**

doers. People who learn best by experiencing something (trial and error). *See also* **experiential learning.**

drills. Repeating a task or exercise to attain a desired performance objective or retain knowledge.

dynamic balance. Balance in motion. *See* **balancing movements.**

dynamic exercise. The process of performing an exercise while in motion. *See also* **static exercise.**

dynamic parallel. Turns with more carving than skidding where the ski is used as a tool and its energy from decambering flows from one turn to the next.

dynamics. A branch of mechanics involving the study of moving objects and the forces acting on them. *See also* **mechanics.**

edge angle. The angle between the base of the ski and the snow surface when the ski is placed on edge. Skis placed flat on the snow have an edge angle of 0°.

edge change. Tilting the ski from one edge to its other edge. This change can apply to both skis simultaneously, such as in a parallel turn, or sequentially, as in a wedge christie. There is no edge change in a wedge turn.

edge-control movements. Movements that increase or decrease edge angles. One of the four basic skills of skiing, edging movements include angulation and inclination.

edge set. A purposeful edge engagement, typically at the end of a turn, that provides a platform for the next turn. *See also* **checking.**

efficiency. The expenditure of only that amount of energy required to accomplish a given task. Efficiency is the ratio of the skier's input energy to the desired output movement. High efficiency implies achieving the desired movement with a minimum input of energy under a given set of conditions.

error correction. An integrated approach to assessing student performance. The instructor evaluates the student's skiing, isolates areas in need of development, devises an instructional plan, and has the student follow the plan.

eversion. The turning or rotation of the foot about its long axis so that the sole points outward.

exercises. Movement patterns that are broken down into component parts and isolated for skill development. Instructors often combine exercises into a progression.

experiential learning. Learning through experience. Instructors create situations in which students perform tasks to learn first-hand how to apply the knowledge presented during the lesson.

extension. Any movement that decreases the angle at a joint. At times, the skier extends the knee, hip, and ankle joints simultaneously. *See also* **flexion.**

extensors. Muscles that enable extension at a joint. For example, the hip muscles act to extend the thigh away from the abdomen, and the trunk muscles cause the spine to arch backward.

extrinsic feedback. Sensations and perceptions about performance that are provided by an external source e.g., an observer. *See also* **feedback.**

fakie. Riding backward on a snowboard in the rider's preferred stance.

falling leaf. An exercise in which the skier alternately sideslips forward and backward to move down the hill.

fall line. The imaginary line, through any single point on the slope, that follows the steepest descent. The fall line is the path on which a ball would roll if it were released down the slope.

far transfer. Transfer of learning from one task to another very different task or setting. *See also* **near transfer** and **teaching for transfer.**

fat skis. A type of ski designed especially for skiing deep powder snow. Fat skis are wider than conventional skis, allowing the skier to "float" higher in the snow. Also known as wide-bodied skis.

feedback. Information students receive about their performance that helps clarify what action they need to take to achieve a desired result. Students obtain feedback from their instructor (*see also* **extrinsic feedback**) or from their own observations and experience (*see also* **intrinsic feedback**).

feelers. People who learn best by experiencing sensations. Feelers depend on kinesthetic or proprioceptive input to make connections between what they are doing and what they understand.

femur. The bone that extends from the pelvis to the knee. The femur is the longest and largest bone in the body.

fibula. The smaller of the two bones in the lower leg. The fibula is located to the outside (laterally) of the larger lower leg bone, the tibia.

flexion. Any movement that decreases the angle at a joint. Often, this entails bending the knee, hip, and ankle joints simultaneously. *See also* **extension.**

flexors. The hip muscles, which act to draw the thigh toward the abdomen, and the trunk muscles, which bend the spine forward into a rounded position.

flow. The continuous movement of the skier's center of mass through a series of linked turns.

foot stance. Foot placement on a snowboard relative to its center (i.e., wide, narrow, etc.) and its major axis (i.e., perpendicular or at an angle).

force. In the external sense, the agent or action that produces a change in the speed and/or direction of a body's motion. External forces include gravity, air resistance, and ski-to-snow and pole-to-snow interactions. Internal force is generated by muscle contractions.

four track. An adaptive skiing technique for people with impaired mobility. There are various designs of four-track equipment, but all consist of two skis and two outriggers, so the skier navigates four separate sliding devices at once to navigate the slope.

free foot. In snowboarding, the rear foot when it is not secured in the binding.

friction. Surface resistance to an object that is sliding across it. A sliding ski experiences very little friction on ice and slightly more friction on smooth snow.

front foot. In snowboarding, the foot closest to the nose of the snowboard.

garlands. Performing the beginning and end of a series of turns, without the middle of the turn. This linked series takes the skier across the slope without crossing the fall line. *See also* **traverse.**

gliding. Forward sliding of the skis, either in a direct line or through a turn. Gliding is used to describe sliding with maximum use of momentum and minimum interference by friction. Its degree is determined by snow conditions, edge penetration in the snow, pressure management, minimal rotary movement, wax, base structure, and ski sole materials.

gliding wedge. When the skis are moving in a convergent position yet with little friction between the edges and the snow. *See also* **braking wedge.**

gluteus maximus. The largest and outermost muscle of each buttock that extends, abducts, and rotates the thigh.

goals. The desired lesson outcomes, which the instructor and students agree upon. Students may achieve outcomes in a variety of ways because of differences in learning preferences, ability level, and other characteristics.

goofy foot. In snowboarding, the directional stance in which the right foot is in front. *See also* **regular foot.**

gravitational force. The force of attraction that the earth exerts on an object. This force acts at the body's center of mass (center of gravity) and points toward the center of the earth.

guided-discovery-style teaching. Student learning through self discovery. The instructor guides students to a specific outcome through a series of activities without explicitly stating the outcome.

guiding or guidance. To use muscular movements to direct motion. Some teachers make the distinction that guiding implies a more subtle action than steering. That is, the effects of the ski-snow interaction are primary, and the skier responds to this interaction with a variety of muscular movements. *See also* **steering.**

hamstring muscle. Any of the three muscles at the back of the upper leg that flex the knee joint, adduct the leg, and extend the thigh.

heel side. The edge of the snowboard under the rider's heels. A heel-side turn refers to the turn direction when the rider sets the edge on the heel side of the snowboard.

herringbone. A diverging ski position useful for climbing hills. The skier faces up the hill and steps upward on alternating feet while edging to avoid slipping back.

This leaves a "herringbone" track in the snow.

high-altitude cerebral edema (HACE). A type of acute mountain sickness characterized by swelling of the brain. *See also* **acute mountain sickness.**

high-altitude pulmonary edema (HAPE). A type of acute mountain sickness characterized by filling of the lungs with edema fluid. *See also* **acute mountain sickness.**

hinge joint. A joint in which a convex part of one bone fits into a concave part of another, allowing motion in only one plane. Knee and finger joints are hinge joints.

hockey stop. A maneuver in which the skier quickly turns the skis sideways to the direction of travel and sets the edges, causing the skis to skid rapidly to a stop.

hop turns. A skiing maneuver in which the skier connects short, angular-shaped turns with a hop. From an edge set and pole plant in one direction, the skier hops up, turns the skis in the air, and lands on new edges in the new direction.

hypothermia. A dangerous condition in which the body core temperature falls below 95°F.

imagery. The process of creating mental pictures of skill performance. Instructors use this technique to have students imagine themselves skiing well and accomplishing specific outcomes.

inclination. Deviation from a vertical body position. Specifically, inclination refers to the angle formed by the head-to-feet axis of the body and the line of gravity. A skier is inclined when angulating or banking.

independent leg action. Activity in which the legs do not make the same movements at the same time; rather, each leg complements or supports the other's movement. Walking, stepping, skating, and stemming are examples of independent leg action.

inertia. The tendency of a body either to remain at rest or to continue in motion in a straight line unless acted on by an external force. The inertia of a body is given by its mass.

instructor behavior. The steps ski instructors take to determine the activities to present in a lesson and the best way to communicate them. Instructors adapt this behavior to the student's needs, based on information they gather from assessing the students. Instructor behavior is an important element of the PSIA Teaching Model. These steps consist of the following: introduce the learning segment; assess the student; determine goals and plan objectives; present and share information; guide practice; check for understanding; and summarize the learning segment. *See also* **teaching cycle.**

International Ski Federation (FIS). The governing body for international ski competition.

International Ski Instructors Association (ISIA). An association that represents professional ski instructors throughout the world. Instructors must hold the highest level of certification available in their own country to be qualified to join ISIA.

Interski. An international educational event for ski instructors that is held every four years at a different site. ISIA-member countries from throughout the world send their demonstration teams and other delegates to this event to compare ski instruction methodologies and exchange information.

intrinsic feedback. A person's sensations or perceptions about performance. A skier gauges his or her own performance and makes any necessary adjustments to achieve desired results. *See also* **feedback.**

inversion. The turning or rotation of the foot about its long axis so that the sole points inward. *See also* **eversion.**

kinesthetic learning. Learning through feelings and sensations (also known as proprioceptive learning). Kinesthetic refers to forces that act outside the body to create a sensation, such as the boot pressing upon the leg.

lateral. Situated at, proceeding from, or directed toward the side. An upright person who leans to one side moves laterally.

lateral learning. A teaching technique in which the instructor has students focus on a broad range of activities within a skiing ability level so they can experience in-depth learning before progressing to the next level. The instructor helps students isolate and develop skills, integrate them fully, and, then apply them to various situations before moving to the next level.

learning partnership. The rapport the instructor forms with the student. Essential to the success of this relationship is the instructor's understanding of the student's needs and expectations and the student's willingness to actively participate in learning.

learning style. A person's dominant or preferred mode of learning or processing information.

lesson planning. The instructor's process of establishing the lesson structure, based on the student goals that the instructor and student have together identified. As defined in the Teaching Model, the lesson duration, snow conditions, student goals and expectations, and numerous other factors contribute to an effective lesson plan.

leverage. Applying pressure in front of or behind the mid-point of the skis. An aid in turning, skiers apply subtle leveraging movements on different parts of the skis.

ligaments. Bands of thick, strong, fibrous tissue that connect bones and serve to strengthen joints.

loading position. The position of a snowboarder's feet on the board

when loading the lift.

mass. The property of a body commonly taken as a measure of the amount of material it contains and causes it to have weight in a gravitational field.

matching. Moving the skis toward a parallel relationship from either a divergent or a convergent position. Skiers match their skis to initiate the christie phase of the wedge-christie turn.

mechanics. The science that deals with the action of forces on bodies. Two principal divisions are statics, when no motion results, and dynamics, when motion results.

medial. Being or occurring in the middle.

meniscus. A cushion of cartilage found in some moveable joints. The top of the tibia is cushioned by meniscal cartilage.

model. An analogy in which concepts are related to a familiar device or system to facilitate understanding. The PSIA Skiing Model, for example, provides descriptions, or models, of skilled, efficient skiing that instructors use as a performance comparison.

modeling. A teaching procedure in which a person demonstrates the correct performance of skills.

mono-ski. An adaptive device designed for people who cannot stand. The mono-ski consists of a seat that is mounted on a wide

single ski with a shock-absorption system. The skier uses shortened outriggers to maintain balance. The term mono-ski also refers to a single ski for able-bodied skiers in which the bindings for both boots are side by side.

motivation. A need or desire that inspires a person to act. To structure lessons effectively, instructors must assess the student's motivations for learning to ski.

motor learning. Movements learned by practice or experience that lead to a relatively permanent gain in performance.

movement analysis. The process of assessing a student's skiing ability—the movement patterns and skill blending—and identifying the correlating cause-and-effect relationships. The instructor analyzes the separate components of the student's skiing to determine how the student's skills compare with Center Line reference maneuvers. The instructor uses this information to determine the focus of the lesson and identify the steps that will produce the desired results. Also known as movement assessment.

muscle. Tissue composed of cells that can shorten or contract and lengthen or relax.

National Ski Areas Association (NSAA). A national trade association for ski area owners and operators.

National Ski Patrol (NSP). An association whose members

support and participate in the ski and outdoor recreation community by providing educational training and emergency care and rescue services.

near transfer. Transfer of learning from one task to another that is very similar. *See also* **far transfer** and **teaching for transfer.**

nordic downhill. Alpine skiing on nordic equipment. The skier may make alpine ski turns as well as telemark turns.

nordic track. Nordic skiing on prepared (groomed) tracks. The skier may use classic technique (traditional diagonal stride) or skate.

objectives. The particular focus a person chooses to reach an overall goal. Objectives pinpoint the actual skills that need to be developed for a goal to be realized. For example, a skier must develop progressive edging skills to reach the goal of making rounded turns.

off piste. Terrain that is not on a prepared ski run. *See also* **piste.**

open question. A question that may elicit a broad range of responses. "What did you feel about your balance in that turn?" is an open question. *See also* **closed question.**

opposing edges. Different edges—the left edge of one ski and the right edge of the other ski, as viewed by the skier. *See also* **corresponding edges.**

orthotic. A device to support and provide correction to the skier's foot so that it maintains a neutral position inside the boot. An orthotic helps the boot transfer movements quickly and powerfully from the foot to the ski. These devices are typically handmade to fit each foot individually.

outcome. The performance capability achieved by the end of a teaching-learning segment. The instructor and student create a goal for each lesson, possibly with intermediate objectives, and use a series of activities that move the student toward the goal. The actual lesson outcome may or may not be the original goal and may be different for each student. *See also* **learning partnership.**

outcome-based education. A system of education in which the learner achieves a series of developmental milestones that lead to an overall goal, or outcome. In the PSIA American Teaching System, each skiing level, 1 through 9, has a specific outcome, defined as skills a student must exhibit before moving from one level to the next.

outriggers. Forearm crutches with ski tips on the bottom. Adaptive skiers use these devices for balance.

pacing. The orchestration of activities that make up a ski lesson—the intensity of the practice period, its duration, and the frequency of repeating practice.

parallel turn. A turn made on corresponding ski edges. It may be more or less carved, depending on the skier's intention and skill.

patella. The kneecap.

pelvis. A cone-shaped bony ring made up of the right and left pelvic bones joined in front and in back.

perpendicular. Meeting a given line or surface at a right (90°) angle. In the ski lodge, skiers stand perpendicular to the floor. *See also* **side-stepping.**

phases of a turn. The four elements of a turn: (1) the preparation phase, when the skier prepares to start a new turn; (2) the initiation phase, when the skier starts a new turn and edge change takes place; (3) the control phase, when the skier guides the skis through the intended arc; and (4) the finishing phase, when the skier stops or traverses. In linked turns (no traverse or stopping) there is no true finishing phase, since it becomes the preparation phase for the new turn.

piste. A European term for a prepared ski run. *See also* **off piste.**

pivoting. Rotating the skis about an axis perpendicular to their base. Pivoting is typically a quick movement performed on a flat ski.

platform. Setting the edges deep enough in the snow to support movements such as stepping, stemming, or rebounding.

pole usage. Pole movements, including pushing, swinging, touching, or planting. In each of these movements, timing, placement, and technique dictate the outcome of the pole use.

posterior. Nearer to the back surface of the body.

practice. Repetition of movement patterns or other activities designed to develop or refine a skill. Student focus and instructor guidance and feedback are important parts of effective practice.

pressure. Force distributed over an area. The force of a skier's weight while standing on skis is distributed over the bottom of the skis as pressure.

pressure-control movements. Movements that create, maintain, reduce, or redirect the pressure of the skis on the snow. Pressure control is one of the four fundamental skiing skills. It is achieved through leverage, extension, flexion, and transfer of pressure from ski to ski, all in combination with edge-control movements. Skier movements, ski characteristics, turn shape, terrain, and snow conditions determine the pressure along the ski at any instant.

pressure transfer. Directing pressure from one ski to the other.

pre-turn. The skier's tightening of the arc at the end of one turn to help a skier slow down. This creates a rebound into the next turn. The slight steering of the skis uphill from a traverse position aids the initiation of a turn across the fall line.

problem-solving-style teaching. A teaching style in which the instructor poses a problem for the students to solve and establishes parameters in which the students must work.

progressions. A sequence of acts, movements, or events oriented toward meeting an educational objective or goal. Progressions are connected from the least complicated to the most difficult. For example, an edging skill development progression might include side stepping up a hill, then sideslipping, followed by side-slipping to an edge-set.

pronation. A flattening of the foot's arch, with the ankle and foot rolling to the inside when the foot is weighted.

proprioception. The sense of the position and movements of the body and body parts. Ski skill development requires the performer to perceive and use proprioceptive information.

PSIA Demonstration Teams. National teams of the Professional Ski Instructors of America whose purpose is demonstration, teaching, and training across the United States. Member instructors are selected for the teams based on performance and teaching ability. The teams are: Alpine, Nordic, Snowboard, and Junior Education Team (JETs) for children's ski instruction.

Q angle. The angle between the extended axes of the femur and the tibia, measured at mid-patella (kneecap). The angle is typically larger for women than men because women have relatively wider pelvic width.

quadriceps. The large extensor muscles at the front of the thigh.

rear foot. The foot nearest to the tail of the snowboard.

rebound. The springing back or recoil from the pressure release of a decambered ski. A skier can control edging, turn shape, and pressure to decamber the skis, and then rebound into the next turn and create a snappy linkage from turn to turn.

reciprocal-style teaching. A teaching style in which the instructor pairs students and outlines specific tasks for each pair. For example, the instructor has a student pair ski through a set of cones, with one student acting as the performer and the other acting as the observer. After discussing the activity, the students switch roles.

regular foot. In snowboarding, the directional stance in which the left foot is in front. *See also* **goofy foot.**

reinforcement. The process of rewarding students for appropriate performance. Recognizing and praising students for reaching their achievements provides even more motivation to them.

retraction. Pulling the legs up under the body by contracting the muscles of the abdomen and hips.

This movement can be used to absorb pressure increases due to terrain changes or turn dynamics.

reverse camber. A ski bent opposite of its natural camber.

revolving line. A class-handling technique. Students separate to form a line down the hill, and the highest student skis from the top of the line in front of the class to the bottom of the line and stops. Subsequent students take turns skiing, and the line "revolves" down the run.

risk management. Using appropriate methods and procedures to reduce risk to customers, guests, and employees at a ski area. Instructors, hill employees, management personnel, and volunteers work together to implement area risk management policies.

rotary movements. Movements that increase, limit, or decrease the rotation of the skis. One of the four basic skills, rotary movements can be grouped into four primary categories: (1) rotation, (a) rotation directly applied to the ski such as with the leg, and (b), rotary momentum transferred to the ski from slowing or stopping torso rotation that was previously established in the turn direction; (2) counter-rotation, twisting the legs and torso in opposite directions; (3) anticipation release, realignment of the torso and legs from the anticipation position; and (4) rotary push-off. *See also* glossary entries for (1) through (4).

rotary push-off. The use of muscular force to project (push) off one or both feet to create rotary movement. Stem turns and step turns are examples of rotary push-off. *See also* **sequential leg rotation.**

rotation. The rotational motion of a body about an axis (including the movement of the body's limbs about their axes). Slowing or stopping body rotation initiated in the direction of the intended turn results in a turning effort that is transferred to the skis. The skier commonly uses the shoulders and hips, either separately or together, to develop the turning effort.

rotators. Muscles that serve to rotate a part of the body. The hip rotators help maintain good alignment while skiing.

safety. Freedom from the occurrence or risk of injury, danger, or loss. The effectiveness and quality of a ski lesson depends on safety awareness, since students will not be receptive to learning if they do not feel safe.

sensorimotor domain. The learning domain related to movement and performance. A beginning skier and an advanced skier can each sense being out of balance. Whereas the motor response of the beginner might be to sit down, the advanced skier might respond by adjusting his or her balance to a centered position. *See also* **affective domain.**

sequential leg rotation. A non-simultaneous rotation of the legs in which one leg is used as a platform from which the opposite leg is rotated. Stemming and stepping are examples of such "one-two" movements. *See also* **rotary push-off.**

Service Model. PSIA's model for providing exceptional customer service. The Service Model provides a framework that instructors can use to determine and satisfy students' wants and needs. Because guests have increasingly sophisticated expectations of ski resorts, this model is the third—and perhaps most important—part of the American Teaching System, which also includes the Skiing Model and the Teaching Model.

shaped skis. A term often used to refer to skis with greater sidecut than conventional skis.

sidecut. The characteristic of skis, when lying flat on the snow and viewed from above, to display greater width at the tips and tails than at the middle.

sideslipping. A method of moving down the hill with the skis perpendicular (or across) the fall line.

side step. A method of moving up the hill. With skis across the fall line, the skier steps up sideways, one ski at a time.

simultaneous leg rotation. Rotation of both legs at the same time. Hop turns display simultaneous leg rotation.

skating. A method of propulsion in which the skier pushes from foot to foot while maintaining the skis in a diverging position. The inside edges of the skis are sequentially engaged as the skier moves forward. In nordic track skating, the skis are positioned into a skating "V" and the skier uses strong push-off from ski to ski. The upper body is typically in a semi-tucked position.

ski brake. A device attached to the ski with prongs that rotate downward below the ski base when the skier's boot leaves the binding. The prongs dig into the snow to stop a ski from sliding away.

skidding. The result of the skis moving forward and sideways simultaneously.

Ski Industries America (SIA). A national, member-owned trade association representing more than 1,000 ski, snowboard, and outdoor product manufacturers, distributors, and suppliers.

Skiing Model. PSIA's reference for identifying and describing the technical and mechanical aspects of student performance. Its components are: the four fundamental skills of skiing and common features of these skills at all levels; the Center Line; and progressions. The Skiing Model is one of the three models in the American Teaching system, along with the Teaching Model and the Service Model.

skill. The capability to bring about a result with maximum certainty, minimum energy, or minimum time.

skill blending. Combining basic skills to create an overall performance. Expert skiers integrate skills depending on the situation or maneuver. Instructors can evaluate students on their ability to blend and apply skills in a variety of situations.

skills concept. The four fundamental skiing skills: balancing, rotary, edge-control, and pressure-control movements. The skills concept, which is an essential aspect of the American Teaching System, provides instructors a base from which to evaluate, prioritize, and develop student performance.

ski pole. A thin pole with a hand grip on one end and a tip with a basket on the other end. Skiers use poles to help obtain balance, propulsion, timing, rhythm, and blocking.

sliding. Movement of the skis in the direction of their longitudinal axis.

slipping. Movement of the skis sideways. Slipping can occur with the skis perpendicular to the line of travel (sideslipping) or in other orientations, such as in a turn.

snowboard. A board for sliding across snow in an angled stance, much like surfing. This device is wide enough to accommodate both feet placed across its width and has characteristics similar to a ski, such as camber and sidecut.

snowplow turn. A turn made in a wide wedge. Snowplow is no

longer a common skiing term; instructors now refer to this maneuver as a wedge turn. *See also* **wedge turn.**

snow types. Approximate classifications of snow. Several types exist: powder—snow that is light, dry, and fluffy; packed powder—snow that is pressed together or groomed; corn—pellet-sized particles that have formed from repetitive thawing, refreezing, and recrystallizing of snow; crud—settling snow that is cut up by skiers; wind-crust—snow with a wind-compacted top layer; cement—uncompacted, heavy snow with a high moisture content; ice—snow that has become very dense and hard.

speed. The rate of motion or progress; the magnitude of velocity.

spine. The bony column that forms the main support for the body and protects the spinal cord. The spine consists of 33 vertebrae.

split. The process of separating a group of students into homogeneous classes. The instructor may group students according to their desired outcomes (e.g., bump skiing versus groomed skiing), skill level (level 1 through 9), preferred learning style (e.g., watcher, thinker, doer, feeler), or any combination of these variables.

stance. How a skier stands on skis. One of the most basic indicators of performance at all levels of skiing, stance affects the application and blending of skills.

star step. A maneuver for beginning skiers to develop a spatial awareness of their skis and change direction on a flat surface. The skier keeps the ski tips in one place while stepping the tails of the skis in a circle around the tips.

static exercise. The process of performing an exercise while standing still. One common static exercise is when students practice rhythmic pole swings while standing still. This is generally followed by practicing the pole swing while linking turns, a dynamic exercise. *See also* **dynamic exercise.**

statics. A branch of mechanics involving the study of bodies that are not moving and the forces that act on them. *See also* **mechanics.**

steering. The use of muscular actions to direct the path of the skis. Some teachers make the distinction that steering means that the skier actively directs the skis to respond to the external conditions (terrain or snow). This is in contrast with guiding, in which the skier responds to these conditions in a more subtle manner. *See also* **guiding.**

stem turns. Turns initiated by stemming the skis. After stemming the uphill ski, the skier transfers weight to that ski to start the turn, then brings the other ski to a matched position.

stemming. The displacement of one ski to a position convergent with the other ski. One result of the stemming is that the skis are on opposing edges.

step turns. A turn in which the skier maintains the downhill ski as a platform and steps the uphill ski into a converging, diverging, or parallel position. This is a quick, dynamic way to initiate a turn.

straight run. Skiing directly down the fall line with the skis in a parallel relationship. Also called schussing (German).

student-centered teaching. Teaching that is determined by the student's needs, desires, expectations, preferred learning styles, and reactions to the learning process. Student-centered teaching is one of the most important underlying philosophies in ATS.

student profile. An element of the PSIA Teaching Model. The student profile is the unique combination of individual characteristics that each student possesses, including his or her physical attributes and background (sports experience), learning preferences, motivation and desire, and emotional state. *See also* **Teaching Model.**

subtalar joint. The ankle joint, which is the primary joint in the foot.

sunburn. A first- or second-degree skin burn caused by exposure to ultraviolet light in the medium-wave range (UVB), with a wavelength of 290 to 320 nanometers.

supination. Elevation of the foot's arch. A supinated foot rolls to the outside when weighted.

synchronization. Group skiing in which skiers maintain formations that are orchestrated with precise timing, rhythm, turn shape, and technique.

tactics. The methods used to gain a desired objective.

targeting. In teaching, focusing the lesson on a specific skill. As an exercise, targeting refers to focusing student attention downhill by assigning the task of skiing toward a target while maintaining a narrow corridor.

task. An assigned activity, for example, skiing toward a target while maintaining a 20-foot-wide corridor.

task-style teaching. A teaching approach in which the instructor assigns a task or activity to the students, then provides them with certain performance boundaries and encourages them to practice on their own.

teaching cycle. A step-by-step guide to creating valid lesson content (*what* to teach) and presenting information in a style that is tailored to student needs (*how* to teach).

teaching for transfer. Drawing upon a student's previous learning to help with present learning, that is, pointing out similarities between familiar movements and new movements. For example, students first learn to create better edge grip for side stepping by rolling their ankles into the hill. Later, students can transfer the movement of rolling the ankles to turning with more edge control. *See also* **far transfer, near transfer,** and **transfer of learning.**

Teaching Model. PSIA's framework for devising ski lessons and making professional decisions about what and how to teach so that instructors can ensure an effective and enjoyable learning experience for students. The Teaching Model consists of two aspects of the teaching and learning process: instructor behavior and student profile. These two parts form, in essence, a learning partnership. The Teaching Model is one of the three basic tenets of the American Teaching System (the Skiing Model and Service Model are the other two). *See also* **learning partnership.**

technique. A movement option for accomplishing a given goal. For instance, the Skiing Model provides a set of movements that represent the appropriate technique for performing parallel turns.

telemark. A position or turn on nordic skis in which the skier's feet are separated longitudinally, with the rear foot bent toward the ski and the rear heel lifted off the ski. The position resembles a genuflect or curtsy.

tether. A strap or rope attached to an adaptive sit-down skiing device or to a small beginning skier. It is used as a teaching aid and for safety purposes.

thinkers. Students who learn best

using cognitive abilities. Thinkers prefer to interpret action and movement verbally, and they generally enjoy descriptions.

three track. An adaptive skiing technique for people with impaired mobility. Three-track equipment consists of one ski and two outriggers for balance.

tibia. The inner and larger bone of the lower leg. Also called the shinbone.

toe side. The edge of the snowboard under the rider's toes. A toe-side turn refers to the turn direction when the rider sets the edge on the toe side of the snowboard.

transfer of learning. The gain (positive transfer) or loss (negative transfer) in proficiency of one task as a result of practice or experience on of another task. *See also* **far transfer, near transfer,** and **teaching for transfer.**

traverse. Skiing across the slope without crossing the fall line. *See also* **garlands.**

turn shape. The form of the turn arc (the exact path the skis travel through the turn). The skier creates turn shape with the unique combination of balancing, rotary, pressure control, and edging movements. Turn shape reflects the skill level of the skier and indicates the timing, intensity, and duration of the skill movements.

United States Ski Association (USSA). An organization that

represents recreational skiing and amateur ski competition in the United States.

United States Ski Coaches Association (USSCA). An association for those who coach skiing in the United States. USSCA provides training and certification programs and establishes coaching standards.

United States Skiing. An organization that represents competitive skiing in the United States.

unweighting. Reducing the pressure on the skis. There are four categories of unweighting: (1) up-unweighting, produced at the end of a rapid upward extension of the body, (2) down-unweighting, produced by a rapid downward flexion of the body, (3) terrain-unweighting, produced as the terrain rapidly falls away from under the skier, and (4) rebound-unweighting, produced after the decambered skis have "kicked back" at the end of a turn.

visual learners. Students who learn best by watching. They prefer demonstrations rather than verbal descriptions or diagrams.

warm-up. A portion of the lesson devoted to preparing for activity. This lesson segment often refers to warming up muscles through light movement and stretching, but instructors also can help students warm up their minds and prepare them to learn.

watchers. Another name for visual learners.

wedge-christie turn. A turn that begins with opposing edges (in a wedge) and finishes with a skidding phase, resulting in corresponding edges (in a parallel). *See also* **christie** and **wedge turn.**

wedge turn. A turn with skis in a converging (wedge) position, with the skier maintaining opposing edges throughout the turn. *See also* **braking wedge, gliding wedge,** and **opposing edges**.

weight transfer. The act of shifting weight, which transfers pressure from one ski to the other. The preferred term is pressure transfer, because weight is only one of the forces that determines the extent of pressure on the skis.

wide track. Parallel turns in which the skis are hip-width apart, leaving a wide track in the snow.

windchill effect. The cooling effect of wind; the coldness felt on exposed skin due to a combination of temperature and wind velocity.

Your Responsibility Code. A code that sets forth the responsibility of each participant for safe conduct on the ski slopes and lifts. There are seven points to the code. It is meant to be a partial list of safe conduct with the message to always be safety conscious. This code is endorsed by NSAA, NSP, and PSIA.

Z turns. Turns with a shape that is angular and harsh rather than rounded and smooth.

Education/ Certification Standards

Revised June 1996

All references to ATS refer to the concepts of the American Teaching System, described in PSIA's *Alpine Manual*. Terminology consistent with the manual is used throughout this document. All references to class level refer to Levels 1 through 9 in *The American Teaching System: Alpine Skiing,* second edition. All references to skills and skill blending refer to balancing movements, rotary movements, edge-control movements, and pressure-control movements. The variety of turn shapes refers to short-, medium-, and long-radius turns.

REGISTERED

No hour requirements have been placed on training for Registered instructors. It has been kept open-ended so that each division and ski school can tailor the instructional material to fit its own format and process. The amount of material to be presented suggests a minimum program of 20 to 30 hours.

Category A: PSIA Education
The instructor is able to...

1. General Information
   a. Introduction to PSIA
      1) discuss the history of PSIA
      2) discuss the organization of PSIA
      3) describe the philosophy of PSIA
      4) understand and discuss the purpose of PSIA
   b. Ski Industry
      1) discuss the role of ski instruction within the ski industry
      2) describe the organization of one's home ski area
      3) understand and discuss the teamwork aspect of home ski area operations
   c. Professionalism
      1) discuss basic principles and philosophies of professionalism
      2) discuss specific behaviors of ski instructor professionalism
      3) demonstrate professionalism at home ski area

Category B: American Teaching Systen (ATS) Education
The instructor is able to...

1. Introduction to ATS
   a. ski Center Line reference maneuvers
      (No specific parameters are set for the performance of the maneuvers until Certified Level I. Registered instructors should be able to ski each maneuver in a basic form that will create understanding and encourage further development.)
      1) ski wedge turns
      2) ski wedge-christie turns with matching early and late in the turn
      3) ski open-parallel turns
      4) ski dynamic-parallel turns
   b. ski variations of reference maneuvers in different on-hill situations
      1) ski wedge turns on both steep or shallow terrain and discuss differences in skill blend
      2) ski wedge-christie turns on both steep and shallow terrain and discuss differences in skill blend and matching

2. Class Organization and Handling
   a. provide individual attention to students in a class lesson
   b. handle a class in a safe and responsible manner
   c. provide a lesson format based on the guidelines of ATS and one's home ski area

3. Risk Management
   a. recite Your Responsibility Code
   b. teach Your Responsibility Code to students at one's home area
   c. practice class handling that demonstrates appropriate decision-making based on risk-management principles

4. Customer Service
   a. discuss the philosophy of a student-centered and customer-service-oriented approach
   b. relate various customer services at one's home ski area to ski school students
   c. demonstrate customer-oriented behaviors with ski school students

CERTIFIED LEVEL I

Category A: Skiing
The instructor is able to...

1. Free Skiing
   a. General
      1) ski open-parallel turns with pole swing and touch on groomed blue terrain
      2) consistently link turns with sustained rhythm
      3) maintain consistent speed by controlling the shape of a turn
      4) maintain a balanced stance throughout a series of turns
   b. Bumps: N/A
   c. Versatility
      1) ski a variety of turn shapes in a series of turns while maintaining speed control on groomed blue terrain

2. Demonstrations
   a. Wedge Turns
      1) demonstrate on the easiest of groomed green terrain
      2) demonstrate a blend of skills
      3) wedge consistently throughout a series of turns
   b. Wedge-Christie Turns
      1) demonstrate on groomed green and the easiest of groomed blue terrain
      2) demonstrate a blend of skills
      3) demonstrate consistently throughout a series of turns
      4) demonstrate matching with active steering of the inside leg

Category B: Teaching
The instructor is able to...

1. Knowledge
   a. recall Your Responsibility Code and discuss how to introduce it when teaching through Level 4
   b. recognize the Teaching Model, Skiing Model, and the philosophy and principles of the ATS, and discuss how to use the system when teaching through Level 4
   c. identify learning styles and give examples of how to recognize a student's learning preference
   d. identify command and task styles of teaching and give examples of how to use them during a lesson
   e. identify the student needs of specific groups, i.e., adults, children, women, or seniors
   f. identify common behavior patterns of children as they develop
   g. describe the components of the Service Model

2. Application
   a. teach the skiing public through Level 4
   b. communicate information using basic techniques, such as eye contact, voice inflection, body language, and appropriate pacing of information
   c. handle a class based on group energy levels; conditions for the day; safety; and lesson content
   d. describe skier services and activities at one's home area

Category C: Technical
The instructor is able to...

1. Terminology
   a. define and explain basic skiing terminology as described in ATS manuals

2. Equipment
   a. identify equipment needs for skiers through Level 4

3. Skiing Model/Skill Development
   a. identify fundamental skiing skills
   b. relate fundamental skills to skill development through Level 4
   c. describe the Center Line reference maneuvers; identify similarities and differences in common skill usage for these maneuvers
   d. identify phases of a turn

4. Movement Analysis
   a. describe the basic movement patterns in skiers through Level 4
   b. determine cause-and-effect relationships, as related to fundamental skills in skiers through Level 4
   c. prescribe what a student should work on by prioritizing skill needs up to Level 4
   d. prepare a lesson plan based upon skill development, including exercises and tasks that target student needs and change the skier's performance

CERTIFIED LEVEL II

Category A: Skiing
The instructor is able to...

1. FREE SKIING
   a. General
      1) ski beginning dynamic-parallel turns on groomed blue and easy black terrain
      2) use ski design and skill blending to shape parallel turns
      3) link turns of consistent rhythm and shape, such as a series of short or long turns
      4) control speed by adjusting turn shape
      5) maintain a balanced stance throughout a series of turns
   b. Bumps
      1) ski blue and easy black bumps that are typical of what students through Level 7 would ski
      2) link turns in or near the fall line for the entire length of the run. Some line change is expected, but rhythm must be maintained without a traverse.
      3) maintain speed control
      4) maintain and recover balance throughout the run without losing fall-line orientation
      5) demonstrate appropriate tactical choices as dictated by terrain
   c. Versatility
      1) demonstrate a variety of turn shapes
      2) apply appropriate tactics and vary skill applications

in a variety of conditions, including ungroomed snow or powder
      3) demonstrate different types of skill blends and movement patterns in exercises, tasks, and turns, upon request

2. Demonstrations
   a. Wedge Turns
      1) demonstrate on the easiest groomed green terrain
      2) demonstrate a balanced stance
      3) demonstrate steering of both legs to create turn shape and speed control
      4) wedge consistently with appropriate skill blending throughout a series of turns
   b. Wedge-Christie Turns
      1) demonstrate on groomed green and easiest groomed blue terrain
      2) demonstrate steering of the inside ski to facilitate matching
      3) demonstrate shaping of the control phase of the turn by blending skills (rotary, edging, and pressure control) and steering both skis
      4) demonstrate matching of the skis in a variety of places in the turn (beginning, middle, end), depending on speed, terrain, or intention
      5) demonstrate consistency for the entire length of the run
   c. Open-Parallel Turns
      1) demonstrate on groomed

or recently groomed (not necessarily smooth) terrain
      2) demonstrate a slight extension at the turn initiation that facilitates a simultaneous edge change
      3) demonstrate a pole swing that facilitates extension and edge change at turn initiation
      4) demonstrate active steering of both legs throughout the turn to facilitate turn shape and speed control
      5) maintain an accurate blending of skills to perform a series of consistent turns

Category B: Teaching
The instructor is able to...

1. Knowledge
   a. recall Your Responsibility Code and discuss how to integrate it into lessons through Level 7
   b. identify the components of the Teaching Model
   c. identify command, task, reciprocal, and small-group teaching styles; identify learning styles; recognize that student behaviors are indicators to adjust teacher behavior appropriately
   d. describe the cognitive, affective, and physical development of students
   e. identify logical steps to teach the skiing public through Level 7
   f. discuss ways to create a learning partnership with students that addresses their

expectations and develops
common goals
  g. describe examples of skier
     services and activities at the
     ski resort that enhance
     student enjoyment
  h. describe and discuss the
     components of the
     Service Model

2. Application
  a. apply the Teaching Model
     effectively to meet the needs
     of students; move from
     linear to circular use of the
     Teaching Model
  b. tailor teaching styles to meet
     the preferred learning style
     of students
  c. work with ranges of student
     performance within a group
     and maintain cohesiveness
  d. modify lesson content to
     meet the needs of children at
     various stages of development
  e. demonstrate how lateral
     learning enhances skill
     development

Category C: Technical
The instructor is able to...

1. Terminology
  a. define and interpret terminol-
     ogy, as presented in ATS
     manuals, and apply it to
     analyzing, understanding,
     and teaching skiers up
     through Level 7
  b. relate basic skiing terminol-
     ogy to students in simple
     language

2. Equipment
  a. describe changing equipment
     needs as students move from

Level 1 through 7

3. Skiing Model/Skill
   Development
  a. describe the fundamental
     skills of the Skiing Model
  b. discuss the common skill
     features of the Skiing Model
  c. identify situational variations
     of skill application through
     Level 7
  d. describe the forces acting on
     a skier in a turn; relate how
     a skier uses muscular effort
     and movements to manage
     these forces

4. Movement Analysis
  a. describe the basic movement
     patterns in skiers through
     Level 7
  b. determine cause-and-effect
     relationships, as related to
     skill usage, in different
     phases of the turn in skiers
     through Level 7
  c. prescribe and justify what a
     student should work on by
     prioritizing skill needs
     through Level 7
  d. develop exercises and tasks
     that target skiers' needs and
     change their performance

CERTIFIED LEVEL III

Category A: Skiing
The instructor is able to...

1. Free Skiing
   a. General
      1) ski dynamic-parallel turns on all mountain terrain
      2) show appropriate skill blending on all mountain terrain, except the most extreme
      3) reduce, generate, or maintain speed without interrupting overall flow or rhythm
   b. Bumps
      1) ski any bumps on the mountain
      2) link turns in the fall line for the entire length of the selected run
      3) reduce, maintain, or generate speed without interrupting the overall flow of the run
      4) maintain turning within a line and intentionally change lines during the run
      5) demonstrate appropriate tactical choices, as dictated by terrain
   c. Versatility
      1) ski a variety of turn shapes (short, medium, long) and apply them to different mountain situations
      2) demonstrate different types of skill blends and movement patterns in exercises, tasks, and turns upon request, and as applied in different mountain situations
      3) maintain turning and speed control while skiing in any snow condition (i.e., powder, crud, bumps, ice, or hard pack)

2. Demonstrations
   a. Wedge Turns
      1) demonstrate wedge turns on any green terrain
      2) demonstrate a balanced stance
      3) demonstrate steering of both legs to create turn shape and control speed
      4) wedge consistently and blend skills throughout a series of turns
   b. Wedge-Christie Turns
      1) demonstrate on any green or blue terrain (not necessarily groomed)
      2) demonstrate a steering of the inside ski to facilitate matching
      3) demonstrate shaping of the turn by blending skills and steering both skis
      4) demonstrate matching in a variety of places in the turn (beginning, middle, end), depending on speed, terrain, and intention
      5) maintain a consistent series of turns
   c. Open-Parallel Turns
      1) demonstrate on any blue (not necessarily groomed) and the easiest of groomed black terrain
      2) demonstrate extension that facilitates an edge change at the beginning of the turn
      3) demonstrate a pole swing that facilitates the exten-

sion and edge change at turn initiation
      4) demonstrate active steering of both legs throughout the turn, resulting in turn shape and speed control
      5) maintain an accurate blending of skills to enhance a series of consistent turns
   d. Dynamic-Parallel Turns
      1) demonstrate dynamic-parallel turns in a variety of terrain and snow conditions
      2) blend skills appropriately, in response to speed, turn radius, tactics, terrain, snow condition, or intention, at any place on the mountain
      3) use ski design and skill blending to carve and shape turns
      4) maintain pressure on the outside ski with dynamic balancing movements
      5) link turns with continuous and accurate movements

Category B: Teaching
The instructor is able to...

1. Knowledge
   a. discuss how to integrate Your Responsibility Code into lessons through Level 9
   b. describe how to use a variety of teaching and learning styles in a group lesson to individualize the lesson
   c. describe elements of teaching and learning theory (such as the parameters for effective teaching, teaching for

transfer, feedback, pacing, and lesson content)

d. identify logical steps to teach the skiing public through Level 9

e. describe in depth the skier services and activities available at one's home area as well as within the ski industry

f. describe and discuss the components of the Service Model and give an example of its application

2. Application

a. use the Teaching Model in lessons through Level 9

b. individualize group and semi-private lessons by using a variety of teaching styles and methodologies

c. arrive at specific outcomes during lessons by using a variety of strategies, including lateral learning to enhance skill development and application in students

d. apply reinforcement, practice, and feedback and other forms of teaching and learning theory to enhance the lesson experience

e. use teaching behaviors that address the individual development needs (cognitive, affective, and physical) of each student

Category C: Technical
The instructor is able to...

1. Terminology

a. discuss all skiing-related concepts from the ATS manual and demonstrate

understanding through skiing performance

b. relate specific skiing terminology to students in simple language

2. Equipment

a. describe, analyze, and prescribe equipment needs for advanced skiers

3. Skiing Model/Skill Development

a. analyze skill blending in skiing

b. describe how skill blending relates to different situations and conditions. Relate skill blending to different populations of skiers (i.e., seniors, women, children, top athletes)

c. relate skill blending to various internal and external forces generated in a variety of skiing situations

4. Movement Analysis

a. describe the basic movement patterns in skiers through Level 9

b. determine cause-and-effect relationships, based on balance, skill blending, tactics, skill deficiencies and proficiencies, and other factors related to the phases of a turn in skiers through Level 9

c. prescribe and justify what a student should work on by prioritizing skill needs through Level 9

d. develop exercises and tasks that target skiers' needs and change their performance

Suggested Reading

The works listed below contain information on topics of relevance and interest to ski teachers. This list does not include all works available on these topics; they are included here to encourage further study and consideration.

Publications Currently In Print

Albrecht, K., 1988. *At America's Service*. Homewood, IL: Dow Jones-Irwin.

Anderson, B., 1980. *Stretching*. Bolinas, CA: Shelter Publications, Inc.

Bailey, C., 1991. *The New Fit or Fat*. Boston: Houghton Mifflin Co.

Brockman, C.F., R. Merrilees, and H.S. Zim., 1968. *A Guide to Field Identification: Trees of North America*. New York: Golden Press.

Burt, W.H. and Grossenheider, R.P., 1980. *A Field Guide to the Mammals*. Boston: Houghton Mifflin Co.

Carbone, C., 1994. *WomenSki*. Boston, MA: World Leisure Corporation.

Carlzon, J., 1987. *Moments of Truth*. Cambridge, MA: Ballinger Books.

Czikszentmihalyi, M., 1990. *Flow: The Psychology of Optimal Experience*. New York: Harper Collins Pubs., Inc.

Donnelly, J.E., 1990. *Living Anatomy,* 2nd ed. Champaign, IL: Leisure Press.

Foster, E.P., 1995. *Technical Skills for Alpine Skiing*. South Hero, VT: Turning Point Ski Foundation.

Foster, E.P., 1994. *Race Skills for Alpine Skiing*. South Hero, VT: Turning Point Ski Foundation.

Foster, E.P., 1993. *Conditioning Skills for Alpine Skiing*. South Hero, VT: Turning Point Ski Foundation.

Foxon, F., 1991. *Skiing: Technique, Tactics, Training*. UK: Crowood Press.

Gagne, R.M., 1988. *The Essentials of Learning for Instruction*. Englewood Cliffs, NJ: Prentice-Hall.

Gamma, K., 1992. *The Handbook of Skiing*. New York: Alfred A. Knopf, Inc.

Glanz, B.A., 1994. *Building Customer Loyalty*. Burr Ridge, IL: Mirror Press.

Hakim, C., 1994. *We Are All Self-Employed*. San Francisco: Berrett-Koehler Pubs.

Howden, M., 1985. *World Class Ski Tuning*. Portland, OR: WCST Publishing.

Jensen, E., 1995. *Super Teaching*. Del Mar, CA: Turning Point Publishing.

Joubert, G., 1980. *Skiing: An Art...A Technique*. La Porte, CO: Poudre Press.

Kubistant, T., 1986. *Performing Your Best*. Champaign, IL: Life Enhancement Publications.

Leach, R.E., ed., 1994. *Alpine Skiing*. Boston, MA: Blackwell Scientific Publications.

LeMaster, R., 1995. *Skiing: The Nuts and Bolts*. Lakewood, CO: PSIA.

Loudis, J.A., Lobitz, W.C., and Singer, K.M., 1986. *Skiing Out of Your Mind*. Champaign, IL: Leisure Press.

MacNeil, D.J., 1994. *Customer Service Excellence*. Burr Ridge, IL: Mirror Press.

McArdle, W., Katch, F., and Katch, V., 1991. *Exercise Physiology: Energy, Nutrition, and Human Performance*. Baltimore: Williams and Wilkins.

Murie, O.J., 1982. *A Field Guide to Animal Tracks*. Boston: Houghton Mifflin Co.

National Ski Patrol, 1994. *Outdoor First Care*. Lakewood, CO: NSP.

Orlick, T., 1986. *Psyching for Sport: Mental Training for Athletes*. Champaign, IL: Leisure Press.

Pearl, B., 1988. *Getting Stronger.* New York: Random House, Inc.

Professional Ski Instructors of America, 1996. *Alpine Level I Study Guide, Level II Study Guide,* and *Level III Study Guide.* Lakewood, CO: PSIA.

PSIA, 1996. *Alpine Handbook.* Lakewood, CO: PSIA.

PSIA, 1996. *Captain Zembo's Ski and Snowboard Teaching Guide for Kids.* Lakewood, CO: PSIA.

PSIA, 1994. *The American Teaching System: Children's Development.* Lakewood, CO: PSIA.

Reichenfeld, R., and Bruechert, A.M., 1992. *Skiing: Step by Step to Success.* UK: Crowood Press.

Rink, J.E., 1985. *Teaching Physical Education for Learning.* St. Louis, MO: Times Mirror/Mosby.

Robbins, C.S., Bruun, B., Zim, H.S., and Singer, A., 1983. *A Guide to Field Identification: Birds of North America.* New York: Golden Press.

Schmidt, R.A., 1991. *Motor Learning and Performance: From Principles to Practice.* Champaign, IL: Human Kinetics Books.

Schwartz, G.H., 1995. *Skiing Literature: A Bibliographical Catalogue.* Mill Valley, CA: Wood River Publishing.

Taylor, J., 1995. *The Mental Edge for Skiing.* Denver, CO: Minuteman Press.

Tejada-Flores, L., 1993. *Breakthrough on Skis.* New York: Vintage Books.

Thomas, G., 1992. *Performance Skiing: Training and Techniques to Make You a Better Alpine Skier.* Harrisburg, PA: Stackpole Books.

United States Ski Coaches Association, 1994. *Rookie Coaches Ski Racing Guide.* Champaign, IL: Human Kinetics Publishers.

Vagners, J., 1995. *A Ski Instructor's Guide to the Physics and Biomechanics of Skiing.* Lakewood, CO: PSIA.

Vermont Safety Research, 1995. ACL Awareness 1996 video and flyer. Underhill Center, VT: Vermont Safety Research.

Witherell, W., and Evrard, D., 1993. *The Athletic Skier.* Boulder, CO: Johnson Books.

Yacenda, J., 1993. *Alpine Skiing: Steps to Success.* Champaign, IL: Human Kinetics Publishers.

Yacenda, J., 1987. *High Performance Skiing.* Champaign, IL: Human Kinetics Publishers.

PSIA Classics

Though out of print, these PSIA classic editions make a worthy addition to your library, if you can find them.

Abraham, H., 1980. *ATM Teaching Concepts.* Boulder, CO: PSIA

Campbell, S., Lundberg, M., and PSIA, 1986. *The Way to Ski.* Tucson, AZ: The Body Press.

PSIA, 1993. *The American Teaching System: Alpine Skiing,* 2nd ed. Lakewood, CO: PSIA.

PSIA, 1993. *The American Teaching System: Alpine Handbook.* Lakewood, CO: PSIA.

PSIA, 1987. *ATS: Strategies for Teaching.* Salt Lake City: Publisher's Press.

Wagnon, J., 1983. *Introduction to Teaching.* PSIA.

Index

Notes

Notes